HELL OR HIGH WATER

JAMES WHITE'S DISPUTED PASSAGE
THROUGH GRAND CANYON
1867

James White at thirty-one

HELL OR HIGH WATER

JAMES WHITE'S DISPUTED PASSAGE THROUGH GRAND CANYON

—

1867

Eilean Adams

UTAH STATE UNIVERSITY PRESS
LOGAN, UTAH

Utah State University Press
Logan, Utah 84322-7800

Cover illustrations:
Front cover lithograph of George Strole falling from James White's and his raft, "The Great Cañon of the Colorado," in A. R. Calhoun, "Passage of the Great Canyon of the Colorado River by James White, Prospector," *Wonderful Adventures* (Philadelphia: J. B. Lippincott & Co., 1874).
Back cover plaque honoring James White, designed by R. E. Adams.
Back cover photo of canyon wall, by Brad Dimock.

Chapter heading illustrations: Panorama of the Grand Cañon from Point Sublime, drawn by W. H. Holmes, in Clarence E. Dutton, *Tertiary History of the Grand Cañon District* (Washington, D.C.: Government Printing Office, 1882), plates xxviii, xxix, and xxx.

Manufactured in the United States of America
Printed on acid-free paper

08 07 06 05 04 03 02 01   1 2 3 4 5 6 7 8

Library of Congress Cataloging-in-Publication Data

Adams, Eilean, 1923–
    James White's disputed passage through Grand Canyon, 1867 / Eilean Adams.
        p. cm.
    Includes bibliographical references and index.
    ISBN 0-87421-425-4 (pbk.) — ISBN 0-87421-426-2 (cloth)
    1. White, James, 1837—Journeys—Colorado River (Colo.-Mexico) 2. White, James, 1827—Journeys—Arizona—Grand Canyon. 3. Colorado River (Colo.-Mexico)—Discovery and exploration. 4. Colorado River (Colo.-Mexico)—Description and travel. 5. Grand Canyon (Ariz.)—Discovery and exploration.. 6. Grand Canyon (Ariz.)—Description and travel. 7. Gold miners—Colorado—Bibliography.
I. Title.
    F788.A36 2001
    917.91'3044—dc21
                            2001004262

To R E A—for more reasons than I can count

CONTENTS

List of Illustrations   viii

Introduction   1

Prologue   8

CHAPTER 1   Callville   11

CHAPTER 2   Who Was James White?   15

CHAPTER 3   White's War   19

CHAPTER 4   The Road to Gold   24

CHAPTER 5   The Rescue   32

CHAPTER 6   Downriver Crier   35

CHAPTER 7   The News Spreads East   42

CHAPTER 8   General Palmer and the Railroad Survey   53

CHAPTER 9   Dr. Parry's Report   59

CHAPTER 10   Major Calhoun's Version   68

CHAPTER 11   Major Powell   77

CHAPTER 12   On the Road Again   84

CHAPTER 13   Powell's Conquest of the Grand Canyon   91

CHAPTER 14   Enter Robert Brewster Stanton   101

CHAPTER 15   Senate Document No. 42   111

CHAPTER 16   Battle of *The Trail*   123

CHAPTER 17   The White Family and Dock Marston   127

CHAPTER 18   Grand Canyon History: Discoveries
and Rediscoveries   133

CHAPTER 19   Bob Euler and Square One   141

CHAPTER 20   In James White's Footsteps   149

CHAPTER 21   Summary and Conclusions: Part A   154

CHAPTER 22   Summary and Conclusions: Part B   160

CHAPTER 23   Summary and Conclusions: Part C   169

CHAPTER 24   Resolution   181

APPENDIX A: James White's 1867 Letter   184

APPENDIX B: James White's 1917 Statement   186

Chapter Notes   192

References and Sources   209

Author's Note   218

LIST OF ILLUSTRATIONS

Frontispiece: James White at thirty-one   ii

1 Lava Falls in the Grand Cañon   7

2 Ruins of Callville, 1926   13

3 AND 4 James White's letter, 1867   49–50

5 James White and his brother, 1869   86

6 James White, wife, and children, ca. 1906   103

7 James White, age seventy, in 1907   109

8 Senate Document No. 42   122

9 Mancos and San Juan Rivers confluence   159

10 Map of western United States, 1869   164

11 Inset from western United States map   165

12 Map of Colorado River Basin   166

13 Map of James White's route   173

14 Anasazi tower, Mancos Canyon   175

15 San Juan River where it enters a canyon   176

16 Comb Wash and Comb Ridge   177

17 Lower Lime Creek forks   177

18 Moqui Canyon   178

19 Deer Creek Falls, Grand Canyon   180

20 Proposed plaque to honor James White   183

INTRODUCTION

Whole I was in the sixth grade, we had a test on the history
of the American West; one of the questions was "Who was the first white
man to go through the Grand Canyon?" The textbook answer was
"Major John Wesley Powell," but I wrote "James White."

Naturally the teacher marked this answer incorrect, but her
curiosity was aroused, for she asked me, "Who, pray tell, is James White?"

"He went through the Grand Canyon in 1867," I said, "two
years before Major Powell." Then I added, "He was my grandfather."

She replied that family loyalty was commendable, but it was not
a substitute for historical fact. She returned my test (with its B+) and
said she would allow me an A, if I corrected my error.

Ignoring the warning signal, I insisted that our textbook was
wrong and I had a book to prove it.

Suddenly, family loyalty became insubordination. Her smile
vanished; she said sternly that I was not there to teach but to learn. She
refused to look at my book.

No doubt imagining myself too noble to consider the cost, I
protested that I *couldn't* change my answer. As it turned out, the cost
was an F; so much for heroism.

But the book I had begged my teacher to read was not a family myth as she supposed. It was very real: a small volume, bound in black Moroccan leather with its title, *The Grand Canyon*, embossed in gold. In the lower right-hand corner was the name Esther M. White, also embossed in gold. Esther M. White was my mother, and she had helped prepare this book.

The overleaf reads,

65th Congress, 1st Session, SENATE Document No. 42

THE GRAND CANYON
An Article
giving the credit of first traversing the Grand Canyon
of the Colorado to James White, a Colorado gold
prospector, who it is claimed made the voyage
two years previous to the expedition under the
direction of Maj. J.W. Powell in 1869.
By
THOMAS F. DAWSON
Presented by Senator Shafroth May 25, 1917

On the next page, it continues,

SENATE RESOLUTION No. 79
Reported by Mr. Smith of Arizona
IN SENATE of the UNITED STATES
June 4, 1917
Resolved, That the manuscript submitted by the Senator
from Colorado (Mr.Shafroth) on May 25, 1917, entitled
"First Through the Grand Canyon" by Thomas F. Dawson,
be printed as a Senate document, with illustration.
Attest: James M. Baker, Secretary

Had the teacher read even the introduction to this book, she might (hopefully) have discovered why I was willing to stand up for my grandfather. This is what she missed:

WHEREFORE
The erection by the National Government of a monument
to the memory of Maj. John W. Powell, as the "first explorer"
of the Grand Canyon of the Colorado, has had the effect of
raising a question among pioneers of the West as to whether
the honor conferred upon Maj. Powell in connection with
the early navigation of the Canyon should not be shared with
another. Mr. Powell's friends claim for him the distinction of
being not only the first to "explore" the canyon but also that

of being the first to pass through it under any circumstances. This claim is challenged on behalf of one James White, a mining prospector, who, they contend, went through the canyon two years previous to the time of the Powell expedition. Powell made his voyage in 1869; White claims to have made his in 1867.

So persistent has been the contention that White was the first to traverse the Canyon that the writer set himself the task of investigating the subject, which he has done as thoroughly as possible consistent with other duties, with the result that he has succeeded at least in convincing himself that White's claim is not unfounded. The undertaking has not been easy; for, while much literature has grown up around Maj. Powell's expedition, comparatively little has been written about White, and that little of the distant past, and now to be found only in publications long since out of print. It is believed that enough of this material has been revived to make a case for White; but if not, it is hoped that at least it may aid the future investigator in arriving at a just conclusion.

In entering into the merits of the controversy it will be well for the reader to bear in mind that the Colorado River is formed in southeastern Utah, by the union of the Grand and the Green, the former rising in northern Colorado and the latter in the adjoining State of Wyoming, and that the stream thus created flows in a general southwestern course into the Gulf of California. Roughly speaking, from the junction to the gulf is a distance of 1,000 miles, the upper half flowing through canyons varying in depth from 1,000 to over 6,000 feet. . . . From the upper to the lower end of this vast stretch of hemmed-in water, there are few crossings, and those difficult and not easily discernable.

The first white men to look into the great gorge were members of the Spanish exploring expedition sent out in 1539 under Coronado; but their investigation was made only from the rim, thousands of feet above the stream. After their casual inspection more than three centuries were permitted to come and go without an exploration of the canyon's depths, and this exploration, like many other things, did not come until after the control of the region had passed from Spain and her heirs into the hands of Americans. Indeed, the canyon plateau was so distant from centers of population, so inhospitable and desolate, and, withal, so inaccessible, before the comparatively recent day of the railroad that it was visited but rarely by any except a few wild Indians. . . . The little knowledge actually existing among white men was confined almost entirely to prospectors, trappers, and a few Government scientists, who had looked into the canyon from one end or the other or had shudderingly peered over the far-away rim into the abyss below. The adventurous frontiersmen were equal to any ordinary task of exploration, but the canyon was too awesome for the vast majority of even this hardy class. True, it was currently reported that at different times some of them had entered the vast inclosure, but none of the reports brought back any of these adventures. Indeed, of these 500 miles of chasm there were vast stretches of which nothing was known. What wonder, then, that the great fissure was regarded as a stupendous mystery and that legend and imagination fill it with untold dangers?

In the face of this universal awe it would have been a brave man indeed who should undertake voluntarily the exploration of the canyon by following the river. Much more probable is it that the first voyage should have been due to accident, as it was if the contention made in behalf of White be correct.

Powell . . . needless to say was well equipped with boats and provisions and . . . was accompanied by a carefully selected body of assistants. He began his first voyage at Green River Station, Wyo., where the Union Pacific Railroad crossed Green River. The start was made on the 24th day of May, 1869, and the end of the journey was reached on the 30th of August following. His party suffered so much hardship and experienced so many narrow escapes from utter destruction that the achievement has been universally and justly exploited as one of the greatest of all feats of daring, skill, endurance, and good fortune. Consequently several books have been written and many stories told about the one-armed ex-Army officer's exploit. And now Congress has decreed that the record which so far has enlivened only the destructible printed page shall be perpetuated in enduring bronze. Very well, so long as the claims in Powell's behalf are confined to his work as a scientific investigator and explorer. But if he is to continue to be heralded forth as the first navigator of the canyoned river, objection probably will continue to be interposed by White's friends in his behalf.

White's trip was the farthest possible from a premeditated proceeding. He had not heard of the canyon, except in general terms, before he found himself locked within its walls, and he continued to the end because he discovered no means of escape from its compelling embrace. Gold was the lure that led him to the Colorado, and pursuit by murderous savages the force which drove him to embark upon its waters.

T.F.D.

I honestly believed that in publishing this little book, the United States Senate was bestowing the seal of truth on my grandfather's journey. I was too young to wonder why, if Mr. Dawson's book had settled a fifty-year-old controversy over the first person through the Grand Canyon, our school textbook remained unchanged fifteen years later. I had, of course, missed the point: Major Powell's expedition had many eyewitnesses; James White fought the river alone, tethered to a crude log raft—his voyage would never make it to the textbook.

Over the next quarter century, my knowledge of my grandfather's story (and even the Grand Canyon itself) remained much as it had been in that sixth-grade classroom. What interest I had was casual and anecdotal, and it might have stayed that way except for a remarkable gentleman named Otis (familiarly known as "Dock") Marston, a dedicated Colorado River runner, Grand Canyon expert and historian, and energetic researcher. He was investigating the history of James White with, he said, a view to either proving or disproving his raft voyage down the Colorado.

My association with Dock Marston and others with similar interests in the Grand Canyon began in 1959, so the reader may wonder why it took so long for this book to evolve. In addition to the usual mundane reasons which manage to sidetrack any project, I harbored the occasional suspicion that White might not have made that trip after all. My doubts were gradually resolved, but as research progressed, a new dilemma arose. Under Dock Marston's aegis, much of my outlook was dominated by the physical aspects of the Colorado River through the Grand Canyon and the opinions of both those who had shaped its nineteenth-century history and Marston himself. I thought almost exclusively in terms of needing to prove that James White's journey had actually happened. But before long, a different picture emerged. The relatively few men who, at first glance, seemed to have legitimately demonstrated the flaws in James White's story had, in fact, engaged in unethical and often licentious means to discredit White's journey by destroying his character.

Unfortunately, my grandfather left behind only one handwritten letter and a colorless, dictated statement about his life, neither of which adequately revealed him as an individual. As is often the case, only family records and oral history could complete such a fragmented story, and it was clear that I had the best access to those who held the memories. My relationship to the leading character might have called my objectivity into question, but I had never known my grandfather personally (he died when I was four), and while I was not entirely without righteous family indignation, I was free of any close, sentimental attachment. I was neither historian nor scholar, but, having been a technical writer for many years, I was determined to maintain the fly-on-the-wall approach inherent in that discipline.

I never viewed James White as a classical hero. I saw instead an unremarkable nineteenth-century pioneer of the American West whose remarkable survival of his Colorado River journey made a contribution of some importance to the history of the Grand Canyon. This book is as much about the men whose paths, for better or worse, crossed White's and about the century-long controversy which brought his journey, and especially his character, under attack. It presents old documents which have only recently come to light and new data about them. It asks a few new questions about old accusations, opinions, theories, and judgments. It offers new research and some excellent detective work, all of which point to a more reasonable answer to an old question:

Who was first through the Grand Canyon?

Figure 1
Lava Falls in the Grand Cañon
(Woodcut, drawn by Thomas Moran from a photograph; in Clarence E.
Dutton, *Tertiary History of the Grand Cañon District* [Washington: GPO, 1882],
plate xix.)

PROLOGUE

The old buzzard drifts high over the river, riding the thermals of a sun-drenched autumn afternoon. As he makes a shallow banking turn, his eye is drawn to the glittering ribbon of the river.

Something is down there, floating on the current. Curious, he moves into a lazy downward spiral. The shape is beyond his experience: long, sturdy, tree branches bunched together, supporting a lumpy, roundish creature with odd-looking limbs. One half of the creature is pale and smooth; the other half is very dark and rough and ends in a mass of long, matted, yellow-white fur. It lies as still as death.

Suddenly, the creature lifts itself from the branches, the fur moves from side to side, the pale limbs twitch. The movement startles the old buzzard. With powerful strokes of his huge wings, he rises and flies off to the west. As he beats his way skyward, he turns his head for a last, brief look at the strange, dwindling figure.

Below, the river current flows strongly, but without turbulence, carrying the flimsy burden of bunched tree branches with its alien passenger. Up close, the branches become cottonwood logs lashed together with ropes to form a crude raft. Here and there, strips of white cloth bind two of the logs in the manner of a repair where the rope has frayed dangerously thin. Up close, the creature becomes a partly naked man, lying prone, arms outstretched to embrace his raft, hands clutching the edges convulsively. The hands are broad, burned very dark, the skin of the blunt fingers shriveled from near constant immersion.

Tied around his waist is a rope, its other end secured to the raft; the intervening length is twenty, maybe thirty, feet; the loop trails in the water—now to one side, now to the other, now directly behind—weaving sinuously as though with a life of its own. It separates the man's naked lower body from his partly clothed upper body and has torn a raw and jagged red line across his waist. There are a thousand tiny scratches from the rough logs on his legs and buttocks and abdomen. There are still-oozing sores with clean white edges, ugly scabbed sores with soft brown edges, and puckered white scars, newly healed but fragile. There are bruises, some small and shallow, some deep and large; some are dark with new blood, some yellow and green and mottled—many days old. The feet are shriveled too, for they hang over the uneven end of the crude raft and drag, unresisting, in the water. There is terrible evidence of the sun's unrelenting work: an angry redness and blisters, some fat with water, some burst and wrinkled and burnt again.

The coat of coarse homespun is shrunken and ripped in many places; the sleeves have been torn away up to the elbows. He wears the tattered remnants of a shirt, most of it long gone to repair the shabby raft. His hair is long and matted and looks like bleached hemp; a tangled beard and mustache eclipse his mouth and chin. What can be seen of his face is burned to the color of old mahogany.

His eyes, pale blue and expressionless, see nothing—not the water or the raft beneath him, not the riverbank with its mesquite and greasewood and scrub, not the dun-colored hills or turquoise blue sky. His focus is on bruised flesh; tortured muscles; burning, blistered skin; suppurating sores and cuts and scratches; empty and spasming stomach; cramped hands. When he lifts his head, it is merely to turn away from the sun, a futile gesture. When he opens his eyes, it is merely an unthinking response to a wave breaking over his head.

All around him the river is a shimmering brown strand, undulating relentlessly. Up ahead is a bend. On a narrow stretch of bottomland on the far side is a low stone structure. Clustered nearby are a few adobe and jacal houses. Nosed against two big logs on the riverbank is a vessel with a crude little cabin; it is long and lies low in the water, and onto it a score of men are loading big burlap bags. Here then is a lifeline for the man on the raft if only he will raise his head—open his eyes—summon the effort to call out. But the eyes stay closed, seeing nothing but their own dark, inward vision.

This shimmering brown strand is the Colorado River. This lonely sliver of civilization clinging to this riverbank in this godforsaken desert is the Mormon settlement of Callville in the newly admitted state of Nevada. The vessel is the barge *Colorado*, recently arrived from downriver. It is Saturday afternoon, September 7, in the year 1867.

CHAPTER I CALLVILLE

W hen Hoover Dam was completed in 1935 and its diversion tunnels closed forever, the waters of the Colorado River began to rise behind the giant structure. They filled the vast, rugged landscape to the north and east, swallowing the mouth of the Virgin River, drowning the little town of St. Thomas, lapping at the foot of the Grand Canyon at Grand Wash Cliffs, and creating Lake Mead, a twentieth-century wonderland of recreational tourism. A few miles upstream from the dam and roughly twenty-five miles east of Las Vegas lie a resort and marina known as Callville Bay, home to cruising houseboats, water-ski power boats, graceful sailboats, and, hopefully, happy tourists.

But hundreds of feet beneath the surface of the glittering waters, buried beyond recognition in the Colorado River's notorious silt, lie the remains of the nineteenth-century Mormon settlement of Callville, its short history virtually unknown to the visitors above.

It was in the year 1864 that Brigham Young, understandably concerned about the safety of his Mormon flock in Utah, sent out a party to investigate the possibility of establishing a port on the Colorado River in what was then Arizona Territory. The party was led by Bishop Anson Call, but its point man was Jacob Hamblin.

Call and Hamblin and a small group of men came down from the town of St. George and set to work finding a suitable site. Nine years earlier, the Mormons had built a small fort at Las Vegas, then abandoned it; a dusty village remained, but it was too far from the river for consideration as a port.

Hamblin's almost encyclopedic knowledge of this country led him to site the settlement on the northwest bank of the river a few miles north of Las Vegas Wash. Washes are inescapable in this country where flash floods are both the lifeblood and scourge of the desert; Las Vegas Wash was notoriously wicked: dry most of the year but deadly when the floodwaters came with a roar that could be heard for miles around, carrying enormous boulders, whole trees, and dead animals down with them. There was no guarantee of safety from the washouts that plagued all such riverside settlements, but Hamblin's choice offered a good chance that Call's Landing would avoid all but the worst of them.

There was little to clear in the sparse landscape; the settlers laid out a plat for a large warehouse, several corrals, and about forty house lots. Despite having to haul nearly all of their building materials from miles away, the settlers built their massive stone warehouse in record time, along with a few small houses. Seventy miles downstream, Bill Hardy's little trading post was fast becoming a town with the predictable name of Hardyville. Call's Landing followed suit with Callville.

Whatever one chose to name it, it was still an isolated outpost lying foursquare and lonely in the harsh Mojave Desert, a land searingly hot and chokingly dry, empty and desolate, with the tortured beauty of relentless sun and pastel shadow, barren rock forms and hidden rattlesnakes, parched scrub and delicate flowers, all blended together in a landscape of awesome dimensions.

For many years, steamboats had been navigating the river from Fort Yuma to the El Dorado Canyon silver mines, carrying goods and people upriver and down; it was not long before they attempted the run to the new settlement. The only real obstacle was Black Canyon; its rapids had run Lieutenant Ives's 1857 iron-hulled steamboat *Explorer* aground during his effort to establish the farthest limit of upstream travel. But Black Canyon could not stop the commercial boats—the rapids just added spice to the trip. By 1867, the *Esmeralda* had come to Callville (and some say the *Nina Tilden* had made it that far as well),

Figure 2
Ruins of Callville, 1926
(Courtesy of Lost City Museum of Archaeology, Overton, Nevada)

but business was not really flourishing. The only materials shipped from Callville between 1865 and 1868 were the salt and lime from Utah Territory needed for the downstream mills that processed gold from the local mines. And for this traffic, barges proved to be more efficient. These dumpy little vessels relied on mule or Indian power; where no towpath existed in the canyon, huge iron ringbolts set in the granite walls, combined with ropes and onboard winches, ingeniously defeated the rapids. Needless to say, the downstream run must have been easy, discounting the odd wayward sandbar or a precarious landing on some tricky piece of riverbank.

By 1867, Callville was on the downhill slope of its short existence. Its connection to the Mormon communities up north was tenuously held via roads barely deserving of the name, over which mail agents rode their own version of the Pony Express. Its link to the south was provided by the swift current of the muddy Colorado or slow, dusty trails past El Dorado Canyon to Hardyville. From there, the river reached south to Fort Yuma, while trails and stagecoach ruts led east to Prescott and west to California.

Callville was never a boomtown, and only a few of the small lots were ever used. Still, it had a bona fide post office (from which nothing was actually postmarked) and enjoyed a brief existence as the seat of Pah Ute County for Arizona Territory until 1866, when the politicians in Washington decided to give everything on the west bank of the Colorado to Nevada and California. Three years later, it no longer mattered to Callville what state it was in; by 1869, it had been abandoned. The completion of the Union Pacific Railroad in that year gave Brigham Young all the access to the outside world he needed; the trains made Callville a ghost town before it even had much of a chance to become a town.

It was here—on September 7, 1867—in this hot, dusty, and remote spot in the Mojave Desert that a raft carrying a man named James White appeared around the bend of the Colorado River, ending a strange voyage and launching more than a century of controversy.

CHAPTER 2   WHO WAS JAMES WHITE?

Despite the bizarre manner of his arrival, Callville's unexpected visitor was, in fact, quite an ordinary thirty-year-old prospector, who, less than four months before, had been making his way through the Rocky Mountains in Colorado Territory in search of gold. Since leaving home to seek his fortune, he had been through a number of adventures not uncommon in the American West, the last of which had consigned him to the silty Colorado.

James White was born on November 19, 1837, in the small town of Rome, New York. Neither his fair complexion, light hair, blue eyes, and sturdy build, nor his surname, nor any sort of family history reveals his ethnic heritage; one guess is as good as another. The only clue is that his grandparents were Connecticut Yankees who had come to the American colonies before the Revolution.

James's father, Daniel, was born in Connecticut in 1789, one-and-a-half years after the state had ratified the new Constitution and six months after George Washington had become the first president of the United States. The 1790 census counted Daniel as one of the 3,929,214 people who constituted the entire known (white) population of the country. The cities of New York and Philadelphia were no larger than towns and the roads that stretched between them merely stagecoach ruts.

James's mother, Mary, was born in 1794. In 1810, she and Daniel married and soon started west. They settled in Rome, New York, where Dan worked as a carpenter. Over the next twenty-six years, Mary produced twelve children, of which James was the youngest.

No family documents or written recollections exist to reveal anything about their lives in Rome, but the town itself and its canal furnish a few general clues. Rome was a growing town, and the decision to build the Erie Canal gave it considerable importance. In 1817, after years of planning, groundbreaking ceremonies for the canal were held in Rome; from then until the official and festive opening in October 1819, the town was alive with the activity and excitement generated by this great engineering feat. The resultant commerce offered plenty of work for a good carpenter. From what little is known, the White family was neither prosperous nor burdened with poverty.

In 1840, Daniel White, possibly encouraged by the great pageant of westward migration before his eyes, decided to move on again. There was less work than in Rome's young heyday, and the promise of more in the new territories of the West must have been a compelling force. Whatever the reason, Daniel, Mary, ten-year-old Joshua, seven-year-old Martha, five-year-old Jane, and baby James, not yet three, settled in Pike Creek Village on the shore of Lake Michigan in Wisconsin Territory after what was, in those days, a difficult and often dangerous journey. In 1848, Wisconsin became a state, the twenty-ninth, and two years later Pike Creek Village became Kenosha.

Kenosha schools were models of excellence in their time, but Joshua and James had scant opportunity to attend them. Daniel put strong emphasis on the nineteenth century work ethic and did not consider even a high school education a priority for his sons. The boys went to work instead. In any case, young James was more interested in physical activities and practical pursuits than in books; he lacked a contemplative nature. He did, however, possess a common-sense intelligence, and this, combined with a stubborn determination, fueled his major ambitions: one, to be free and independent and, two, to make his fortune in gold out West. In 1861, he left Kenosha. Leaving the family home announced that he was no longer his mother's baby James or his father's run-of-the-mill carpenter's apprentice, but his own man, eager for adventure, with a modest "grubstake" eked out of hard-earned and slowly acquired savings.

His railroad ticket took him as far as the line went: St. Joseph, Missouri. There, Russell, Majors, and Waddell advertised their Overland Coach to Denver: for $125 they would take a lucky passenger over the Oregon Trail to Ft. Kearney, along the South Platte River to the Upper California Crossing, and then to the way station at Julesburg, where the Denver stages turned south. It was a fast journey, a mere twenty bone-shaking days, but it was too expensive a waste of White's money.

The alternative was joining one of the wagon trains which started at St. Joseph to go to Colorado, Wyoming, and along the trail to Oregon. There was always room for another hand, someone willing to do chores, scout the trail, fix broken wagons, shoot game, or handle any of the other jobs that were part of the westward push in the 1860s.

White arrived at last in Denver, that ultimate of Wild West towns. Denver! It had everything: bankers and merchants, blacksmiths and carpenters, joiners, coopers, painters and stonecutters, not to mention saloons, houses of ill repute, gambling dens, and lynchings, even an enterprising carpenter named Joe Walley, maker of "pinch-toe" coffins for prospectors who left town feet first. Fashionable Larimer Street boasted "smart" establishments whose wicked attractions gave the Ladies Aid Society severe competition. By the time White got there, however, the much heralded Pike's Peak gold "find" had been exposed as a hoax; there were almost as many "Go Backs" headed east as newcomers on the road west.

There is little question that White was a greenhorn with a hole in his pocket. His money trickled away, spent on "bargain" prospecting tools and mining claims urged on new suckers by old ones. He departed the magic city just one step ahead of total pennilessness and made his way (with a few thousand others) to Virginia City, Nevada, land of the Comstock Lode.

Virginia City was nothing more than an enormous mining camp clinging precariously to a hillside. It had a huge population in constant flux; if you weren't looking for silver, you were looking for a way out. Neither activity was very rewarding. And those awful little mines everywhere, hellholes waiting to collapse on unsuspecting heads—which they did with terrible frequency. You wonder how many dreams vanished amid the rubble of that incredible community.

But—sound the trumpet—the army actually came to the rescue! It was almost farcical. In the late fall of 1861, the Fifth California Volunteer Infantry came to town, looking to enlist the broke, the hungry, and the disillusioned into the Union Army, offering a hundred dollars to anyone who would sign on the dotted line. The recruiters were smart; they arrived during the first winter snowfall. They were even smarter when they told the lucky enlistees, after they had signed up, that they wouldn't get their bonus until they mustered out in three years. Still, things must have been bad; they had plenty of takers, and James White was one of them. The experience would not be edifying.

CHAPTER 3 WHITE'S WAR

The stagecoach conveyed White to the army fort at Sacramento. He was shortly transformed into an infantry private, described for the official records as: "Ht: 5' 7"—Eyes: blue—Complexion: Fair." Posted to San Francisco, he found his brief stay memorable only because he spent it standing guard at the military stockade on Alcatraz Island. In February 1862, his outfit sailed down the coast to San Diego and Camp Wright, his first and only voyage on the Pacific Ocean. In May the unit marched over the mountains and through the sand dunes to Fort Yuma.

As a teamster in the Quartermaster Corps, White spent a lot of time waiting around on the riverbank, getting acquainted with the steamboats and hearing vague bits of trivia about remote upriver settlements. And of course he learned the ubiquitous joke about the Fort Yuma soldier who died and went to hell but came back the next day for his blanket.

In February of 1863, his outfit made the long march from Fort Yuma to Tucson, then, in the following May, to Cooke's Spring, New Mexico Territory. That June the soldiers ended up in Franklin (now El Paso), Texas. White had a brief stint riding herd on army cattle at Las Cruces, New Mexico, in July, the only break from the monotonous, boring, and repetitive wartime activities of an army unit that encounters no enemy and does no action. It was a strange war for these forgotten soldiers. But, in the end, White did find himself engaged in a battle, not against the Confederacy, but against the military itself. The opening shot came in early September 1864; he had only three months left on his enlistment.

White was on guard duty at the post stockade when the lieutenant appeared with a small Mexican boy in tow and ordered all guards and prisoners lined up outside; the officer asked the boy, "Which one?" After a brief hesitation, the boy pointed at James. The officer immediately ordered White to a cell in the stockade.

It would be useless to speculate on White's state of mind at that moment—shock, fear, anger, or confusion. As was his way, he went to the cell in silence. Within an hour, he was joined by a Private Higgins and another soldier; they soon heard the charges against them: stealing two hundred pounds of coffee from the post commissary, taking it across the Rio Grande into El Paso (now Juarez), Mexico, and trading it for whiskey. It was stated, with remarkable vagueness, that the crime had occurred on either September 8, 9, or 10.

The three men spent a month in the stockade listening to the rumors: Mexican border guards had seen several soldiers crossing the Rio Grande with sacks, which they dropped when shouted at; the guards did not know the soldiers; the dealer who had received the coffee said he knew them; this dealer, Butshoffsky, was an American, a former army man who had apparently helped build the commissary and later deserted and skipped over the border to safety.

The soldiers at Franklin had always crossed to the Mexican border town freely, drawn by friendly people, cheap Mexican goods, and the colorful sights, especially the brightly dressed women and children. Most of them knew who Butshoffsky was; they bought goods from his store but were not on friendly terms with the man.

The accused soldiers maintained their innocence, but no one was listening. On October 13, a special order convened a court martial. The prisoners were advised they could call their own witnesses and question the army's witnesses; each prisoner was required to defend himself and prove where he had been and what he had been doing on each of the three nights specified.

Two depositions were taken on October 20 at Franklin, Texas. One came from a border guard, Selferino Silvas (in Spanish, duly translated by the commissary sergeant); the guard was vague: He did not know the soldiers, he did not remember the date. The other was from Butshoffsky, whose status as a deserter was conveniently overlooked by army prosecutors. He claimed to have been awakened (at midnight or maybe 1:00 A.M.) by three (or four) soldiers who wanted whiskey in exchange for some coffee. He said he had given the men the whiskey, but the next day he found that the coffee had been confiscated and was being held in the Customs House; when he went to claim it, he was told he could not have it until he paid *double duty* and then only after the case was investigated. In his statement, Butshoffsky admitted receiving 75 pounds of the illicit coffee (apparently no one inquired about the other 125 pounds) and pointed to the three prisoners as the men to whom he had traded the whiskey.

The attempts by these men to question the whiskey dealer were ludicrous; the clever Butshoffsky had them beat by a country mile. The witnesses went back to Mexico; the prisoners were sent to Las Cruces to await trial. Ten days later, the court was duly convened.

The transcript (handwritten in the most exquisite script imaginable) of these depositions and the ensuing trial present an almost unbelievable picture. It should be required reading for the army's judge advocate general and all civilian law schools. The ACLU would love it.

The formal charge was that White had "burglariously entered the Commissary, stealing 200 pounds of coffee from the United States Army, and transporting it into Mexico." The prosecution divulged several interesting pieces of evidence:

1. Private Nutt kept the key to the commissary in the pocket of his "pantaloons" that hung on the head of his bed in the yard. He admitted that "someone *could* have taken the key" without his knowledge.
2. The commissary sergeant testified that "some" coffee was missing on the morning of September 11; the "200 pounds" was "deduced" by the sergeant by calculating the amount he "thought" he had dispensed on September 4. (No written records or accounts were produced to support this testimony.)

3. Army officials had demanded the return of the stolen coffee, but Butshoffsky offered to identify the miscreants *only on condition that he could keep the coffee*; the officials agreed. However, when asked for the names, Butshoffsky had said he did not know but would "ask around and find out."

4. Although offered a pass to come onto the post to make his identification, Butshoffsky declined and sent a "small Mexican boy" who "knew the men." (This identification was duly entered in evidence.)

5. It was Butshoffsky who had advised the army officials how the key had been obtained and the commissary entered.

The prosecution rested; White ("the accused") was now invited to call his witnesses. His roommate, Dan Applegate, testified to White's whereabouts on September 8, 9 and 10. Sergeant John Hance testified that on September 10, White had gone to his room about 10:00 P.M. and later, around 1:00 A.M., had come looking for a candle. White asked both men if they had ever seen him drinking; both said no. White himself testified that, early in September when he had been on duty, he had found the commissary door unlocked and had reported it to the corporal of the guard. Two witnesses confirmed this.

The court then delivered what had to be—for James White—a devastating coup de grâce: He was ordered to appear the next day and present them with a *written* statement of his defense. In retrospect, one might think that White could have swallowed his pride long enough to admit he was semiliterate rather than face the consequences of a court martial, but it is possible that White, knowing himself to be innocent and his witnesses' testimony strong, was actually naïve enough to believe that the verdict could not possibly rest exclusively on a piece of paper.

When the morning arrived, he respectfully told the court that he would stand on the defense as he had presented it. It was then November 1, 1864, three years to the day from his enlistment in Virginia City, the day he was to have become a civilian again. Instead, the court, having struck out the term "burglariously" for some odd (but undisclosed) reason, found him guilty.

Once more White waited, this time for a period of three weeks, for the court to sentence him. On November 19, he turned twenty-seven; under the circumstances, the birthday probably remained uncelebrated. His sentence was droned out by a sergeant while White stood at attention before the presiding officers: "to be confined [at Fort Craig] at hard labor for one year; to wear a 24 pound ball attached to his left leg by a 3 foot chain; to forfeit all pay except the just dues of the sutler and laundress; and at the end of the sentence to be dishonorably discharged from the Army of the United States."

On April 24, 1865, after five months of incarceration, General Order No. 25 spelled amnesty for all Union prisoners in confinement. White returned to Franklin and received the hundred-dollar bonus promised in Virginia City, some traveling money, and more importantly, an honorable discharge.

Neither Mexico to the south nor the defeated Confederacy to the east held any interest for him; California would remind him of his army service, and Texas of its humiliations. He bought a horse and saddle and followed the Rio Grande north to Colorado.

Chapter 4 The Road to Gold

The major trail through New Mexico Territory led past the hated Fort Craig stockade at Las Cruces, along the Rio Grande, and finally to Santa Fe. White continued along the Santa Fe Trail, by way of the mountain leg that runs through Trinidad in Colorado Territory, and returned to Denver. He found nothing to keep him there, and, in the fall, he went east to Atchison, Kansas, in the company of a Captain Turnley and his family. Either that winter or the following spring, White went on to Fort Dodge, where he hired on to drive stage on the Santa Fe Trail for the Barlow and Sanderson Line.

White covered the run from Fort Dodge to Cimarron Crossing, the point where the trail divided, going south across the Arkansas River and into the shortcut known as the Cimarron Cutoff, or west along the mountain leg. Among his acquaintances was another young gold seeker named George Strole.

The two men became friends, having in common both the search for gold and fortune and the acceptance of mundane jobs when luck deserted them. Few young men came west seeking to be stagecoach drivers. They asked no questions of each other and shared only sparse glimpses into their pasts; they spent much of their time cussing Indians (and learning which tribe was which) and discussing gold prospecting.

Since White had already experienced the joys and disappointments of Cripple Creek, Denver, and Virginia City, he tended to be more skeptical, but he was not altogether immune to the lure of prospecting.

Just such a lure presented itself in the person of one Captain Charles Baker, who showed up in Fort Dodge in the spring of 1867. James White later said he knew little about the captain's past, and that was not surprising; Baker was—and still is—a mysterious figure. As late as 1971, Colorado historians believed he was a southerner and ipso facto a Confederate officer, but after considerable research they were apparently not even certain of his real identity. Regardless of the holes in Baker's past, however, his activities in the early 1860s were no mystery.

By the start of that decade, a number of gold seekers had gone into the San Juan Mountains via northern New Mexico Territory, traveling from Santa Fe to Abiquiu, along the Trappers' Trail and over Sangre de Cristo Pass, thence onto the Spanish route to the San Juan country. Two of them, Albert Pfeiffer and a Mr. Mercure, in their notes on the San Juan Mountains, published by the *Santa Fe Gazette* in the spring of 1860, spoke of its many gold deposits, echoing William Gilpin's descriptions of the San Juan's "metalliferous band of metals" which appeared in an 1859 publication, *Guide to the Kansas Gold Mines at Pike's Peak*. Historians believe that Baker learned of the gold potential from these sources, but even they admit to a certain vagueness about Baker's first foray into that area.

More interesting are two accounts of that trip, one of which expresses definite opinions about Baker's character: "In 1860 California Gulch was swarming with placer miners. Among them . . . was Charles Baker, a restless, adventurous, inpecunious man who was always in search of something new. He entertained extravagant theories about the riches of the country beyond and at last prevailed upon S. B. Kellogg and F. R. Rice to outfit him for a prospecting expedition."

The second was Baker's own account of his journey, written in a letter to the *Santa Fe Gazette* on November 29, 1860. After a description of some preliminary efforts near the Sierra La Plata, he says,

> I ascended Lake Fork to its head and crossed the range to
> the head waters of the Rio de los Animos, which stream
> flows south into the Rio San Juan . . . . In these moun-
> tains, on the waters of the Rio de los Animos are the gold

mines discovered by myself and party in August last. They are extensive gulches and bar diggings, and I believe them to be richer than any mines hitherto discovered to the North-East.

In October, Baker arrived in Abiquiu, and

in order to determine the practicability of reaching these mines from some central points on the frontier of New Mexico . . . I met with a cordial reception from H. Mercure, who kindly furnished me with all the necessary information, and in ten days after we reached the mines, about one hundred and seventy-five miles distant . . . over the only good practical road to this district . . . organized in accordance with the usual mining customs—claimed a town site in a beautiful park in the center of the mining district.

He writes that he then went to the San Miguel River, thence to the Dolores River and Rio de los Marcus (Mancos), and finally back to the Rio de los Animos "amid falling snow."

Other accounts reveal several tidbits of additional facts, such as the main field was located in Baker's Park (now the site of Silverton) and its environs, where eleven districts with some two hundred claims were organized, several town sites were laid out, and various claims made to open a toll road over the old trail from Baker's Park to Abiquiu. Whatever their merit, these accounts gave Baker enough credibility that some even urged the abrogation of Indian title to the lands being settled there.

Baker left Denver in December of 1860 with an entourage which included women and children. After enduring incredible weather conditions over the Continental Divide (it was amazing both that the group kept on and that they had such faith in Baker), those members of the party who did not turn back reached the Rio de los Animos (the Animas River) in March, built a bridge, and started north toward Baker's Park. Most of the company stopped at Castle Rock, where the ladies were "made comfortable"; they called the place Camp Pleasant.

Baker and some of the men continued north. Several of the men who had remained with the ladies set out in the spring to search for Baker and his party; they reported that "they were living in brush shanties and had so wintered. Their diggings were nine miles upriver where is now Eureka . . . they made some sluices, but had collected very little gold." These joyless events, amid some harrowing experiences with the wild winter snows and various alarms about the Utes, turned the whole venture into a fiasco, and the adventurous group scattered, east to Denver or south to Santa Fe. Baker and a few others remained at Eureka Gulch until fall; historians believe Baker left to join the Rebs, but the reports are vague. There is apparently no record of Charles Baker from 1862 until he turned up in Fort Dodge in the early spring of 1867.

Whatever had happened in those five years, Baker had not lost his enthusiasm for the San Juan Mountains, but he had revised his requirement for followers. He applied his silver tongue to the Barlow and Sanderson men for good reason; he had a problem. Indians, he said, had stolen his horses and supplies, and he needed help to replace them. His plan for accomplishing this was to steal as many horses as possible from a small band of Indians camping on Mulberry Creek a short distance southeast of Fort Dodge. Although this was apparently a common way to acquire horses, the fact that White and Strole agreed readily to the idea indicates either that Baker was a consummate Pied Piper or, more likely, that Indians were always considered fair game for anything.

Besides White and Strole, another adventurous young man named Joe Goodfellow signed on for both the raid and the prospecting trip into the San Juan country. Baker scouted the Indian camp and convinced the three men that the job was child's play. So they met to carry out their dubious plan; however, Goodfellow came up missing at the crucial moment. The other three went on without him.

They arrived at a small willow grove near Mulberry Creek; the "hostiles," as promised, were in camp and apparently rather careless with their security measures. The men tethered their horses and after dark crept closer to wait for the camp to settle down. They needed light for their raid, so it was not until near midnight, when the moon rose, that they were able to move in among the horses. Their own expertise with horses allowed them to move about without spooking the animals. They knew that none of them was as skilled as the Indians in bareback riding, but they had the element of surprise in their favor. And if they could capture a few head and scatter the rest, they were certain they could escape.

And so they did. They cut out the desired horses and let the others go, rode hellbent for the willow grove, where they transferred to their own mounts, and rode on with their four-legged loot. They kept up a steady pace, eventually crossed the Arkansas, and continued to a prearranged campground beyond Cimarron Crossing. The Indians, alerted by the white men's shots that had sent their remaining horses in all directions, tried to follow, but it was useless; Baker and company had too good a head start.

After a short rest, the men continued along the mountain leg of the Santa Fe Trail toward Bent's Fort. At a well-hidden camp near the Caches, they were rewarded with the sudden appearance of Joe Goodfellow, full of friendly enthusiasm for their upcoming prospecting trip and airily expecting the other three to share the Indian stock with him on even terms. His inclusion in the party was naturally the captain's decision as its leader; Baker okayed Goodfellow's coming with them but refused to give him even one animal. Not surprisingly, White and Strole were in complete agreement.

There is an interesting postscript to the Mulberry Creek raid: a rumor that the Indians in retaliation set fire to the Barlow and Sanderson stables at Fort Dodge and helped themselves to the horses; it's a great story, apocryphal or not.

The four men, with their stolen Indian horses, rode to Colorado City, a sort of gateway to the San Juan country, where good provisions and animals could be bought or traded. When it was all sorted out, Goodfellow had been forced to pay hard cash to the others for his mount and pack animal, and Baker had instructed them all in exactly what they needed for prospecting. There was never any doubt who was in charge.

After about a week, the party arrived at a small settlement on the upper Arkansas named Brown's Creek. A storm blew in on their first night, leaving them snowbound and forcing them to lay over in the local schoolhouse for several days. This delay apparently exacerbated the tensions that had been building since the incident at Mulberry Creek; when the weather cleared and the party was preparing to leave, some trivial dispute erupted into a shooting match between Joe Goodfellow and White. Apparently a number of shots were exchanged, but the two must have been poor marksmen, for only Joe Goodfellow was hit and

only in his foot. Captain Baker arranged to leave Goodfellow to recu-
perate with a family named Sprague. The other three continued on over
the Continental Divide and into the San Juan Valley, along the Animas
River, and thence to Baker's Park.

Here Captain Baker was on familiar turf. The party prospected in Eureka Gulch and Baker's Park itself, but their luck was minimal. Baker proposed going via the Dolores and the Mancos down to
the San Juan River, where he believed the placer diggings would be
better than the Animas. White and Strole, unfamiliar with the territory, naturally bowed to Baker's greater experience and knowledge.
He carried a compass and a memorandum notebook and assured
them that from the San Juan, they could head north for further
prospecting on the Grand River. The Grand (which on today's map
appears as the upper reach of the Colorado) rises in the Rocky
Mountains and flows southwest to join the Green River from
Wyoming. Baker was confident and convincing, and the lure of the
yellow metal remained unabated.

They gathered animals, tools, and provisions and headed for the
San Juan River. By now July was coming to a close. They had cele-
brated Independence Day in Baker's Park, gone fishing in a couple of
the many mountain lakes near the Dolores's headwaters, and followed
the Mancos River Valley, where they admired the ruins of Indian cliff
houses below Mesa Verde without knowing what they were. Finally,
they came to the San Juan River near Four Corners, where today
Utah, Arizona, Colorado, and New Mexico meet.

The men got to work on placer diggings along the riverbanks,
moving northwest by west and following the meandering river. Where
the river entered a steep-walled and forbidding canyon, they came to
an abrupt and discouraging halt. There was no place to walk or ride
and no bottomland for prospecting.

This apparent dead end called for a crucial decision by Baker.
They could, of course, retrace their steps to Baker's Park and follow a
known route to the Grand River, but the captain's intuition (or possibly his ego) convinced him that they could get to the Grand from this
point on the San Juan. It was simply a matter of finding the shortest
overland route to the north that would allow them to strike either the
Colorado or the Grand at the nearest point. The prospect of travel

through this rugged and desolate country was daunting, but White and Strole apparently remained willing to follow Baker's lead.

The most obvious route lay through a large wash just a short distance from the San Juan's canyon. Along its eastern edge ran an imposing ridge; to the west were smaller ridges and canyons in a great jumble. It was rough country, and water would be scarce, but it must have seemed worth the risk, for they swam the horses across to the north bank and left the San Juan behind.

Baker kept an eye out for any breaks which could lead them generally northwest, the direction where he was certain the river lay. At the first break, they turned west. The contours of the land took them over near-mountainous terrain that was hard on the horses' legs and feet; they were funneled into cul-de-sacs and forced in ever-changing directions. They occasionally stumbled upon Indian trails. They spent a night on the trail. Finally, despite the detours and delays, they found a river, but Baker was unwilling to commit to giving it a name. In any case, this river was hundreds of feet below them down a sheer cliff, and from their vantage point, they could see that it offered scant bottom-land along its course. A side canyon presented itself, and their pressing need for water drove them to find a way down its steep slopes.

There was water at the bottom; it was not a running stream but a spring healthy enough to satisfy both men and animals. Their short stay in this little canyon provided rest and gave Baker a chance to explore the possibility of exiting it to the north to reach a more accessible part of the river. Unfortunately, the north slope of the side canyon was too sheer to allow them a way out. Once again it became necessary for Baker to reassess their position. He finally determined that their only choice was to retrace their steps to the San Juan. It was a disappointing decision.

The following day they packed the animals and started out of the canyon by the same route they had entered, with Baker, as usual, leading the way up the steep slope and over the top. Without warning, shots broke the silence. Ambush! Baker fell, mortally wounded, before the Indians' guns. White and Strole, far enough behind to have escaped the first shots, peered over the top and realized immediately that the captain was dead and they were hopelessly outnumbered. All they could do was retreat into the canyon and try to save themselves.

The two men did not panic, but they lost no time in removing as much as possible from the horses before abandoning them: overcoats, lariats, guns, ammunition, and flour. From what Baker had told them about the Indians in this territory, they were sure their attackers were Utes and would pause long enough to claim the horses, possibly even to mutilate Baker's body, giving them time to escape by the only route open to them—down the canyon to the river.

They made reasonably good time, pausing occasionally to listen for sounds of pursuit and encouraged by the silence. As the sun set and the darkness approached, the moon gave them enough light to make it to the river's edge. This river, whatever its name, was broader and deeper than the San Juan, but it was smooth and unthreatening. A hurried discussion brought them quickly to the conclusion that the river offered the only hope of survival. They hastily gathered some driftwood logs and, using their lariat ropes, made a crude raft. It was, they thought, just good enough to keep them afloat, and they were anxious to leave this side canyon behind as quickly as possible. White remembered from his days in the army at Fort Yuma that there were many upriver settlements where, with luck, they would be rescued. Strole, from St. Louis, was no stranger to rivers; each carried his own brand of optimism into the currents of the muddy river on that quiet, moonlit night.

CHAPTER 5   THE RESCUE

O n that furnace-hot afternoon of September 7, 1867, Callville was the scene of considerable activity. The barge *Colorado* lay firmly snubbed up against the riverbank, the muddy waves of the Colorado River lapping at its hull. Its owner, Captain L. C. Wilburn, was directing the loading of bags of salt for delivery to the downstream mills; the Mormon men and Paiute Indians formed a human chain from the big stone warehouse to the barge, heaving the bags hand over hand. They were sweating in the heat and tired, but the work went doggedly on.

Suddenly, one of the Paiutes dropped a bag, pointed to the river, and shouted, *"Haiko, haiko."* This Paiute word for "white man" was a natural attention getter, but when the men looked toward the river, all they could see was a bunch of logs floating on the current. Captain Wilburn, from atop of the barge's little wheelhouse, could see that there was something—perhaps a man—on the logs.

Two of the men, responding to Wilburn's shouts, quickly took off their boots and waded into the river. As they came closer, they stared in disbelief at the creature lying prone on the crudely tied logs. The rescuers, John Tillman and Charley McAllister, grabbed the raft quickly and began to pull it out of the main current. The rest reached out to help bring it ashore. They all gawked at the nearly naked body, the sores and scratches, and the sun-bleached hair and beard. The man was as still as death.

A sudden movement of his head showed that he was alive. When his eyes opened, they were filmy, veined with red, and without focus, like windows in an empty house. When his mouth opened and he tried to speak, only a few strangled sounds emerged. The rescuers watched in silence; then one of them whispered, "By God, he's some loco'd."

That stung the men into action; they beached the raft quickly and fumbled to untie the rope that fastened the man to it. When it would not yield to their clumsy efforts, anxiety overcame thrift, and someone produced a knife. They turned the man over and revealed another landscape of sores and bruises. He groaned as they tried to lift him. He was unable to stand erect, so severe were the cramps that knotted his leg and back muscles, but he made a shaky effort. He struggled again to speak, but no one could understand him.

James Ferry, Callville's mail agent, came to the rescue with a blanket; he and Captain Wilburn took charge. They put the man on the blanket as carefully as possible. Ferry dispatched Charley McAllister to round up some oil and lime for the sores. Then the others carried the man up the hill to Ferry's house.

All these men had seen worse injuries. Death was not a stranger in that harsh and hostile land, but it usually came from disease, or, more often, from the desert: from exposure, starvation, or heat prostration; from the sting of the scorpion or the bite of the diamondback; from a bullet or an arrow. The odds of this man's arrival by way of the river were about the same as his falling from the sky. Because it shocked and surprised them, it would long remain vivid in their memories.

At Ferry's house, the men removed the remnants of the man's clothes, dressed his sores, and tried to make him comfortable. As they worked, they grew more and more curious. Who was this man? Where had he come from? What had happened to bring him to Callville?

When the man's eyes opened again, there was a faint spark of life in them. One of the men, startled, asked the question that was uppermost in all their minds: "Who are you?" Barely coherent, the man rasped out the answer, "James White."

But the men had to contain their curiosity; their mysterious visitor had relapsed into an unconscious state. Captain Wilburn and the rest, anxious to finish before dark, returned to the loading. Soon the spectacular sunset was turning the drab hills to a smoky purple and the muddy Colorado to copper. The breeze died to a whisper. The makeshift raft lay under a mesquite; it would not long survive Callville's need for firewood.

Jim Ferry, concerned about White's condition, remained near-by to come to his aid; the generous residents of the settlement were equally helpful: The men gathered clothes they thought would fit White, and the women prepared nourishing food, later reminding Ferry to ration the portions.

Going in later to light a lamp, Ferry found his charge awake and surprisingly alert. He immediately told White where he was and how he'd been rescued; even better, he brought him a supper consisting of a small piece of mutton, a middling-sized dumpling, and half an ear of corn. Ferry explained the small portions as rationing necessary for those who—like White—were on the verge of starvation. Although he was ravenous, White had to bow to this wisdom; it was a supper he remembered *in every detail* for the rest of his life.

White was more than grateful for his rescue by the settlers and for their compassion and consideration, but he was reluctant to talk to them about his river experience that evening as Ferry suggested. Ferry had heard the words "some loco'd" applied to White that afternoon, but it is doubtful that he considered it more than the usual comment on difficult, strange, or incomprehensible behavior. He was familiar with the obvious signs of starvation and injury, and, to some degree, the phe-nomenon of delirium; he understood the reasons for rationing well enough but knew nothing at all about what we now call traumatic shock. White, trying to cope with its crippling effects, was equally igno-rant. Despite the confusion he must have felt, one thing was paramount: his strong obligation to his rescuers. His conscience would not allow him to refuse Ferry's request. He reluctantly agreed and, later that evening, his rescuers began the first of many friendly interrogations.

CHAPTER 6 DOWNRIVER CRIER

The next morning, September 8, at first light, the barge *Colorado* cast off, caught the current smartly, and was soon on her way downriver amid farewells from shore.

Captain Wilburn was pleased; last night the entire male population of Callville, plus Tillman, McAllister, and himself, had crowded into Ferry's little house and listened to White's account of his raft voyage. Curiosity overwhelmed their natural concern for an injured man, and they were eager to hear his story.

Ferry had spruced White up, helped him into a clean shirt, and propped him up on his cot. What the men saw now was a man of medium height, about five foot, seven inches, with a broad stocky build and massive chest; despite obvious weight loss, he was well muscled, attesting to recent hard physical labor. He had a broad, high forehead, a wide mouth, fleshy lobed ears laid flat against a large skull, and a strong, aquiline nose. His complexion was fair, with deeply set, heavily lidded blue eyes, shielded by unruly eyebrows bleached nearly to invisibility. His demeanor apparently held no clues to his thoughts.

Like Ferry, the settlers and riverboat men had the usual frontier experience with physical illness and a typical nineteenth-century attitude toward the delicate subject of insanity. At the moment of White's

35

rescue, they had all seen signs which prompted one of them to offer the homely diagnosis of "some loco'd"; even the Paiutes called the *haiko* Ya-Na, which meant "crazy." But now he *seemed* completely normal; he spoke coherently, if with hestitation, apparently in full possession of his wits. In any case, the men took him at face value, ready to forget their earlier impressions.

White's story was brief: He told them about the prospecting party and the two other men with him, about digging for gold along the San Juan River, about turning north to find a shortcut to the Grand River; described their ambush by the Indians, and how Captain Baker was killed coming out of a side canyon. He told them that he and his friend, George, had taken ropes and supplies from the horses and escaped by walking down to the river, where they built their raft and set off; that they had had good sailing for awhile, until George was washed off in a rapid and drowned. He paused, the men waited for him to continue, but White merely stared off into the distance and remained silent.

So the questions began. The settlers were curious about the river upstream and the rapids White had been through, and for very good reason. Just a few months earlier, Jacob Hamblin and a couple of other Mormon men had come downriver from the Grand Wash Cliffs, through Boulder Canyon, to Callville—roughly a sixty-mile trip—in two days. Their little jaunt had produced none of the effects the men had seen in White. That trip had not resulted in anyone being injured or driven anyone "loco." So they wondered exactly *where* White had come from and how far he had traveled. No one knew what was upstream of Grand Wash; it was that completely unknown territory called Big Cañon. If that was where White had been, it surely meant that he had to be the first person to see this mysterious canyon. They wanted every last drop of information about it.

They asked first where he and his partners came from, then who the Indians were and why they did not follow the escaping men to the river. How had he built his raft? What did he mean by "rapids"; how many were there and how big were they? If he was in a canyon, how high were the walls and was there any way out? What did he have to eat? White's answers were hesitant and vague. When they asked how long he had been on his raft, his obvious weariness cut off further questions.

Most of the men were satisfied, knowing there would be opportunities later to find out more, but Wilburn knew he had no other chance to find out the details White had omitted, especially and specifically how long he had been on the river. When Ferry left the settlement—curious to investigate White's statement that Indians had taken his gun in exchange for some dog meat—Wilburn convinced White to tell him more about the river voyage.

When Ferry returned later that night, he heard what the captain had managed to elicit from an exhausted White: fourteen days on the raft, hair-raising descriptions of turbulent rapids, and the awesome canyon landscape. These, and White's condition when rescued, strongly convinced them that this stranger had come through the unknown Big Cañon. They were sobered by the implications, believing firmly that this was more than an ordinary journey. After rehashing what they had learned, they agreed that Ferry should question White further to settle some of the confusing points before making his usual mail run to Hardyville.

Wilburn arrived at the mining town of El Dorado Canyon by afternoon. Here a lively audience could usually be found: miners, workers from the stamp mill, a couple of old timers from the Techatticup mine, steamboat crews, and the occasional stranger—like the gentleman named E. B. Grandin.

Captain Wilburn related White's adventures in a straightforward, undramatic manner. The usual lore of the Colorado consisted of tales of Indian raids and ambushes, flash floods that wiped out whole towns, mine and mill accidents by the dozens. But the story of White and his raft was different. Here was a man just like themselves who had solved, however unintentionally, the mystery of Big Cañon, beaten the odds *and* Mother Nature, and lived to tell about it.

Later that evening Grandin wrote a letter to his friend, Frank Alling, back in San Francisco:

> El Dorado Canyon, Sept.
> A man by the name of White arrived at Callville on the 7th instant, who has come all the way from Green River on a raft. He was badly bruised, nearly starved, and almost entirely naked. Judging by his appearance he has had a rough time, and according to his statements he has had many hairbreadth escapes. He gives the following

account: He was in company with two men, who were formerly residents of St. Louis, Missouri; one of them was known as Captain Baker and the other was named George Strode [*sic*]. They were prospecting together on a branch of the Colorado that they called San Juan River. It is between the Little Colorado and the Green Rivers. I think it is sometimes called "The Blue." About the 24th of last month they were attacked by Indians. Captain Baker was killed at the first fire, White and Strode got away, and succeeded in gathering some rope and some ten pounds of flour, and with their guns made for the river. At the river they were fortunate enough to find some drift wood, with which they made a raft, and embarked, prefering to trust to the river rather than to stay there and lose their scalps. Some three days after starting Strode was washed overboard and lost. White continued on alone and after running fourteen days reached Callville. Soon after starting the flour was either washed overboard or spoiled by getting wet, and he was seven days at one time with nothing to eat. Then he luckily struck some Indians, from whom he bought a dog, giving the Indians his revolver. He managed to make out on dog meat until he reached Callville.

He describes the Big Cañon of the Colorado as terrific, a succession of rapids and falls. Some of the falls, he thinks, are fully ten feet perpendicular. His raft would plunge over such places, rolling over and over, and he was compelled to lash himself fast to keep from being washed away from it altogether. He says that there are rocky cliffs overhanging the river that he believes to be a mile and a half high.

White thinks that they were in the vicinity of what will prove to be good mines there, on the San Juan River, judging from the prospects they obtained.

Yrs, etc. E. B. Grandin

Next morning Captain Wilburn set off on his run to Hardyville; it was late afternoon when he nosed the *Colorado* into the muddy riverbank by the town. Here he found the usual bustle of activity: barges and steamboats either docked or heading in and out—upstream or more likely downstream; the stagecoach from California headed east to Prescott; miners, surveyors, ranchers, soldiers, and transients busily transacting their business. After taking advantage of the amenities of Hardyville (which included a bath, clean clothes, and a good meal), he was soon telling White's story to a new audience.

He provided accurate information where he could and made guesses about things to which he had paid scant attention during his talk with White. He had good reason to stick to the truth; his listeners were by and large natural skeptics, suspicious of tall tales. But they found his graphic description of White's physical condition, spectral appearance, tangled white-hemp hair and beard, and empty eyes—all of which he had seen himself—authentic. One particularly avid listener was J. B. Kipp, a regular traveler between San Bernardino and Prescott, who asked a lot of questions.

That night Kipp wrote a letter to Simon Wolff in San Bernardino, giving him all the details he could recall:

> Hardyville, Sept. 10
> Sir:
> Capt. Wilbern [*sic*] arrived here last night from Callville
> with a load of salt and lime, and reports the arrival of a
> man by the name of James White, at that place, who has
> traveled some seven hundred miles on a raft, where a
> white man has never traveled before, and who sets the
> question forever at rest about the big Canon spoken of by
> Capt. Ives as being navigable. He says no boat can ever be
> got through the canon, as he passed over rapids ten feet
> in height.
> Mr. White says his company consisted of Captain
> Baker, George Strobe [*sic*] and himself. Capt. Baker and
> George Strobe were from St. Louis; Mr. White is from
> Panosha, Iowa. The party left Colorado city to find placer
> diggings; they arrived at the San Juan river without acci-
> dent, and commenced prospecting; sunk a shaft fifteen
> feet deep but found no bed rock; they tried the dirt and
> got twenty-five cents to the pan; a short distance from that
> place they sunk another shaft and found a hard cement,
> in which they obtained gold. Shortly after this they were
> attacked by about fifty Indians, and Capt. Baker and the
> mules were killed at the first fire. Mr. White and Mr.
> Strobe caught up some ropes, a hatchet and about twelve
> pounds of flour and ran for their lives toward the river.
> On their arrival at that point, they had but little time to
> consider over their misfortunes, as they expected the
> Indians to make their appearance every minute, and they
> immediately constructed a rude raft and started on their

perilous journey down the Colorado, some seven hundred miles. Three days after they started, in going over a rapid, Mr. Strobe lost his hold, fell off from the raft and was drowned. The flour, all the food they started with, was also washed off, and Mr. White was left without a mouthful of anything to eat. Mr. White lashed himself to the raft, and, as he describes his feelings, "he was bound to keep above the water dead or alive." He traveled from twelve to fourteen hours each day, and at night he would tie up his raft to some shelving rocks and fasten himself to it, knowing that if it got away from him, there was no hope of his saving his life, as it was impossible for him to climb the walls of the canon—there was but one way for him, and that was to continue his course down the river. He saw some lizards in the canon, and caught a few and ate them. He lived on two rawhide knife-scabbards for two days, and for seven days he had nothing to eat, but continued his course. At times in going over the rapids, he was under water so long that he had no strength to assist himself, but the friendly rope kept him safe until his strength again returned. His hair and beard has turned a reddish white from exposure; he is about thirty-five years old, but looks as if he was seventy; he cannot stand erect, on account of the position he was in on the raft; he is one sore from his hips to his feet. On his arrival at the mouth of the Rio Virgin he saw some Indians, one of whom swam off to him and pushed his raft ashore; he had two pistols; the Indians stole one of them and also his hatchet, the other he traded for the hind-quarters of a dog, one of which he ate for supper, and the other he had for breakfast on the day of his arrival at Callville. On his arrival, Mr. Ferry summoned the chiefs to appear at his house, and when they came he told them of the treatment Mr. White had met with from the Indians, and told them unless they sent and got the pistol and hatchet, he would send to Fort Mohave for one hundred soldiers. The chiefs immediately sent Indians out for the missing articles.

Mr. Ferry will attend to all the wants of Mr. White, as his hand is always open to suffering humanity. Mr. White wishes the papers to publish his account, so that the friends of Baker and Strobe may hear of their sad fate.

Yours, J. B. Kipp

Living so close to the mystery of Big Cañon, Wilburn's audiences in Hardyville were like those of El Dorado Canyon: They saw in

White a frontiersman like themselves—a man of the West, not an eastern scientist or explorer—and they identified with him and the harrowing escape that had brought him down the river to Callville.

The steamboats and other barges soon departed, carrying the exciting news of the raft voyage to the downriver Colorado River community—Fort Mohave, Iretaba City, Liverpool Landing, Aubrey City, Ehrenberg, Mineral City, Castle Dome, Fort Yuma, and Arizona City.

CHAPTER 7   THE NEWS SPREADS EAST

O f all the Colorado River towns flourishing in 1867, few were more colorful than Hardyville. Created only three years earlier by an unlikely, but energetic, entrepreneur named William Harrison Hardy and backed by steamboat pioneer George Johnson, it soon grew from a simple trading post into a bustling crossroads community, with a ferry that linked the state of California to Arizona Territory and points east.

The steamboats and barges that opened the mines and settlements along the Colorado River included such wonderful ladies as the old *Colorado, Mohave, Esmerelda, Nina Tilden,* and *Cocopah I* and had recently been joined by the *Cocopah II,* whose clean lines, shiny paint, large paddle wheel, and shallow draft made her the newest "Queen" of the Colorado. The steamboats and their ungainly sisters, the barges, had carried soldiers, miners, ranchers, and merchants, as well as their equipment and products, into the territory and carried out millions of dollars in gold, silver, copper, and lead from mines hundreds of miles upriver.

These steamboats were remarkable; built in San Francisco or Sacramento, they were dismantled, loaded into sturdy brigs, and sailed around the Baja and up the Mar de Cortez (later renamed the Gulf of California) to the fanning delta of the Colorado River, where they were reassembled in the estuary. The shifting currents and the daily tidal bore—

that broad, six-foot wall of seawater whose roar was like a locomotive and whose inexorable power could and did capsize or ground small vessels—transformed these efforts into a dangerous and exciting business.

The rewards of this river commerce were great. The Picacho placers, the Planet Lode north of La Paz, El Dorado Canyon, Techatticup, and Queen City—all these and more were magnets that drew thousands to the Colorado River. But there were also disasters: the flood that swept away an entire town within a few hours, the erratic current that shifted and carved a new channel, leaving La Paz high and dry, miles from the new riverbank.

The joys, follies, and perils of steamboating on the Colorado were very different from those of the Mississippi or the Sacramento; on the Colorado, you could run aground even if your boat drew only two feet. The Colorado was disgustingly shallow and wildly capricious about the way it rearranged its sandbars. The one you avoided yesterday was gone today, but over there was a new one where none had ever been before. And navigating at night? Ah, well, that was foolhardy at best and disastrous at worst, which was why all boats headed for shore at sunset. Or a new rock just under the surface could sink your boat in minutes. It often seemed that steamboating on the Colorado was a form of entertainment; indeed, a captain's most fervent prayer was that when he made a fool of himself (and he surely would sooner or later), it would not be in full view of a bunch of hooting spectators.

Hardyville had grown with the steamboats, and Hardy's influence and reputation had increased with it. His appearance did not match his importance. A short, wiry fellow with a long, narrow head, big nose, jug-like ears, and a mouth well hidden behind a scruffy beard and mustache, he dressed like an ordinary worker and kept his straw-colored hair hidden under a battered felt hat. None of this fooled anyone; he had a finger in every pie and knew everyone in town and nearly all who passed through it, whether by ferry, steamboat, stagecoach, on horseback, or afoot.

Jim Ferry rode into Hardyville on September 10, made his usual stop at the post office, took advantage of the same amenities that Wilburn had enjoyed, and joined the captain and Bill Hardy over supper for another discussion of White. As expected, Hardy was avidly interested in the story; within a few months he would play a significant role in spreading it back east.

Later, Ferry and Wilburn met a young man named William Beggs, who, like everyone else on the river, was fascinated with James White and his raft voyage. Beggs wanted a scoop, and he intended to get it from these two rescuers who had heard the story straight from White himself. Beggs bragged that he could take the story straight to Prescott and get it published in the *Arizona Miner*—even promised to send the men copies of the newspaper that carried his article.

Beggs kept Ferry and Wilburn busy with questions. As Wilburn had discovered with Grandin and Kipp earlier, he and Ferry were still hazy about a few details, but their answers were straightforward, and credible to Beggs. After a couple of hours spent exhausting the men's knowledge, he went back to his room and drafted his account. There should be no delay getting to Prescott now that the San Bernardino stage was back on a schedule; this year it had been interrupted often by the Colorado floods, the worst since 1862. He was sure that John Marion, the *Miner*'s new editor, would appreciate this story.

September 14, 1867, was a red-letter day for the new editor of the *Arizona Miner*. Marion, a dark, homely man of thirty, was an intense fighter against moral wrongs and mortal mistakes, whether just in Prescott or across the entire United States. He had come to the territory in 1863 on the brig *Hidalgo*, landing across the river from Fort Yuma in Arizona City, still queasy from the ride. There had been interesting options; he had investigated the new strike in Prescott, had hunted and mined gold, but had soon decided that he would rather be a newspaperman. In '64, he became the new typesetter for the new *Arizona Miner*. Now he was both owner and editor.

His purchase of the newspaper was closely tied to the fact that in 1866, Pai Indians living in and around the south rim of Big Cañon had literally declared war on every white man in Arizona Territory. The Walapai attack in early February of '67 had led directly to the unfortunate death of Marion's predecessor, Emmet Bentley. Bentley's arrow wound was not considered serious at the time, but tetanus, the common and deadly companion of such wounds, had killed him before the month was out.

Many of Marion's observations as he walked along Montezuma Street that fall morning—like the patchy frost on the ground and the absurdity of Sheriff Bourke's fall from his horse the night before—

would find their way into that day's edition. And he clearly enjoyed contemplating the delicious jabs he would take, in print, at Jack Moore's political aspirations.

The *Miner*, originally a biweekly, had just become a weekly. This created more work but did not affect the local news of the territory; it was the outside news that was the problem. Strange as it may seem, the national news traveled from the East all the way to California and then, by stagecoach, back to Prescott. When the Colorado was in flood, as it had been this spring, the coaches could not make the crossing, and the news had been limited to the local Indian predations, mining stories, and general trivia. But now things were back to normal; as a bonus, he had the governor's message to offer this week. And he looked forward to the extension of the telegraph lines that would make this news gathering a less awkward and frustrating exercise.

William Beggs arrived in Prescott just in time to make the deadline for the September 14 edition. As predicted, Marion was more than ready to accept White's route from the Green-Grand River area through Big Cañon as a completely reasonable one. Marion was an avid reader of Denver's *Rocky Mountain News,* whose coverage of Colorado's mountain regions was excellent, and he had a good grasp of western geography. Although he claimed no special knowledge of the unexplored parts of the West, he was aware that there were few routes open to White that could bring him to Callville on a raft. The events of the past year, with the Pai on the warpath (and who knew better than he?), had shown with great clarity what a price any white man paid for being caught in their territory south of Big Cañon, even in groups and with armed escorts. He had little trouble believing that the Colorado River, however cruel or turbulent, offered a lone white man better odds than the Walapai.

Beggs's article was set almost immediately in a prominent position on page two:

NAVIGATION OF THE BIG CAÑON
A TERRIBLE VOYAGE

Sept. 14, 1867
Wm. J. Beggs, who arrived here today from Hardyville,
brings us the following account of the first passage, so far
as is known, of any human being through the Big Cañon

of the Colorado. He derived the particulars from Captain
Wilburn of the barge *Colorado*, who arrived at Hardyville
on Monday last, and James Ferry of Callville, who arrived
on Tuesday:

In April last a party, consisting of Captain Baker, an old
Colorado prospector and formerly a resident of St. Louis,
George Strobe [*sic*], also from St. Louis, and James White,
formerly of Penosha, Iowa, and late of Company H, Fifth
California Cavalry, left Colorado City to prospect on San
Juan River, which empties into the Colorado between the
junction of Green and Grand rivers and the Big Cañon.
They prospected until the middle of August with satisfactory success, and then decided to return to Colorado City
for a supply of provisions and a larger company. They set
out to go by the mouth of the San Juan, with the double
purpose of finding a more practicable route to Green
river than the one they had traversed, and of visiting some
localities which Captain Baker had prospected some years
previously. On the morning of the 24th of August, while
encamped about a mile from the Colorado, they were
attacked by a band of about fifty Utes. Captain Baker was
killed, but Strobe and White secured their carbines and
revolvers, some ropes and a sack containing ten pounds of
flour, and ran to the Colorado, where they found a few
small drift logs, which they hastily lashed together, and
embarking on the frail raft, started down the river in the
hope of reaching Callville. On the second day they came
to the first rapids, in passing over which they lost their
flour. On the third day they went over a fall ten feet high,
and Strobe was washed from the raft and drowned. White
had lashed himself to the raft, which although shattered
by the shock, sustained him, and he hauled it up on an
island below the fall, repaired it, and proceeded alone. He
had not much hope of getting through alive, but he
thought his body might go through, and, being found,
furnish a clue by which his friends might learn his fate.
He describes the course of the river as very tortuous, with
a constant succession of rapids and falls, the latter varying
in height from four to ten or twelve feet. Sometimes when
he plunged over a fall the raft would turn over upon him,
and he would have much difficulty in extricating himself
from his perilous position. For a few days he found on
bars and islands in the river sufficient mesquite to allay
the pangs of hunger, but for seven days he had nothing to
eat but a leather knife scabbard. He saw a few lizards but
was unable to catch them; and he looked from side to side
in vain for any mode of egress from the Cañon, the

perpendicular walls of which were in many places a mile and a half, as well as he could estimate, in height.

He floated on an average, about ten hours a day, hauling up at night on the bars which were formed by the eddies below the falls. For about ten days he was without hat, pants or boots, having lost them while going over a fall. On the afternoon of the 6th inst. he passed the mouth of the Virgin river, and a party of Pah-Utes swam off and pushed his raft ashore. They stole one of two pistols which he had managed to preserve, and he bartered the other to them for the hind quarters of a dog, one of which he ate for supper and the other for breakfast. On the 7th he reached Callville, and was taken care of by Captain Wilburn and Mr. Ferry. He was much emaciated, his legs and feet were blistered and blackened by the sun; his hair and beard, which had been dark, were turned white, and he walked with difficulty, being unable to stand erect. He remains at Callville, and although in a precarious condition, will probably recover.

From his actual traveling time, and the rapidity of the current, it is estimated the distance through the cañon, from the mouth of the San Juan to Callville, is not much short of five hundred miles.

Beggs was as good as his word; he sent the promised copies of the September 14 issue to Wilburn and Ferry in Hardyville on the next westbound stage.

Back in Callville, White got to know Ferry's assistant mail agent, Adam Simon, which led to a fine friendship in the long run but at the time seemed about as exciting as watching the mesquite grow. There was nothing to delay his recovery and few distractions. He grew restless and decided to write to his brother back home in Kenosha, Wisconsin, although he did not exactly look forward to the task.

Many of the problems that eventually surrounded White's raft trip lay in his inability to translate his thoughts and experiences into written words. The inevitable result was that much of that traumatic event remained forever locked away in his memory. This simple fact made him vulnerable to criticism and disbelief. He had grit and courage in abundance, but neither could replace the education he did not have; now that he had something worthwhile to write home about, he found he did not have the words to do it justice.

The letter he finally wrote still exists in the Bancroft Library in Berkeley, California, and is reproduced here (see figures 3 and 4).

Here, complete with its literary warts, is a straight translation from the handwritten text (an edited version of the letter appears in appendix A):

> Navigation of the Big Canon
> A terrible voyage
> Callville   September.26. 1867.
>   Dear Brother it has ben some time senCe i have heard frome you i got no anCe from the last letter that i roat to you for i left soon after i rote i Went prospeCted with Captin Baker and gorge strole in the San Won montin Wee found vry god prospeCk but noth that Would pay. then Wee stare Down the San Won river wee travel down a bout 200 miles then Wee Cross over on Coloreado and Camp We lad over one day Wee ~~found that~~ found out that Wee Cold not travel down the river and our horse Wass sore fite and Wee had may up our mines to turene baCk When Wee Was attaCked by 15 or 20 utes indes they kill Baker and gorge Strole and my self tok fore ropes off from our hourse and a ax ten pounds of flour and our gunns Wee had 15 milles to woak ~~before~~ to Colarado Wee got to the river Jest at ~~dalk~~ night Wee bilt a raft that night Wee got it bilt abot teen oClock tha night Wee saile all that night Wee had good Sailing fro three days and the ~~third days~~ fore day gorge strole Was Wash of from the raft and down that left me alone i though that it Wold be my time next i then pool off my boos and pands i then tide a rope to my Wase i Wend over folls from 10 to 15 feet hie my raft Wold tip over three and fore time a day the thurd day Wee loss our flour flour and fore ~~days~~ seven days i had noth to eat to ralhhide nife Caber the 8.9 days i got some musKit beens the 13 days a party of indis frendey thay ~~Walk~~ Wold not give me noth eat so i give my ~~revl~~ pistols for hine pards of a dog i ead one of for super and the other breakfast the 14 days i rive at Callville Whare i Was tak Care of by James ferry i Was ten days With out pants or boos or hat i Was soon bornt so i Cold hadly Wolk the ingis tok 7 head horse from us Josh i can rite yu Halfe i under Went i see the hardes time that eny man ever did in the World but thank god that i got thrught saft i am Well again and i hope the few lines will fine [illegible] you all Well i sned my beCk respeCk to all Josh anCer this When you git it.
>   DreCk you letter to Callville ~~Are~~ Arizona
>   ....James White

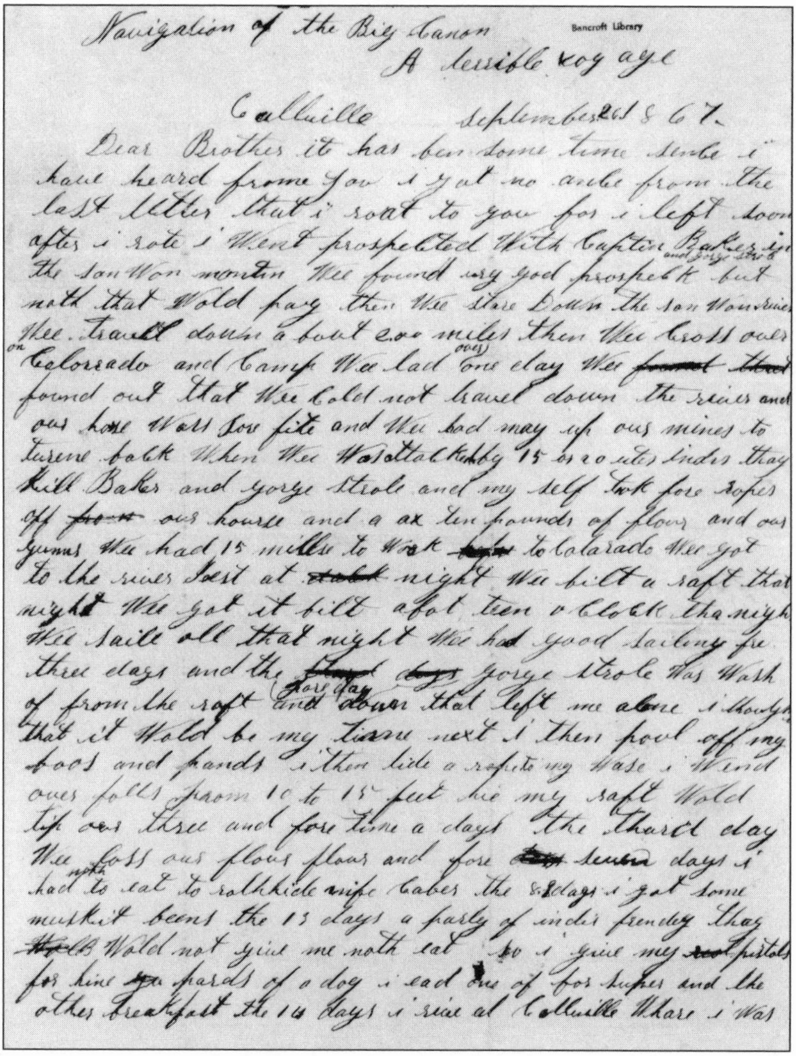

Figure 3.
James White's letter to his brother Joshua, 1867
(Courtesy of the Bancroft Library)

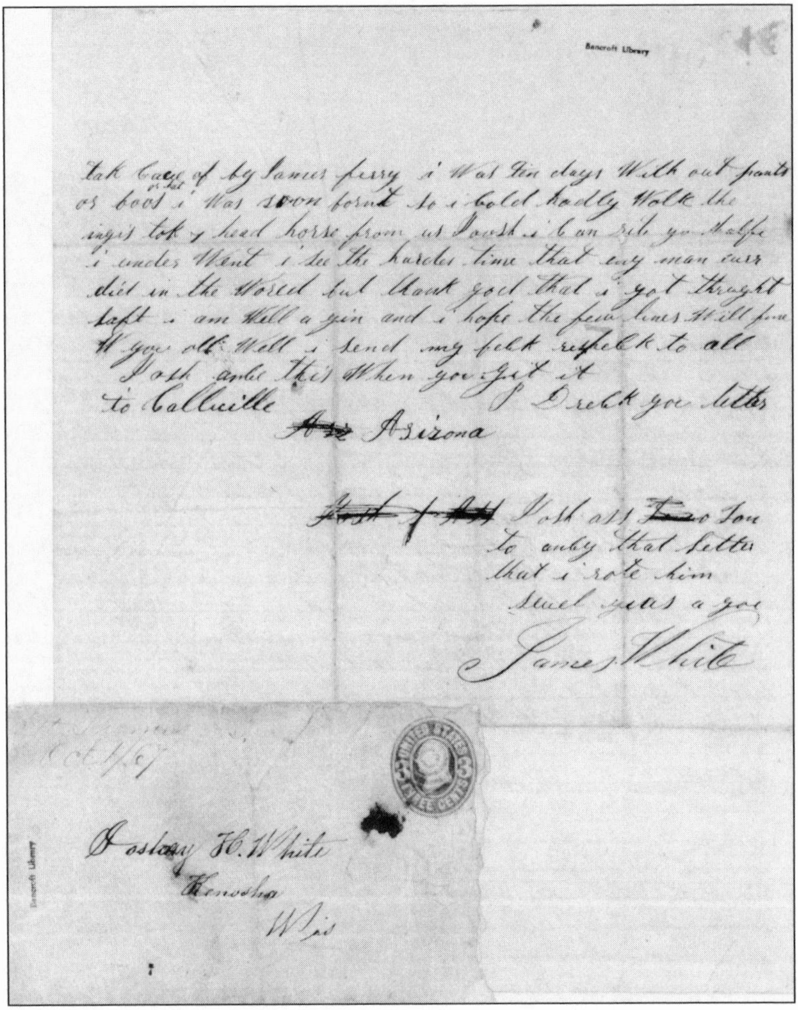

Figure 4.
Second page and envelope of James White's letter
(Courtesy of the Bancroft Library)

This was the only account White ever wrote; there were no other letters, no diaries, no journals. The letter's fourth-grade spelling and grammar unfortunately tend to obscure an innate, practical intelligence. The letter conveys a powerful sense of White's mental distress in dealing with the death of his partners, as well as his confusion over dates. The story he relates is dramatic but not imaginative.

The headline that is so prominently and meticulously written at the top of the letter is obviously from Beggs's article in the September 14 *Arizona Miner;* since it is in White's handwriting, it seems safe to conclude that he copied it there himself. The date, 26, was clearly squeezed into the gap between September and 1867, so a good guess is that the headline was added at the same time. There are several logical scenarios that would account for his being sufficiently impressed with the headline to add it to his letter. Whatever the reason, he certainly recognized the truth of the words—it had indeed been a terrible voyage.

About this time, Ferry offered White a job carrying the mail between Callville and Hardyville/Fort Mohave. White's recovery had been swift but unremarkable. Once he was rescued, his physical injuries were no longer life threatening; nineteenth-century frontier medicine took care of the sores and bruises, and the Mormon settlers fed him well. All things considered, he seems to have handled his emotional trauma remarkably well; whatever it may have cost him internally, he managed to present to the world the culturally correct, stoical image of the macho frontiersman.

Ferry's offer was a second rescue for White, who was growing desperate. He had lost everything, and his prospects in Callville were hopelessly dead-ended. No amount of work performed in aid of the settlers, whether carrying heavy loads or currying horses, repairing damaged wagons or shoring up jerry-built houses, could distract him from worrying about how to get back on his feet.

With Ferry's job, there was hope. Almost immediately, Ferry encouraged White to ride to Hardyville with him. There he enjoyed the lively activities that were missing in Callville: the rough-and-tumble population, the colorful parade of steamboats and barges on the river, and the familiar rumble of the stagecoaches as they passed through town on their way between Prescott and San Bernardino.

His reception in Hardyville was respectful; people were generally awed by his survival. As far as the usual questions were concerned, White had become comfortable with his two-week schedule and the events he so neatly fitted into them; he was also getting adept at evading or blurring the memories he needed to put behind him.

Bill Hardy was convinced, along with everyone else in town, that White had made the journey through Big Cañon. Hardy knew a railroad survey was in progress in the territory and that the surveyors were interested in any information about the Colorado River and Big Cañon. General Palmer, the leader of the survey, and several members of his party had been in and out of Hardyville at various times, and Hardy was quick to pass White's Big Cañon story on to them.

Hardy boasted about his knowledge of the survey and said that the general himself had been very interested in interviewing White. Hardy's lively description of Palmer was typical: a general in the Pennsylvania Cavalry at the youthful age of twenty-nine, prominent in some eastern railroad or other (the Pennsylvania), and now a real big shot with the Kansas-Pacific. Hardy also bragged that he could arrange for White to meet the general.

In late September, the two letters written by Grandin and Kipp appeared in some California newspapers. These and the *Miner* article were the earliest published accounts, but their circulation appears to have been confined largely to the West. White's own letter would not surface until 1907.

Chapter 8   General Palmer and the Railroad Survey

Despite White's success in putting his army experience behind him and burying his court martial and imprisonment, he was fated to have his name and his Colorado River journey forever linked to two prominent army officers. These interconnections would create an indelible question mark over Grand Canyon history.

The first was General William Jackson Palmer. Despite his considerable accomplishments, he is not widely known. He was born in September 1836 in Pennsylvania, the eldest son of well-educated Quaker parents. He was a precocious child and had the advantage of an excellent early education; his parents were not considered well-to-do, but their families had many influential friends—and he was blessed with a rich uncle. His education as an engineer began at seventeen, sponsored by this uncle, who not only gave him a job but sent him abroad for further study. Palmer distinguished himself as a superb officer on the battlefield during the Civil War and even volunteered for more dangerous exploits, acting twice as a spy for the Union Army. He was captured but escaped before the Rebs learned his rank—to become a hero and a general at 29.

After the war, still under the aegis of his uncle but now recognized for his own talents, he went to work for the Pennsylvania Railroad, then for the Kansas-Pacific. Later on, he branched out to create the Denver and Rio Grande Railroad, which had a checkered existence, surviving a long and monumental war with the Santa Fe. He then became the driving force and primary builder of the Mexican National Railroad during the Diaz presidency. During his western travels, he fell hopelessly in love with the Rocky Mountains, founded the city of Colorado Springs, and became its premier citizen.

During the year of 1867, Palmer led extensive surveys along the thirty-second and thirty-fifth parallels for the Kansas-Pacific Railroad (better known as the Union Pacific-Eastern Division). His activities on the survey were almost as adventurous as those he'd had during the war; he and his men were pursued and attacked by Apaches in the Little Colorado area, surviving by hairbreadth escapes and introducing his survey team to western American realities.

It was during this survey that General Palmer and various members of his team found themselves in Hardyville. The town was something of a hub, and, since the survey tended to fort-hop across the country, its proximity to Fort Mohave made it a logical meeting place for the team's often scattered members. James White's raft journey was major news in Hardyville; Palmer recognized its potential for broadening the survey data by including an eyewitness account of an area completely unknown not only to them but to the world. He was naturally eager to take advantage of such a fortuitous circumstance.

He wished to meet White and interrogate him himself, but the variables of distance and schedule could not be reconciled. Failing that, the general assigned a member of his party to interview White whenever it could be arranged. Of course, Bill Hardy was happy to oblige everyone in such an arrangement.

Two likely team members for the assignment were Dr. Charles Christopher Parry, a scientist with some prior knowledge of the territory, and Major Arthur R. Calhoun, a journalist. Not a lot is known about them. Dr. Parry, although reportedly a medical doctor, was actually signed on as the survey's botanist. His duties were diverse and he apparently considered himself a geologist. Major Calhoun had been a member of General Palmer's Fifteenth Pennsylvania Cavalry (where he lost a leg in battle), which may explain his inclusion in the survey, but not his function on the team. There seems to be a difference of opinion as to who was actually assigned by the general to interview White; however, since Palmer's interest in White's journey was primarily in its usefulness to the survey, the choice of a scientist over a journalist appears logical. Whatever the reason, it was Parry who wrote the official survey report; Calhoun, who was not present at Parry's interview, wrote an account of his own, which was published in both Philadelphia and England.

It was not until January 1868 that one of White's visits to Hardyville finally coincided with one of Dr. Parry's. The meeting produced the only recorded face-to-face interview in those early days; its subsequent publication in an academic journal influenced Colorado River and Grand Canyon history. By a strange twist of fate, it also provided some of the ammunition used to destroy the credibility of White and his voyage.

Although it was Parry who conducted the interview, White forever believed that it was General Palmer—a misapprehension perhaps caused by Hardy telling White that the general intended to interview him directly and failing to mention Parry.

The focus of Parry's interview was naturally on the physical aspects of White's journey, and he was determined to report all information as accurately and precisely as posssible. Like any private about to be questioned by a brigadier general, White was eager to oblige; unfortunately, his recollections were not as precise as Parry had hoped.

Parry started with background questions, some of which (city, state, and the men's names) had been incorrect in the *Arizona Miner* article; he put dates on the times of departure from Dodge and Colorado City, although it is likely that Parry defined these himself— White's "middle of the month" became Parry's "thirteenth"—dates were a matter of indifference to White. Strole's name was corrected from Strobe (although George became Henry, for some odd reason), and the number of men in the prospecting party was corrected from three to four without Parry asking for further detail.

Like any good scientist, Parry took notes during his interview. They read as follows:

James—White—Kenosha Wisconsin—Started from Ft
Dodge—13 April—with a prospecting party under Capt
Baker Came to Colorado City—left 20th May—for San
Juan—struck Animas—Dolores—Mancos Canon followed
to San Juan down that 200 miles crossed to north side
crossed over Mts to Colorado—50 miles went up 12 miles
to canon. went down to Colorado—12.

   Henry Strole. Capt Baker killed—went back into
Canon unpacked took 10 lb flour & coffee—24 Aug
fight—went to mouth canon. built raft—8 inch 10 ft 3.
tied up with lariats river wide and still small bottom. 25.th
stopped. and repaired raft passed Green 30 miles—after
leaving Green Canon travelled 40 miles to San Juan. laid
up night 26th travelled all night 40 miles 27th all night—
28th 4th—came to rapids and Strun [*sic*] was washed off &
drowned 3P.M. lost provisions kept passing rapids—25 or
30 a day passed Colorado Chiquito 4th in evening continuous rapids—to 100 miles above Callville—Rock in Canon.
White Sand Stone 2 days in foot of Canon Volcanic reach
Callville 8th [*sic*] Sept—line of high water mark 30 to 40 ft
width of river in canon narrowest 100 ft height 3000 ft
rapids caused by fallen rocks one fall 10 ft ?—many
whirlpools & eddies stopped in an edy [*sic*] mouth of C
chiq 2 hours prayed out shape of Canon perpendicular for
several 100 ft then flares out course of river very
crooked—raft bumping on rocks—Same character of rock
through the main Canon.

White had no trouble defining the early stages of the prospectors' route: from Colorado City to the San Juan Mountains and the
Animas River, across to the Dolores River, and thence down the
Mancos Valley to the San Juan River, then traveling west along the
river (with a brief description of activities), and finally turning north
when they were unable to continue along the San Juan. He gave a
brief and vague description of the terrain over which they traveled to
the side canyon of the river, estimating several distances, probably at
Parry's prompting. The notes state, "went up 12 miles to canon. went
down to Colorado—12." White's letter of September 1867 clearly
called this river the Colorado; so must he have named it to Parry in
January 1868.

   In most situations, the interviewer leads the subject, and this
was no exception. After White's bare-bones recital of the Ute ambush,
Baker's death, and the escape to the river, Parry first tried to pin down

the exact date of the Indian attack. As we have seen, White's dates were vague since they were useless on the trail; however, the date of his rescue at Callville was well known, and that, combined with White's absolute insistence that he was on the river for *exactly* fourteen days (which Parry, like White's rescuers, accepted without question) led to August 24 as the day he began his voyage. But White's answers, beginning with the description of Baker's death, and especially the time after Strole's death, became increasingly sketchy and vague; however, the interrogation elicited some estimates as to the width of the river, rate of flow, and other details.

Parry now attempted to nail down exactly where White and Strole began their voyage, considering such information crucial to a railroad survey. White doubtless told Parry that the Grand River was Baker's ultimate destination, and Parry began to focus upon the descriptions and distances which might establish their actual point of embarkation. Parry knew, academically, that the Grand and Green Rivers join to form the Colorado, but beyond that, his actual knowledge, like everyone else's at that time, was purely speculative. There are several rivers which enter the Colorado between the Green-Grand confluence and Callville (later bearing historical names like Escalante and more colorful ones like Dirty Devil and Bright Angel), as well as numerous streams (Navajo Creek and Diamond Creek). Any of them might have been the ones White described. At that time, neither White nor Parry, nor anyone else, could possibly have known one from the other. That, and Parry's assertion that the men embarked on the Grand, indicated by his notation, "passed Green 30 miles—after leaving Green canon," casts doubt on the process by which he concluded that the prospecting party had reached the Grand instead of the Colorado. It was a classic case of the blind leading the blind.

White's description of the canyon was wildly variable. Elements like the distances run, rate of travel, character of the river course, fall of the river through a rapid, or cause of a rapid were pure guesses. High water marks and the whirlpool at the mouth of a stream were unambiguous and clearly described; overwhelming phenomena such as the number and size of the continuous rapids, height of the awesome walls and cliffs, and his vague and highly unlikely identification of the canyon walls as white sandstone were muddled and uncertain.

It was unfortunate that Parry, notwithstanding his scientific education, knew no more about stress, starvation, and sheer terror than the local river men. But it was the nineteenth century, and Parry's expertise—or lack thereof—was standard.

Parry's confident assertion that White and Strole had entered the river some thirty miles up the Grand from the Green-Grand junction produced the original error which in turn spawned the cumulative downstream errors. But flaws and errors aside, Parry managed to get a remarkable amount of information that was not challenged by later explorers. The interview itself, because of its closeness in time to the event and White's willingness to answer questions on the mistaken assumption that the interviewer was General Palmer, probably represented White's core expression of his experience insofar as he himself knew or understood it.

Using his extremely sketchy notes, and apparently a lot of information that does not appear in them, Parry wrote a comprehensive official report.

Chapter 9   Dr. Parry's Report

Parry's report was different from the newspaper articles of the time in that it was the result of a firsthand interview and represented the findings of a commercial survey rather than the usual piece of western journalism. It was strongly supported by a natural science society and subsequently published in its official journal. It began:

> Account of the passage through the Great Cañon of the Colorado of the west, from above the mouth of Green River to the head of steamboat navigation at Callville, in the months of August and September, 1867, by James White, now living at Callville. Reported Jan. 6, 1868, to J. D. Perry, Esq., Pres't of the Union Pacific Railway, Eastern Division, by C. C. Parry, Ass't Geologist, U.P.R.R. Survey.

The report was divided into three parts: cover letter, narrative, and conclusions. Only the last two carry significant data, but the eloquent letter to J. D. Perry so beautifully exemplifies the nineteenth century approach to scientific endeavor that it would be a sin to omit it. Parry wrote:

> Sir—The Railroad survey now in progress under your direction has afforded many opportunities for acquiring valuable additions to our geographical knowledge of the unexplored regions of the far West from original sources

not accessible to ordinary map compilers. Mining prospectors within the last twenty years, more adventurous even
than the noted trappers of the Rocky Mountains, have
scarcely left a mountain slope unvisited, or a water-course
unexamined, over the wide expanse extending from the
Mississippi River to the Pacific Ocean. Could the varied
and adventurous experience of these mountain men be
brought into an accessible form, we should know nearly as
much of these western wilds, as we now do of the settled
portions of our country.

Among the geographical problems remaining for the
longest time unsolved, was the actual character of the stupendous chasms, or cañons, through which the Colorado
of the west cleaves its way from its snowy source to its exit
into the California Gulf. Within the last ten years public
attention has been frequently directed to this subject, and
various Government expeditions have imparted reliable
information in reference to the upper and lower course of
this remarkable river. Lieutenant Ives, in 1857-8, made a
satisfactory exploration of the navigable portion of the
Colorado, extending from its mouth to the Great Cañon,
and since then a regular line of light draft boats have been
successfully traversing these inland waters. Still the *Great
Cañon* remained a myth; its actual length, the character of
the stream, the nature of its banks, and the depth of its vertical walls, were subjects for speculation, and afforded a fine
field for exaggerated description, in which natural bridges,
cavernous tunnels, and fearful cataracts formed a prominent feature. Now, at last, we have a perfectly authentic
account from an individual who actually traversed its formidable depths, and who, fortunately for science, still lives to
detail his trustworthy observations of this most remarkable
voyage. Happening to fall in with this man during my
recent stay of a few days at Hardyville, on the Colorado, I
drew from him the following connected statement in
answer to direct questions noted down at the time.

Following this eloquent prologue, Parry revealed his enthusiasm
for and obvious belief in White's journey in his presentation of the
results of his interview:

NARRATIVE

James White, now living at Callville, on the Colorado
River, formerly a resident of Kenosha, Wisconsin, was
induced to join a small party for the San Juan region, west
of the Rocky Mountains, in search of placer gold diggings.

The original party was composed of four men, under the
command of a Capt. Baker.

The party left Fort Dodge on the 13th of last April,
and after crossing the plains, completed their outfit for
the San Juan country in Colorado City, leaving that place
on the 20th of May. Proceeding by way of South Park and
the Upper Arkansas, they crossed the Rocky Mountains,
passing round the head waters of the Rio Grande, till they
reached the *Animas* branch of the San Juan River. Here
their prospecting for gold commenced, and being only
partially successful, they continued still farther to the west,
passing the *Dolores* and reaching the *Mancas*, which latter
stream was followed down to the main valley of the San
Juan. Crossing the San Juan at this point, they continued
down the valley in a westerly direction for about 200
miles, when the river entered a cañon. Here they again
crossed to the north bank, and leaving the river passed
across a mountain ridge aiming to reach the Colorado
River. In a distance of 50 miles over a very rugged country, they reached this latter stream, or rather its main eastern tributary, Grand River.

It is essential to pause here to introduce eight highly significant
words:"or rather its main eastern tributary, Grand River." Parry's interview notes, from which he produced his report, state: "crossed over
Mts to Colorado" and "went down to Colorado," describing the party's
land journey, and clearly referring to the Colorado *River*, specifically
that portion of the river formed by the confluence of the Grand
(which rose in Colorado Territory) and the Green (which rose in
Wyoming Territory). In the portion of the notes covering their river
travel, however, the phrase "passed Green 30 miles" suddenly appears,
indicating that the men had been on the Grand—despite the fact that
there is no mention of that river in the notes. In the report, Parry,
without any explanation of how he arrived at this conclusion, places
White and Strole's point of embarkation on the Grand River, a statement that fueled more than a century of controversy over who was
first through the Grand Canyon.

At the point where they first struck the river it was
inaccessible on account of its steep rocky banks; they
accordingly followed up the stream in search of a place
where water could be procured. At an estimated distance
of 12 miles they came upon a side cañon down which

they succeeded in descending with their animals, and
procuring a supply of water. They camped at the bottom
of this ravine on the night of the 23rd of August, and on
the morning of the 24th, started to ascend the right
bank to the table land. In making this ascent they were
attacked by Indians, and Capt. Baker, being in advance,
was killed at the first fire. The two remaining men, James
White and Henry Strole, after ascertaining the fate of
their comrade, fought their way back into the cañon,
and getting beyond the reach of the Indians, hastily
unpacked their animals, securing their arms and a small
supply of provisions, and proceeded on foot down to the
banks of Grand River. Here they constructed a raft of dry
cottonwood, composed of three sticks, 10 feet in length
and 8 inches in diameter, securely tied together by lariat
ropes, and having stored away their arms and provisions,
they embarked at midnight on their adventurous voyage.

The following morning, being on the 25th of
August, they made a landing, repaired their raft by some
additional pieces of dry cedar, and continued on their
course. The river here was about two hundred yards
wide, flowing regularly at a rate of 2-1/2 to 3 miles per
hour. According to their estimate they reached the
mouth of Green River, and entered the main Colorado
30 miles from the point of starting. Below the junction
the stream narrows, and is confined between perpendicular rocky walls, gradually increasing in elevation. At an
estimated distance of 40 miles from Green River they
passed the mouth of the San Juan, both streams being
here hemmed in by perpendicular walls. From this point
the cañon was continued, with only occasional breaks
formed by small side cañons equally inaccessible with the
main chasm. Still they experienced no difficulty in continuing their voyage, and were elated with the prospect
of soon reaching the settlements on the Colorado, below
the Great Cañon.

The report continues with the crescendo of high drama:

On the 28th, being the fourth day of their journey,
they encountered the first severe rapids, in passing one of
which, Henry Strole was washed off, and sank in a
whirlpool below. The small stock of provision was also lost,
and when White emerged from the foaming rapids, he
found himself alone, without food, and with gloomy
prospects before him for completing his adventurous journey. His course now led through the sullen depths of the

Great Cañon, which was a succession of fearful rapids, blocked up with masses of rock, over which his frail raft thumped and whirled, so that he had to adopt the precaution of tying himself fast to the rocking timbers. In passing one of these rapids, his raft parted, and he was forced to hold on to the fragments by main strength, until he effected a landing below in a shallow eddy, where he succeeded, standing waist deep in water, in making necessary repairs, and started again. One can hardly imagine the gloomy feelings of this lone traveler, with no human voice to cheer his solitude, hungry, yet hopeful and resolute, closed in on every side by the beetling cliffs that shut out sunlight for the greater part of the long summer day, drenched to the skin, sweeping down the resistless current, shooting over foaming rapids, and whirling below in tumultuous whirlpools, ignorant of what fearful cataracts might yet be on his unswerving track, down which he must plunge to almost certain destruction; still, day after day, buoyed up with the hope of finally emerging from his prison walls, and feasting his eyes on an open country, with shaded groves, green fields, and human habitation.

If you compare Parry's opening paragraphs and this passage with James White's letter to his brother, the poetic license which dramatizes this report and colored Parry's scientific precision might seem amusing. Still, the nineteenth century rhetoric does not eclipse the value of the report.

The mouth of the Colorado Chiquito was passed on the fourth day, in the evening, the general appearance of which was particularly noted, as he was here entangled in an eddy for two hours, until rescued, as he says, "by the direct interposition of Providence." The general course of the river was noted as very crooked, with numerous sharp turns, the river on every side being shut in by precipitous walls of "white sand rock." These wals [*sic*] present a smooth, perpendicular and, occasionully [*sic*], over-hanging surface, extending upward to a variable height, and showing a distant line of high-water mark thirty to forty feet above the then water level.

His estimate of the average height of the Cañon was 3,000 feet, the upper edge of which flared out about half way from the bottom, thus presenting a rugged crest. The last two days in the Cañon, dark-colored ingenious [probably igneous] rocks took the place of the "white sandstone," which finally showed distinct breaks on either side,

till he reached a more open country, containing small
patches of bottom land, and inhabited by bands of
Indians. Here he succeeded in procuring a scanty supply
of Mezquite bread, barely sufficient to sustain life till he
reached Callville, on the 8th [*sic*] of September, just fourteen days from the time of starting, during seven of which
he had no food of any description.

When finally rescued, this man presented a pitiable
object, emaciated and haggard from abstinence, his bare
feet litterly [*sic*] flayed from constant exposure to drenching
water, aggravated by occasional scorchings of a vertical sun;
his mental faculties, though still sound, liable to wander,
and verging close on the brink of insanity. Being, however,
of a naturally strong constitution, he soon recovered his
usual health, and is now a stout, hearty, thick-set man. His
narrative throughout bears all the evidences of entire relia-
bility, and is sustained by collateral evidence, so that there is
not the least reason to doubt that he actually accomplished
the journey in the manner and time mentioned by him.

This report became the basis for a multitude of spin-off
accounts, used alternately as proof that James White did not traverse
the Great Cañon of the Colorado of the West and proof that he did.

From the specific details elicited from White, Parry drew the
following conclusions:

CONCLUSIONS

The following may be summed up as some of the new
facts to be derived from this remarkable voyage, as additions to our present geographical knowledge of the
Hydrography of the Colorado River:

1st. The actual location of the mouth of the San Juan,
forty miles below Green River junction, and its entrance
by a cañon continuous with that of the Colorado.

2d. From the mouth of the San Juan to the Colorado
Chiquito, three days' travel in the swiftest portion of the
current, allowing a rate of four miles per hour, for fifteen
hours, or sixty miles per day, would give an estimated distance of one hundred and eighty miles, including the
most inaccessible portion of the Great Cañon.

3d. From Colorado Chiquito to Callville, ten days'
travel was expended. As this portion of the route was
more open, and probably comprised long stretches of still
water, it would not be safe to allow a distance of more
than thirty miles per day, or three hundred miles for this

interval. Thus, the whole distance travelled would amount
to five hundred and fifty miles, or something over five
hundred miles from Grand River junction to head of
steamboat navigation at Calville [*sic*].

4th. The absence of any distinct cataract, or perpendicular falls, would seem to warrant the conclusion that in
time of high water, by proper appliances in the way of
boats, good, resolute oarsmen, and provisions secured in
water-proof bags the same passage might be safely made,
and the actual course of the river with its peculiar geological features properly determined.

5th. The construction of bridges by a single span
would be rendered difficult of execution on account of
the usual flaring shape of the upper summits; possibly,
however, points might be found where the high mases
[*sic*] come near together.

6th. The estimated average elevation of the Canon at
3,000 feet, is less than that given on the authority of Ives
and Newberry, but may be nearer the actual truth, as the
result of more continuous observation.

7th. The width of the river at its narrowest points was
estimated at 100 feet, and the line of high water mark
thirty to forty feet above the average stage in August.

8th. The long continued uniformity of the geological
formation, termed "white sandstone" (probably
Cretaceous), is remarkable, but under this term may have
been comprised some of the lower stratified formations.
The contrast, on reaching the dark igneous rocks, was so
marked that it could not fail to be noticed.

9th. Any prospect for useful navigation up or down
this cañon during the season of high water, or transportation of lumber from the upper pine regions of Green or
Grand Rivers, could not be regarded as feasible, considering the long distance and the inaccessible character of the
river margin for the greater part of its course.

10th. No other satisfactory method of exploration,
except along the course of the river, could be adopted to
determine its actual course, and peculiar natural features,
and James White, as the pioneer of this enterprise, will
probably retain the honor of being the only man who has
traversed, through its whole course, the Great Cañon of
the Colorado, and lived to recount his observations on
this perilous voyage.

The report contains two intriguing statements: "I drew from him
the following connected statement in answer to direct questions *noted*

down at the time," and "His narrative throughout bears all the evidences of entire reliablility, and is *sustained by collateral evidence*" (italics are mine). The notes do not support these observations. Critics often point to this discrepancy as evidence of falsification by Parry, but the other contemporary reports by Grandin, Kipp, and Beggs are too similar to Parry's to seriously credit such an allegation. Parry's first statement is admittedly untrue, unless he made other notes which have not turned up—unlikely but not impossible; the second may well have been true, but since White's voyage was accepted without question at the time, it probably didn't seem necessary to include the details within the report.

As for Parry's conclusions, no matter how they were formulated, they are equally intriguing:

First, the distance from the Green-Grand confluence to the San Juan is 138.5 miles, not 40, a mistake of considerable magnitude; however, the point of embarkation proposed in this book is 47.5 miles upstream of the San Juan.

Second, from the mouth of the San Juan to the Little Colorado is 140 miles, not 180; this was not a bad guess.

Third, the distance from the Green-Grand confluence to Callville is 620 miles; given Parry's precision, 120 miles seems excessive to be described as "something over five hundred miles." Moving the point of entry just under one hundred miles downstream, however, makes the five hundred remarkably close.

Fourth, concluding that the absence of cataracts or perpendicular falls meant that the river could be safely navigated with proper provisions, boats, and "resolute oarsmen" is obviously reasonable, considering that is what Major Powell did in 1869.

Fifth, concluding that bridge construction in the Grand Canyon would be difficult is also reasonable when you consider that the original Navajo Bridge across Marble Canyon, built in 1929, and the new one, built next to it seventy years later, are unique in the canyon.

Sixth, concluding that White's estimates of elevation might be nearer the actual truth than those of Ives and Newberry is, of course, nonsense; the latter gentlemen were on an official scientific exploration. White was at every moment in danger of losing his life and in no condition to be accurate about anything within the canyon, let alone the perpendicular and flaring walls. His guesses are irrelevant.

Seventh, the estimates of the narrowest river width and high water marks are reasonable, even if they were simply guesses by White.

Eighth, the description of white sandstone walls was the result of White's desperate condition and was accepted by a man who lacked the knowledge to recognize the problem. Parry's speculation of what type of rock this might be merely reveals that he, along with the rest of the world, knew nothing of the Grand Canyon's inner geology and incredible technicolor display.

Ninth, to conclude that "useful navigation" (profitable?) or "transportation of lumber" would not be feasible because of the "long distance and inaccessible character of the river margin" is reasonable. Indeed, no one transports lumber or anything else—except people—through the Grand Canyon, and Parry could hardly have foreseen today's multi-million-dollar river-running industry.

Tenth, concluding that only exploration "along the course of the river" would be satisfactory "to determine its actual course and peculiar natural features" is also entirely reasonable; as for White being the only one to make the trip, that is romantic speculation, as Major Powell was shortly to prove.

Chapter 10 Major Calhoun's Version

An astonishingly detailed account of White's journey was written by Major A. R. Calhoun and published as "Passage of the Great Canyon of the Colorado River by James White, the Prospector," the first of a series of stories that appeared in 1868 in a book called *Wonderful Adventures*. As a journalist, Calhoun would certainly have viewed the journey as good copy, but it was entirely as a "wonderful adventure" that it was presented here.

Calhoun begins with a vague description of the general region around the Colorado River and Grand Canyon as a romantic prologue for the story of James White and his raft.

> Twenty years ago the trapper and the hunter were the romantic characters of the far West. They still figure in fiction, and there is a fascination about their daring deeds which is scarcely undeserved. They have trapped on every stream and hunted on every mountain side despite the opposition of the Indian and the barrier of winter snows. They have formed the skirmish line of the great army of occupation which is daily pushing westward, and they have taught the savage to respect the white man's courage and to fear the white man's power.
> While the field for the trapper and hunter has been gradually growing less another class of adventurers has

come into existence—the prospectors in search of pre-
cious metals. Within the last quarter of a century these
men have traversed every mountain slope from the
rugged peaks of British Columbia to the rich plateaus of
Old Mexico and have searched the sands of every stream
from the Mississippi to the shores of the Pacific, stimulat-
ed by the same hope of reward that led the early
Spaniards to explore inhospitable wilds in their search for
an Eldorado. Could the varied and adventurous experiences of these searchers for gold be written we should
have a record of daring that no fiction could approach,
and the very sight of gold would suggest to our minds
some story of hairbreadth escapes.

It has fallen to the lot of one of these prospectors to
be the hero of an adventure more thrilling than any
heretofore recorded, while at the same time he has solved
a geographical problem which has long attracted the attention of the learned at home and abroad, who could but
theorize before his journey as to the length and nature of
the stupendous chasms or canyons through which the
Colorado cleaves its central course. While on the survey
before referred to and while stopping for a few days at Fort
Mojave, Dr. W. A. Bell, Dr. C. C. Parry, and myself met this
man, whose name is James White, and from his lips, the
only living man who had actually traversed its formidable
depths, we learned the story of the Great Canyon.

Calhoun's claim that he, Parry, and Bell all participated in the
interview at Hardyville was later denied by both Bell and White. Bell
was not in Hardyville at the time of the interview, and White did not
recall meeting or talking to Calhoun or anyone remotely like him.
Because of the major's obviously artificial leg, he would have been difficult to miss or forget. There were, however, several ways for Calhoun
to have obtained his information other than the January 2, 1868, interview: the *Arizona Miner*, Bill Hardy, and/or Parry's notes and survey
report. It appears that all of the dates he used were taken from either
the notes or the report; his distance estimates are either close to Parry's
or exaggerated. The *Miner* story included no specific dates and only
two estimates, which probably indicates that Calhoun did not read
William Beggs's account of the raft journey.

The account continues,

James White now lives at Callville, Arizona Territory,
the present head of navigation of the Colorado River. He

is 32 years of age, and in person is a good type of the Saxon, being of medium height and heavy build, with light hair and blue eyes. He is a man of average intelligence, simple and unassuming in his manner and address, and without any of the swagger or bravado peculiar to the majority of frontier men. Like thousands of our young men, well enough off at home, he grew weary of the slow but certain methods of earning his bread by regular employment at a stated salary. He had heard of men leaping into wealth at a single bound in the western gold fields, and for years he yearned to go to the land where fortune was so lavish of her favors. Accordingly, he readily consented to be one of a party from his neighborhood which, in the spring of 1867, started for the plains and the gold fields beyond. When they left Fort Dodge, on the Arkansas River, April 13, 1867, the party consisted of four men, of whom Capt. Baker, an old miner and an ex-officer of the Confederate Army, was the acknowledged leader. The destination of this little party was the San Juan Valley, west of the Rocky Mountains, about the gold fields of which prospectors spoke in the most extravagant terms, stating that they were deterred from working the rich placers of the San Juan only by fear of the Indians.

Baker and his companions reached Colorado City, at the foot of Pike's Peak, in safety. This place was and still is, the depot for supplying the miners who work the diggings scattered through the South Park and is the more important from being situated at the entrance to the Ute Pass, through which there is a wagon road crossing the Rocky Mountains and descending to the plateau beyond. The people of Colorado City tried to dissuade Baker from what they considered a rash project, but he was determined to carry out his original plan. These representations, however, affected one of the party so much that he left, but the others, Capt. Baker, James White, and Henry Stroll [*sic*], completed their outfit for the prospecting tour.

There are several pieces of incorrect and misleading information here. The first is age; he was not thirty-two; he had in fact turned thirty just two months after his rescue at Callville. Another is the implication that this foray into gold prospecting with Captain Baker was his first, omitting White's travels in the West over the previous six years. A third is the identification of Captain Baker as an ex-officer of the Confederate army: even today Baker's background is hazy in that regard. The most fanciful is the representation that the people of

Colorado City attempted to dissuade the party from continuing and the fourth man was so affected that he dropped out. Had Calhoun interrogated White directly, he would have produced a decidedly different account.

Calhoun continues in much the same vein:

> On the 25th of May they left Colorado City and, crossing the Rocky Mountains through the Ute Pass, entered South Park, being still on the Atlantic slope of the continent. After traveling 90 miles across the park they reached the Upper Arkansas, near the Twin Lakes. They then crossed the Snowy Range, or Sierra Madre, and descended toward the west. Turning southerly they passed around the headwaters of the Rio Grande de Norte, and after a journey of 400 miles from Colorado City they reached the Animas Branch of the San Juan River, which flows into the Great Colorado from the east.
>
> They were now in the land where their hopes centered, and to reach which they had crossed plains and mountains and forded rapid streams, leaving the nearest abodes of the white man hundreds of miles to the east. Their work of prospecting for gold began in the Animas, and though they were partially successful, the result did not by any means answer their expectations. They therefore moved still farther to the west, crossing the Dolores Branch of Grand River to the Mancos Branch of the San Juan. Following the Mancos to its mouth, they crossed to the left bank of the San Juan and began their search in the sands. There was gold there, but not in the quantity they expected; so they gradually moved west along the beautiful valley for 200 miles, when they found the San Juan disappeared between the lofty walls of a deep and gloomy canyon. To avoid this they again forded the river to the right bank and struck across rough, timbered country, directing their course toward the great Colorado. Having traveled through this rough country for a distance estimated at 50 miles they reached Grand River, being still above the junction of Green River, the united waters of which two streams form the Colorado proper.

Some of the dates and distances match Parry's, as does the designation of Grand River; however, Calhoun cannot resist the kind of embellishment that implies close personal knowledge of the prospectors' activities.

At the point where they struck the river the banks were masses of perpendicular rock, down which they could gaze at the coveted water, dashing and foaming like an agitated white band, 200 feet below. Men and animals were now suffering for water, so they pushed up the stream along the uneven edge of the chasm, hoping to find a place where they could descend to the river. After a day spent in clambering over and around the huge rocks that impeded their advance, they came to a side canyon, where a tributary joined the main stream, to which they succeeded in descending with their animals and thus obtained the water of which all stood so much in need.

The night of the 23rd of August they encamped at the bottom of the Canyon where they found plenty of fuel and grass in abundance for their animals. So they sat around the camp fire lamenting their failure in the San Juan country, and Stroll began to regret that they had undertaken the expedition. But Baker, who was a brave, sanguine fellow, spoke of placers up the river, about which he had heard, and promised his companions that all their hopes should be realized and that they should return to their homes to enjoy their gains and to laugh at the trials of the trip. So glowingly did he picture the future that his companions even speculated as to how they should spend their princely fortunes when they returned to the "States." Baker sang songs of home and hope, and the others lent their voices to the chorus till far in the night, when, unguarded, they sank to sleep to dream of coming opulence and to rise refreshed for the morrow's journey.

But the best is yet to come.

Early next morning they breakfasted and began the ascent of the side canyon up the bank opposite to that by which they had entered it. Baker was in advance, with his rifle slung at his back, gayly springing up the rocks toward the table-land above. Behind him came White and Stroll, with the mules brought up the rear. Nothing disturbed the stillness of the beautiful summer morning but the tramping of the mules and the short, heavy breathing of the climbers. They had ascended about half the distance to the top when, stopping a moment to rest, suddenly the war whoop of a band of savages rang out, sounding as if every rock had a demon's voice. Simultaneously with the first whoop a shower of arrows and bullets was poured into the little party. With the first fire Baker fell against a rock; but, rallying for a moment, he unslung his rifle and fired at the

Indians, who began to show themselves in large numbers, and then, with blood flowing from his mouth, he fell to the ground. White, firing at the Indians as he advanced, and followed by Stroll, hurried to the aid of his wounded leader. Baker with an effort turned to his comrades and in a voice still strong, said: "Back, boys; back; save yourselves; I am dying." To the credit of White and Stroll be it said they faced the savages and fought till the last tremor of the powerful frame told that the gallant Baker was dead. Then slowly they began to retreat, followed by the exultant Indians, who, stopping to strip and mutilate the dead body in their path, gave the white men a chance to secure their animals and retrace their steps into the side canyon beyond the immediate reach of the Indian's arrows.

Great drama, suitable for any adventure series, but not very accurate. Still, it has the flavor, as does most of Calhoun's narrative, of being a firsthand debriefing of the central character. The most interesting statement involves the party's ascent up the opposite bank of the side canyon; at a later date, this piece of misinformation was corrected by White when he maintained that there was no way out of this canyon except by the way they had entered; a fact suggested by White in his letter to his brother: "Wee had may up our mines to turne back." Parry's report says, "[they] started to ascend the right bank to the table-land," which indicates more than anything else that details of the Indian ambush were missing from all the early accounts, including White's. The *Miner* article makes no specific mention of it.

Calhoun continues,

Here they held a hurried conversation as to the best course they could pursue. To the east for 300 miles stretched an uninhabited country, over which if they attempted escape in that direction the Indians, like bloodhounds, would follow their track. North, south, and west was the Colorado with its tributaries, all flowing at the bottom of deep chasms, across which it would be impossible for men or animals to travel. Their deliberations were necessarily short, and resulted in their deciding to abandon their animals, first securing their arms and a small stock of provisions and the ropes off the mules. Through the side canyon they traveled due west for four hours and emerged at last on a low strip of bottom land on Grand River, above which for 2,000 feet on either bank the cold gray walls rose to block their path, leaving to them but one avenue

of escape, the foaming current of the river flowing along
the dark channel through unknown dangers.

Note that Calhoun tells us that the Colorado with its tributaries lay north, south, and west, but by traveling "due west," the men came
upon the Grand and its "foaming current." The narrative goes on to
describe the raft building; the number and dimensions of the logs agree
with Parry's notations, but then Calhoun describes their embarkation
upon "angry waters" and "amid blacking shadows" that do not appear
in anyone else's descriptions. Calhoun adds even more details:

> then, seizing the poles, they untied the rope that held the
> raft, which, tossed about by the current, rushed through
> the yawning canyon on the adventurous voyage to any
> unknown landing. Through the long night they clung to
> the raft as it dashed against half-concealed rocks or
> whirled about like a plaything in some eddy, whose white
> foam was perceptible even in the intense darkness.

He describes the following day with estimates that agree with
Parry and places the two men at the confluence of the Grand and the
Green Rivers, where he states,

> At the junction, the walls were estimated at 4,000 feet
> in height, but detached pinnacles rose 1,000 feet higher
> from amidst huge masses of detached rock confusedly
> piled, like grand monuments, to commemorate this meet-
> ing of the waters. The fugitives felt the sublimity of the
> scene, and in contemplating its stupendous and unearthly
> grandeur they forgot for the time their own sorrows.

At this point, Calhoun indicates that the men have "entered the
Grand Canyon" with its "gray sandstone walls" increasing in height.
He states that "Baker had informed his comrades as to the geography
of the country, and while floating down they remembered that
Callville was at the mouth of the Canyon, which could not be far off
. . . a few days would take them to Callville." This is an interesting
observation since Callville was only founded in 1864 and then only as
a small Mormon settlement; it was highly unlikely to have been
important enough to have filtered east to Captain Baker's attention.
    Calhoun's narrative continues, using Parry's numbers and basic
information but embellishing the story, especially the death of Strole.

After this event, he quotes White as resolving "to die hard and like a man." The next event was the whirlpool at the mouth of the Colorado Chiquito. Parry's notes state succinctly that White "prayed out" of this whirlpool; in his formal report, Parry expands this to say that White was "entangled in an eddy for two hours," quoting him as saying that he was rescued "by the direct interposition of Providence." Major Calhoun heightens the event with his usual exciting prose, ending with

> Then, for the first time, he remembered that there was a Strength greater than that of a man, a Power that "holds the ocean in the hollow of His hand." "I fell on my knees," he said, "and as the raft swept around in the current I asked God to aid me. I spoke as if from my very soul and said, 'O God, if there is a way out of this fearful place guide me to it.'"
>
> Here White's voice became husky as he narrated the circumstances, and his somewhat heavy features quivered as he related that he presently felt a different movement in the raft, and, turning to look at the whirlpool, saw it was some distance behind, and that he was floating down the smoothest current he had yet seen in the Canyon.

The remainder of the account is relatively straightforward except for the identification of the Indians at the mouth of the Virgin River as Yampais. The *Arizona Miner* article identified them as Pah-Utes and mentioned that they had given White parts of a dog to eat. Since Calhoun supplies his own Indian tribe and makes no mention of a dog (which would surely have appealed to him), it is safe to assume that he did not read that paper.

William Bell, a fellow survey member, included Calhoun's account as part of his book, *New Tracks in North America*, which he compiled and subsequently published in 1870. He made two additions to Calhoun's account. One is a description of White's physical condition when rescued, which was, surprisingly, omitted from the earlier publication. The second involves the whirlpool:

> This statement is the only information White volunteered; all the rest was obtained by close questioning. One of his friends who was present during the examination smiled when White repeated his prayer. He noticed it, and said with some feeling: "It's true, Bob, and I'm sure God took me out."

Although probably not intended, these accounts had a negative effect on the credibility of James White's story and his journey; for one thing, Calhoun insisted that he had met White in person and learned his story "from his own lips," and two, his consistent inclusion of supposedly actual quotes from White's own testimony persuaded many critics to accept Calhoun's exaggerations and vivid rhetoric as White's, giving them an excuse to call White a liar, "yarn spinner," and "monumental prevaricator," probably the only time the messenger was spared and the message vilified.

CHAPTER 11 MAJOR POWELL

The second army officer with whom James White's life would become inextricably linked was Major John Wesley Powell. In a strange series of interwoven coincidences, White and Powell each played a role in the exploration of the American West, but only one of them emerged with glory and made it into the history books.

Powell was the son of a well-educated English emigrant, a Methodist-Episcopal preacher who named his firstborn John Wesley as a rather broad hint that he was expected to walk in his father's footsteps. He received a good education at home and at whatever frontier schools presented themselves during the family's frequent moves.

As the time approached for college, it became clear that young Wes preferred science to religion; when he declined to follow the religious path, he found himself financially on his own. He taught in several different schools and broadened his education in the natural sciences through reading. With his brother-in-law's assistance, he finally entered Wheaton College and later Oberlin. When the Civil War erupted, he enlisted as a private but was soon promoted to lieutenant, largely because of his education; at Shiloh he lost his right arm to a minié ball and, after a long recuperation, returned as a captain of artillery and was honorably discharged as a major in September of 1864.

The Powell family had followed the Erie Canal immigration trail during the same years that the White family had lived in Rome, New York. Powell was born in nearby Castile, and both men in their youth resided in the same corner of Wisconsin in the 1840s, another set of coincidences. They could not, however, have been further apart in every other way.

By November of 1866, Major Powell was a professor at Illinois Normal University and the secretary of the Illinois Natural History Society. He was selected by both Normal and Wesleyan Universities to lobby the Illinois legislature on behalf of the society for funding for a natural history museum. He went to Springfield on three occasions that winter, and in his final proposal, he told the legislators,

> In order that the Society may carry out its purposes, it should have a general commissioner and curator, who can give his whole time to the work of the society; and whose duty it would be to superintend the researches and collections, take charge of the museum, carry on the exchanges, and make the distributions.

By February 26, 1867, the state's house and senate had passed a bill incorporating Powell's exact words; on March 26, 1867, Professor Powell was appointed curator of the new museum by the Illinois Board of Education.

Powell now turned his attention to a natural history expedition into the Rocky Mountains, which he had organized and set for that summer. Between March and June, he went hunting for the necessary funds: to Washington to obtain rations and an army escort through the good offices of his old commander, General Grant; to the various railroads for free transportation for his group and his expected specimens; to the Smithsonian for the loan of a few of their scientific instruments; and to several scientific institutions for additional support, preferably cash.

By October 1867, Powell had successfully completed his field trip along the front range of the Rockies. He had climbed Pike's Peak, proving conclusively that the amputation of his right arm was no impediment to physical achievement. His guides were Jack Sumner, O. G. Howland, Billy Hawkins, and Bill Dunn, all experienced men and all shortly to become well-known names in Colorado River and Grand Canyon history.

Powell's original plan for this summer of 1867 had included travel through the Dakotas. He had been promised a military escort from Fort Laramie through the Badlands, but General Sherman advised against stirring up the Sioux and recommended the southern route into the Rocky Mountains instead. Any disappointment Powell might have felt about this change soon vanished; he was fast becoming enchanted with this part of the country and its splendid possibilities.

The success of this trip encouraged him to make more ambitious plans for the following summer. In organizing this first trip, he had learned several lessons, especially about getting support for an expedition. In short he had learned the value of lobbying.

William Byers, editor of the *Rocky Mountain News,* had earlier proposed that Powell use his brother-in-law, Jack Sumner, as a guide and thus had both a personal and professional interest in the major's activities. When, in a lecture on November 4, 1867, Powell announced his next summer's goal was the Grand River, Byers's newspaper published the major's plans in its November 6, 1867, issue. Powell's biographer records that "Powell spent the winter of 1867–1868 making preparations for a more ambitious expedition to culminate in a passage of the Grand River to its junction with the Colorado."

In March 1868, Powell traveled to Washington to ask General Grant for army rations but for an expedition to a new destination. Grant told him to put his request in writing, and on April 2, 1868, Powell wrote him the following letter:

> GENERAL: A party of naturalists, under the auspices of the State Normal University of Illinois, wish to make a scientific survey of the *Colorado River of the West.* This work is to be a continuation of work done last year in north, middle, and south parks.
>
> It is hoped that a survey of that river can be made from its source to the point where the survey made by Lieutenant Ives was stopped.
>
> In addition to the general scientific survey a topographical survey of the region visited will be made. The services of two civil engineers have been secured for this purpose.
>
> I most respectfully request that the proper officers be instructed to issue rations to this party to consist of not more than twenty-five persons.
>
> I need not urge upon your attention the importance of the general scientific survey to the increase of knowledge. It

is believed that the grand cañon of the Colorado will give
the best geological section on the continent.

Nor is it necessary to plead the value to the War
Department of a topographical survey of that wonderful
region, inhabited as it is by powerful tribes of Indians, that
will doubtless become hostile as the prospector and the
pioneer encroach upon their hunting grounds.

You will also observe that the aid asked of the
Government is trivial in comparison with what such expeditions have usually cost it. The usual appropriation for
such an exploration has been many thousands of dollars.

Invoking your favorable consideration of this request,
I am, with great respect, your obedient servant[.]

This letter reveals Powell's new plan. He does not indicate why
his goal has changed from "passage to the Grand River to its junction
with the Colorado" to "a scientific survey of the Colorado River from
its source to the point where the survey made by Lieutenant Ives survey was stopped"—in other words, the Grand Canyon.

As in so many similar instances, Major Powell left no written
record which specifically revealed his knowledge of Parry's report, but
there is evidence to indicate that the major was well aware of White
and his journey when he wrote his letter to General Grant. Parry's
report, dated January 6, 1868, was presented by Dr. George Engleman
on February 17, 1868, at a meeting of the organization variously
referred to as the St. Louis Academy of Science, the St. Louis Academy
of Natural Science, and the Academy of Science of St. Louis. St. Louis
is about two hundred miles from Powell's home in Normal, Illinois;
the St. Louis Academy of Science is a next-door neighbor to the
Illinois Natural Science Society. Professor Powell, as secretary of the
society and also curator of its museum, was, in his own words, charged
with the responsibility to "carry on the exchanges," which must have
included fellow institutions.

Given Powell's compelling interest in the subject, it is more logical to give him credit for knowing about Parry's report than insult
him by assuming that he remained ignorant of it. Also his activities in
the immediate wake of the report certainly seem to confirm such
knowledge.

Once the April 1868 letter to General Grant had been written,
Powell dusted off his lobbying skills and proceeded to line up support

from his Illinois congressional members, Rep. Shelby Cullom and Sen. Lyman Trumbull, to obtain the required legislative approval for federal assistance. On April 15, Cullom introduced House Resolution 251, which called for the authorization by the secretary of war to furnish supplies for Powell's endeavor. The House, sitting as a Committee of the Whole, passed the resolution and sent it on to the Senate. There was, however, a delay of nearly six weeks during which the Senate conducted its momentous impeachment trial of President Andrew Johnson. At the end of the trial, this exhausted body took a nine-day breather before resuming more mundane deliberations. In the meantime, the usual behind-the-scenes activity led to the enlistment of new supporters. One of them was Representative Garfield, whom the sponsors hoped might put in a good word with his Ohio colleague, Senator Sherman, a member of the all-important Senate Appropriations Committee.

The Powell resolution came to the Senate floor on May 25. The *Congressional Globe*, forerunner of the *Congressional Record*, covered the proceedings. For some reason, it was Senator Wilson of Massachusetts who introduced HR 251. Vermont Senator Edmunds immediately interrupted to ask who Professor Powell was, and Wilson supplied a brief sketch but admitted to being personally unacquainted with Powell. Edmunds went on to object at length to the expenditure of government funds for an apparently private expedition but finally said, "I turn it over to my friend from Ohio, who knows whether we can afford it."

Senator Sherman, Edmunds's friend from Ohio, obliged by bemoaning the expense, in general, of government-funded surveys and explorations in the West and then stated, "The eastern division of the Pacific railroad, as it is called, is now engaged in exploring its route under a very competent man, General Palmer, from Santa Fe or Albuquerque, westward. These surveys cannot be of any service to it."

Senator Trumbull of Illinois now rose for the first time and, without referring to Sherman's statement, began to describe Professor Powell and his 1867 explorations in Colorado. His final words led to the following interesting exchange:

> MR. TRUMBULL (Illinois): He [Professor Powell] proposes this year to survey the Colorado River. The Colorado river, as laid down upon our maps, for some six or seven hundred miles has never been seen by a civilized man.

MR. SHERMAN (Ohio): It was run recently, during
the last fall, I believe, by three men to escape the Indians
and one of them got through alive.
MR. TRUMBULL: The whole distance?
MR. SHERMAN: Yes, to the Great Cañon.
MR. TRUMBULL: I was not aware of it. Is that
authenticated?
MR. SHERMAN: Yes, the man lives. He went in at one
end and came through at the other.

Trumbull made no further response and resumed his disserta-
tion on Powell as though Sherman had never interrupted. This strongly suggests that Trumbull may well have been hearing about these
"three men" for the first time.

But while Trumbull remained silent on the subject, his ally from
California promptly emphasized the point:

MR. CONNESS (California): I had some conversation
with General Palmer on the subject and he furnished me
with an article contributed to a magazine, giving an
account of what is known of the Colorado river, of the
upper part of it, and also an account of the progress of
the three men spoken of through a portion of the cañon
of the river.

Since this information had reached Sherman and Conness, it
seems certain that Powell knew it as well, which makes Trumbull's
apparent ignorance of the report somewhat puzzling.

After a sharp exchange between Senators Conness and Howe,
Trumbull rather brusquely interrupted to state that he had "communications which will explain very fully this whole transaction if Senators
will pay attention." He then read into the record Powell's letter to Grant
with the General's endorsement; the report of the commissary general,
subsistance, to the secretary of war; and a letter from Professor Henry
of the Smithsonian Institution. The debate ended with the usual fiscal
concerns. In this regard, it is tempting to speculate that the references
to General Palmer and "the progress of the three men ... through a portion of the cañon of the river" may have helped reassure the penny-
pinchers in that august body that they were not risking taxpayers'
money on a first-time, hopelessly dangerous, or even impossible project. At any rate, with twenty-five "Yeas," including Trumbull, Conness,

and Wilson, seven "Nays" including the redoubtable Sherman, and twenty-two absent, the senators voted Powell his assistance. Powell later rewarded Trumbull by naming a mountain after him.

In August 1868, Powell was back in Middle Park in the Colorado Rockies, where he met Samuel Bowles, later the author of two books about his travels in the West: *The Switzerland of America* and *Our New West*. Bowles describes the major's upcoming expedition and James White's 1867 journey in almost the same breath. He refers to White's trip as "a fact that calls keenly for further exploration and description" and then mentions Powell's long-range plans. Curiously, however, Bowles comments, "before even this experience was known, Professsor Powell . . . had secured government assistance in a personal plan for exploring the Parks and Mountains of Colorado, and then going down the Canyon of the Colorado." Bowles could only have received this information from Powell himself, and there is no suggestion that Bowles had surprised Powell with news of White's "experience." His comments, coupled with the evidence from the *Congressional Globe,* appear in fact to confirm Powell's determination to promote the idea that he had for many years considered the Grand Canyon his goal, not the "passage of the Grand River to its junction with the Colorado" noted in the *Rocky Mountain News* of November 6, 1867, and confirmed by Powell's biographer, William Culp Darrah, in *Powell of the Colorado.*

Some historians and river runners believe that Powell's change of plans was Jack Sumner's idea. But while the possibility of exploring the Colorado River through the Grand Canyon might have been in many minds, the fact remains that until White's journey in 1867 became known, no one, including Powell, attempted it.

CHAPTER 12   ON THE ROAD AGAIN

Ⅰn the spring of 1868, many of the young men of the Colorado River community began to set their sights on new and distant goals. In Callville Jim Ferry was the first; he sold his mail contract to Jim Hinton and headed for California. Hinton lasted only a few months before he, too, wanted out. Rumors of gold strikes up north in Sweetwater, spread by Adam Simon's ex-army friend, Jeff Stanford, lured Simon and Hinton into the search for the yellow metal. Even James White was willing to give it another try. There were placer diggings nearby, but plenty of prospectors were filling up this local landscape, including soldiers from Fort Mohave and even the stalwart Captain L. C. Wilburn; it was getting too crowded. Sweetwater seemed to offer less competition; apparently it did not occur to them to wonder why.

By mid-May, the three men were in St. George, buying prospecting gear; for White it must have been a case of deja vu. What turned out to be even more so was learning, halfway to their destination, that Sweetwater was a bust. Stanford turned west; the others kept going north.

Along the way, they heard about the Union Pacific Railroad—it was big news in that territory. Their savings were dwindling along with their prospects, and this mammoth enterprise offered a choice of work. As they neared Salt Lake City, they discovered what it was: railbed grading (about which they knew nothing) or cutting and dressing railroad ties (about which they needed to know nothing). By the time they reached Ogden, they agreed that one of them should contract with the Union Pacific to cut ties; White was elected and lined up jobs to the north around Bear River.

It was backbreaking work and lasted through the summer. Decision time came when the roadbed moved farther west. By then they had accumulated some money and were sick of cutting ties. Hinton moved on to California; Simon bought White's mule and went even further north to Montana; White stayed on as a Union Pacific wagon boss. Later, he drifted to Corinne, Utah, on the Bear River, where he bought a saloon.

The town of Corinne was like one big camp and, except that it was flat instead of hilly, may have reminded White of Virginia City. But where that crazy town had existed for silver mines, this one was dedicated to trains. The "buildings" were mostly box tents—flimsy wood frames, with or without plank flooring, to which canvas walls were nailed; his saloon was probably indistinguishable from the rest. But he soon found that the saloon business was worse than cutting ties and running wagons. In mid-November, he put it up for sale and gladly took what he could get from the first buyer to appear. It was nearly Christmas, and White was restless, possibly homesick. He headed east.

In the intervening seven years, Kenosha, Wisconsin, had changed, but the lake and the snow and his parents' home had not. His father had died in 1865, but his seventy-five-year-old mother was in good health and living with his brother Josh, Josh's wife, Margaret, and their sister Jane in the family home. His family was eager to hear what had happened to him through the years. His 1867 letter had given them some idea of his adventure, and they had more or less filled in the blanks by reading the account in the October 1 issue of the *Kenosha Telegraph,* which began,

> Interesting Narrative of the Adventures of a former resi-
> dent of Kenosha through the Great Cañon of the
> Colorado of the West . . . Mr. J. D. Perry Esq., President of
> the Union Pacific Railway, has furnished the following nar-
> rative of explorations, in a hitherto unexplored region,
> for the St. Louis Academy of Natural Science.

Figure 5.
James White with Joshua White and wife, 1869
(Photo courtesy of the White family)

This was Parry's report, and James had little to add to it. But, because they were family, they wanted to hear all the details.

So White attempted to tell them about the chaotic town of Denver, the crazy days of Cripple Creek, the weeks on the trail, the freezing cold of Virginia City, the raid on Mulberry Creek, and the burning heat and desolation of the western desert; needless to say, his brief mention of the army did not include the court martial. He had traveled over much of the vast country: from Kenosha to Denver; to Virginia City; to Sacramento, San Diego, Yuma, Tucson; to Texas and New Mexico. He told them about Eureka Gulch, Baker's Park, the San Juan, and—probably with more vagueness than the *Kenosha Telegraph*—the raft, the muddy Colorado, and the rescue at Callville.

The article which appeared in the *Kenosha Telegraph* was one of a second round of accounts keeping White's raft voyage fresh in people's minds, most of them based on Dr. Parry's report. The first was written in February 1868 by none other than Parry himself for the *Weekly Gazette* of Davenport, Iowa; others then cropped up sporadically in newspapers and periodicals across the West, Midwest, and East—notably *Lippincott's Magazine,* the *Rocky Mountain Herald,* the *Chicago Tribune,* the *Daily Pantagraph,* the *Rocky Mountain News,* and the *New York Sun.* Except for the article shown to him by his family, White was unaware of these publications. He would be an old man before even a few of them were brought to his attention.

One small mystery is how James White's 1867 letter to Josh ended up in the possession of Dr. Parry. Only one possibility makes sense: Parry, leaving no stone unturned, must have asked White whether he had written anything about his trip. When White acknowledged the letter, Parry probably asked if he could have it to complete his survey report, and White, thinking Parry was General Palmer, agreed. Josh duly sent the letter to Parry. Whatever the scenario, it ended up in Parry's files.

White's devotion to his family did not include remaining in Kenosha. In the spring of 1869, he was once again on his way west; the rough familiarity of the western territories and Barlow and Sanderson's stagecoaches beckoned. By late that summer, White had settled into a much quieter job than driving stage: tending stock and coaches at Barlow and Sanderson's Half Mile Station on the Arkansas River near Bent's Fort in Colorado Territory, still on his old stamping ground, the Santa Fe Trail.

On August 9, he had visitors. General William Palmer was on his way from Colorado Springs to Fort Lyon and Sheridan along with a friend, Mr. Carr. Learning from their driver that White was at Half Mile Station, the general was determined to stop and meet the prospector who had run the mighty Colorado River and Grand Canyon. Palmer was already a believer in White's voyage, but having missed him in Hardyville, he wished to meet White directly. White, who always believed it was Palmer who had interviewed him there, was pleased to see the general for what he thought was a second time. We can only conclude that either Parry bore a surface resemblance to

Palmer or White had a bad memory for faces because he persisted in
his mistake for the rest of his life. He, Palmer, Carr, and the coach driver had a sort of picnic at the station.

When the general was once again on the road, he wrote a letter to his fiancée, Queen Mellen, about the meeting.

<blockquote>

On the coach between Ft. Lyon and Sheridan
August 9th/69

My darling Queen
When Mr. Carr and I reached Bent's Fort on the
Arkansas yesterday, we found unexpectedly that there was
no coach to Sheridan until Monday morning—so we
stopped at the Fort all night—took a delightful and
refreshing bath in the Arkansas River the next morning,
and after breakfast got the stage people to drive us down
in a buggy to Fort Lyon (18 miles). —It was a very warm
day, but that pleasant breeze which so constantly blows
across the plains, cheered us and made the ride of three
hours as delightful as we could have wished. —On the way
we stopped at a stage station known as "1/2 mile Point",
where we had an interview of three hours with a very
remarkable character. I do not know that you have ever
heard me tell of James White—the man who came
through the Colorado Canon alone on a raft just two years
ago. —and whom our surveying party met in Arizona
shortly after—when we learned his story—The account he
gave was so wonderful and dramatic that very few people
in the United States have ever believed the story or the
fact that he ever really traversed this terrible cañon—four
hundred miles of journey at the bottom of a trough of
rock, from 20 to 30 times as deep as Niagara is high and
with walls nearly precipitous and affording no outlet for
nearly two weeks as he sailed on a raft of rude logs tied
together with lariats. —I did not get to see White in
Arizona, so I was very glad to have the opportunity of
meeting him here—where I could ask him questions to
my heart's desire and satisfy myself from his replies and
manner as to whether or not the perilous journey on
which Powell has since set out had actually been made
alone by this man. —I cannot of course tell you his story
by letter, but I will, sometime when it will not have so far
to travel—there were many interesting points brought out
as we sat on the sill of the stable for which he was acting as
stocktender—matters that have never been referred to
before, and very likely that it had never occurred to him
to mention before. Suffice it to say that from his entire

</blockquote>

appearance and manner and his prompt, spontaneous way
of replying to sudden questions, Mr. Carr and I came to
the conclusion that without doubt this man was telling us
the truth. Then there was outside confirmatory evidence
in the fact that our driver knew him when he left the valley of the Arkansas where he was driving coach in
March/67 . . . and three frontiersmen . . . picked him up
in a starved almost insane condition at Colville [*sic*] in the
following August after he had completed the strange passage, with no clothing on him but a coat and shirt, the
rest of his body being one mass of blister, from the scorch-
ing rays of the sun . . . and from the buffeting of the water
in "running the rapids" . . . sometimes there were dozens
of these rapids to "run" in a single day . . . . There were
four of them in the little party that started in the Spring
from Fort Dodge—one was killed by Indians, one was
drowned from the raft in descending the cañon. —The
fourth I had never heard accounted for, and had often
wondered why White had never referred to him. One gentleman in my presence threw doubts upon the whole
story, because this last individual was never accounted
for—I availed myself of this opportunity to ask White the
question direct—"What became of the fourth man". He
hesitated a moment and then said "I shot him" —It was in
a quarrel on the Arkansas in which he said the other had
given the first and repeated provocation. This accounted
for his never having mentioned him before.

An account of the shooting turned up in a letter written to
James White in 1916 by T. J. Ehrhart, then chairman of the Colorado
State Highway Commission. Ehrhart was a young boy in 1867 when
his family was living at Brown's Creek; the curious T. J. was an eyewitness and in this letter described the shooting. Ehrhart apparently did
not know who the shooter was. He said he later learned of the
prospecting party's disaster and of White's survival and when, in 1916,
he saw a newspaper article stating that White was living in Trinidad, he
"wrote Mr. White something about my impressions concerning the
party while camped in the old schoolhouse on Browns Creek, to
which Mr. White replied, proving to me, without question of doubt,
that Mr. White was a member of this party."

Critics have suggested that the shooting proves White had a
violent temper and that he, not Indians, killed Baker and Strole. It is
true that White never mentioned Joe Goodfellow in his first talks with

Ferry and Wilburn; the Grandin and Kipp letters and the Beggs article, all based on what these two men related, list White, Baker, and
Strole as the only members of the prospecting party; Parry's account
reports four men but lets the fourth disappear without further mention. In 1917, with Ehrhart's letter in hand and the shooting confirmed
(but the shooter still unidentified), White stated only that Goodfellow
had been shot and left behind at a farmhouse. Rather than assigning a
sinister motive to White's failure to mention his role in the shooting,
it seems likely that he was following his usual path: offer little information, answer only what is asked, and stick to the truth. Had he been
attempting to hide the episode, White could easily have made
Goodfellow vanish altogether simply by never mentioning a fourth
man to Parry at all.

The general, having mentioned earlier in his letter "the perilous
journey on which Powell has since set out," now told Miss Mellen,

> White said that Professor Powell had endeavored to see
> him before starting on his expedition this Spring, to
> induce him to go along—but they had failed to meet. He
> said he would have gone willingly—and would have gone
> again through the cañon, as he thought from his experi-
> ence he could make the trip safely,—he was just the kind
> of adventurous man that I know would have hailed such a
> renewal of danger with delight.

General Palmer's Civil War experience as the commander of a
difficult and rebellious cavalry unit had shown him to be an able judge
of men. His previous acceptance of White's journey had rested largely
on his confidence in Parry's opinion; this face-to-face meeting convinced him that White "was the very opposite in every way of a man
who would either think of, or be able to concoct, such a story out of
whole cloth." He accepted White's statement about Powell and his
expedition without question. How and where White acquired this
knowledge, Palmer apparently did not think it important to inquire—
although one might wish that he had.

CHAPTER 13   POWELL'S CONQUEST OF THE GRAND CANYON

The paramount message of James White's 1867 voyage was that *there were no insurmountable obstacles in the Grand Canyon to bar exploration.* Did Major Powell believe it? He certainly had no specific knowledge to weigh against it and no evidence to prove it false. Even if he had been skeptical or suspicious, the very nature and scope of the publicity given to White's journey meant that it was perceived as fact, which in itself was powerful enough to make another attempt at the canyon inevitable. It was, after all, the age of exploration and adventure, and there were undoubtedly many who were eager to try. It was highly fortuitous that Powell's earlier activities and his preparations for an assault on the Grand River, coupled with his curatorship of the Illinois Natural History Society, placed him in a perfect position to make the rapid shift to exploring the Grand Canyon.

Despite Powell's silence on any knowledge of White's journey, diaries kept by two of his expedition members while actually on the river in 1869 point to the inescapable conclusion that Powell claimed not only to have known about White but to have had a face-to-face meeting with him, passing the raft story on to the team as firsthand information. Jack Sumner's entry for August 13, 1869 (after a particularly nasty rapid) says, "How anyone can ride that on a raft is more than I can see. Mr. White may have done so but I can't believe it." George Bradley's August 10 entry reads, "This point has not been determined though it is said a man went through from here on a raft to Callville in eleven days. If so we have little to fear from waterfalls below . . . his story has been published with much show of reason and Major has seen the man." Since neither Sumner nor Bradley ever claimed acquaintance with White, where else could their information have come from except Powell?

William Culp Darrah, in his biography *Powell of the Colorado,* states, "The Major sought out James White, who, it had been reported, came through the canyons from the San Juan River to Callville on a raft in eleven days, but the fellow's simple story seemed too vague to credit." This claim of a meeting probably came from the Sumner and Bradley diaries, which Darrah had edited for publication, but it is hardly convincing evidence that such a meeting ever took place. Where the offhand dismissal of White's story came from is anyone's guess.

While Sumner and Bradley were making their notes, General Palmer was hearing a different story from White.

Whatever else these vague statements do, they fail to explain where or when White learned about Powell or whether these men had any opportunity to meet. Of course, one can always come up with a logical, if not provable, possibility. Like the fortuitous coincidence that placed James White, General Palmer, Dr. Parry, and Major Calhoun together in the vicinity of Hardyville in the fall and winter of 1867 and led to Parry's interview, it is possible that in the spring of 1869, White was in the vicinity of Green River City, Wyoming, the starting point for Powell's expedition.

The preparations there during 1869 must have made the expedition a lively topic of conversation in that remote and sparsely populated area. White, after visiting his home in Kenosha in January 1869, returned to the West that spring. Because he had worked for the Union Pacific Railroad in Utah for several months in 1868, it is not unreasonable to assume that he had a pass for the train. The trains stopped at Green River City, where, in those early days, passengers had their meals at the station. These were typically friendly occasions for exchanging news. What would have been more newsworthy than the forthcoming Grand Canyon expedition? What would have been more natural than for White, hearing about Powell, to offer his own Grand Canyon story? This proximity of time and place suggests a reasonable hypothesis, but like so many other questions about White and Powell, it is simply a tantalizing guess.

Powell's Grand Canyon expedition began at Green River City on May 24, 1869, with four stout boats and ten strong, adventurous men. The descriptions of the team and its equipment might prompt a wild speculation that Powell had adopted Parry's fourth conclusion: "In time of high water, by proper appliances in the way of boats, good, resolute oarsmen, and provisions secured in water-proof bags the same passage might be safely made, and the actual course of the river with its peculiar geological features properly determined."

By July 21, 1869, the expedition had passed the confluence of the Green and Grand Rivers and entered Cataract Canyon. The team members found the beauty of this canyonland awe-inspiring but soon viewed the Colorado River with less exalted emotions.

That morning the rapids forced them to portage their boats along the slender strip of sand that edged the river. In the afternoon, Powell, in the *Emma Dean,* decided to run a rapid; however, the boat was soon swamped and overturned, dumping the three men into the turbulent river. The rest of the team landed their craft above the rapid and made a safe portage. The crew of the *Emma Dean*—Jack Sumner, Bill Dunn, and the major—wet but unharmed, managed to get their boat ashore, undamaged except for the loss of its oars and some equipment. They might have shrugged this mishap off, but they had already lost one of their boats back on the Green and could not afford to lose another. More to the point, this part of the Colorado River, where Parry's report had placed White and Strole on their raft, was supposed to be smooth sailing. These terrible and furious rapids must have been quite a shock to the expedition and obviously destroyed whatever credence these men had given White's journey up to then.

A month later, the explorers had apparently become even more cynical. Darrah tells us that "the men took turns ridiculing the story of Mr. White and his raft. Assuredly he had not gone through this place." After all, Powell's expedition had been one long, terrifying ordeal; it had survived near catastrophe; the men were exhausted by physical exertion, sick to death of the dismal diet of coffee, spoiled flour, and dried apples, and irritable from the alternate soaking in the silty water and steaming in the blazing sun.

On August 28, the Howland brothers and Bill Dunn left the river at Separation Rapid. They climbed to the plateau above—just a few miles short of the end of the Grand Canyon—and were killed, supposedly by Shivwits Indians. The rest completed the short distance to the end of the Grand Canyon at Grand Wash Cliffs. Powell and his brother left the expedition at the mouth of the Virgin River; Jack Sumner, Andy Hall, Billy Hawkins, and George Bradley continued downriver, stopping at Hardyville, the first town after the Virgin River—a visit recalled by Bill Hardy. Considering Hardy's proprietary interest in White, he might even have treated them to his version of the story. Two of the men left the river at Yuma, and the other two continued to the head of the Gulf of California.

When Powell arrived in Salt Lake City on September 15, the press was waiting to cover his successful Grand Canyon expedition. That same day the official report that O. G. and Seneca Howland and Bill Dunn had been killed by Shivwits Indians was relayed to Powell. His statement regarding this tragedy was carried within days by the Cheyenne *Leader* and the *Chicago Tribune*, as was another intriguing news item. In what was possibly the first indication of Powell's post-expedition attitude toward James White and his raft journey, this September 16 article stated, "Colonel [*sic*] Powell pronounces the reported adventures of the man White, who furnished the data for the article in *Lippincott's Magazine*, on the Grand Canyon of the Colorado, a complete fiction."

Powell left shortly thereafter for home and on the way found himself involved in another one of the remarkable coincidences that seemed to dog this odd, triangular association. He met by chance with none other than General Palmer. In a letter written some years later in response to a request by a Colonel Robert C. Clowry for information on James White's raft journey, Palmer wrote, "It gives me great pleasure to send you a copy of my report of the survey made for the Kansas Pacific Railroad, across the Continent in 1867." After a short description of White's journey and rescue, the general continued,

That adventure was in the autumn of 1867. Some two or
three years later I was going from Denver to the East, by
way of Cheyenne, when I met on the Union Pacific
Railway, coming home from his exploration of the Grand
Canon, Major Powell, with whom I had a long talk.

Palmer and Powell had not met before this time, although they
possessed some knowledge of each other's Union Army activities and
reputations during the Civil War. Powell was doubtless aware of
Palmer's survey sponsorship of Parry's report on James White, and
Palmer clearly had great interest in Powell's Grand Canyon expedition.
But one can guess that Powell found this "long talk" with Palmer something of a mixed blessing. Questions posed by anyone else might have
been summarily dismissed, but it was only four years since the end of
America's devastating Civil War, and even officers who were not career
army were careful to maintain the rigid rank-conscious deference of
majors to generals. Powell was no exception. He was diplomatic and
respectful, but he was clearly determined to deny White's voyage.

Palmer's letter continued,

I found [Powell] to be disposed to be quite incredu-
lous with regards to White's adventure, saying that it was
as much as he could do with his large party, ropes, boats,
and all the assistance of the U. S. Government to make
the passage of that Cañon safely, and it was simply impossible for a man, lashed to a raft, to have done so. I replied,
"Major, I have a copy, fortunately, of my report of the
Kansas Pacific Surveys . . . in my satchel. White mentions a
great many detailed circumstances. You have certainly
been through the Cañon, and he says he has been
through, so there is a good opportunity for you to check
these statements, many of which are of a nature not at all
likely to be invented or imagined by an illiterate man,
such as White". I then went over the report, sentence by
sentence, and as anything was stated as facts, or approximate facts, I appealed to know if that was right. For
instance I said, "Now, Major, here he says, 'The walls
seemed to be at times three to four thousand feet high.'
"Well, said the Major, they are higher than that at places."
"And the river seems to be 200 feet wide in such
places",—he said, "That is about right". I said "he speaks
about a certain white sandstone that prevails in certain
places".—"Correct", said Powell. "And he speaks of the
high water mark made by the river as approximately 30 to

40 feet above the stream". Powell said, "This is about
right" and so forth. The result was that if I had any doubt
before I was absolutely convinced now not only that White
had traversed the Cañon, but also of the substantial accuracy of his report. Major Powell, however, would not give
in, and still claimed that he had been the first man to
have made that wonderful and perilous passage.

Just one month before this, Palmer's meeting with White had
strengthened his belief in the man himself. His statement, "if I had any
doubt before I was absolutely convinced now not only that White had
traversed the Cañon, but also of the substantial accuracy of his report,"
was clear evidence of Palmer's careful evaluation of all available aspects
of the story. He concluded the letter with "I am therefore as fully persuaded that White did, in 1867, pass through that Grand Cañon on a
raft, as I am that Columbus ever crossed the Atlantic."

This letter seems to confirm Powell's intent, beginning with his
statement on the *Lippincott's* article, to exploit his fame not only as an
eminent explorer but as the first to conquer the Grand Canyon, despite
the fact that all publications at that time were giving James White this
honor. Once Powell had brought his own expedition to its successful
conclusion, however, he could not help but realize that the circumstances
of White's voyage—he was an uneducated prospector, the sole survivor
of an escape from hostile Indians on a flimsy log raft—might easily ren-
der early accounts of his trip suspect. After all, the Cataract Canyon rapids
pointed to a glaring flaw in Parry's report and, by inference, cast doubt
on White's entire journey. This, of course, is exactly what happened.

Powell went on to make public appearances in Detroit,
Cincinnati, Chicago, Bloomington, and points east. Heavily supported
by the press, his colorful names for Grand Canyon landmarks, like
Bright Angel and Dirty Devil, were widely quoted. He used all this
publicity to good advantage.

In 1871, the major embarked on a second Grand Canyon expedition but considered it merely a routine surveying and mapping effort.
It began at the same place and on nearly the same date as the 1869
expedition, but the major spent a great deal of time exploring the surrounding country, which stretched this expedition into a second year.

Early in 1872, Powell left the team on the river and went to
Washington, D.C., to raise money for future scientific endeavors. He

rejoined his expedition in August and spent one month with the men before they all left the river at Kanab Creek, well shy of completing a Grand Canyon transit.

In 1875, he published his account of his expeditions. An examination of this report, titled *Exploration of the Colorado River of the West and Its Tributaries Explored in 1869, 1870, 1871 and 1872 Under the Direction of the Secretary of the Smithsonian Institution,* reveals several inexplicable discrepancies. Although the report's title includes Powell's second expedition, he did not refer to it directly; other than casual praise for a land trip to the mouth of the Dirty Devil River made by A. H. Thompson, he did not even identify the team members. Instead, he credited information which was acquired in 1871–72 to the 1869 expedition and combined portions of his own diary with parts of Jack Sumner's diary and several letters written to the *Chicago Tribune.* All this is evidence of selective editing.

Excerpts from what he claimed was his original 1869 diary contain statements like "We are now ready to start on our way down the Great Unknown . . . we have . . . an unknown river yet to explore . . . what falls there are, we know not; what rocks beset the channel, we know not; what walls rise over the river, we know not. . . . Ah, well! we may conjecture many things." These phrases create the impression that he had never heard of James White or Dr. Parry. While still on the river in 1869, Powell had probably discarded the raft story, maybe considering that he had good reason to do so. By 1875, he was sufficiently sure of his preeminence in the Grand Canyon to make statements like this without any fear of contradiction.

Without denigrating the purpose served by this document, an objective analysis reveals it as an extensively edited work containing many self-serving statements, errors, and misdirections.

In 1878–79, Powell became heavily involved in the creation of the United States Geological Survey (USGS), as well as the Bureau of American Ethnology; not surprisingly, he was appointed director of both organizations. He continued to achieve political importance throughout the closing years of the nineteenth century, steadily acquiring power in government and scientific circles. His most ambitious goal, founding the Bureau of Reclamation, was realized just before his death in 1902.

In 1917, an enormous bronze plaque was erected at Grand Canyon for his achievement of 1869. And in 1964, as an even grander monument to him, the huge reservoir rising behind Glen Canyon Dam was named Lake Powell.

While Powell did not commit himself in print on the subject of James White, it is undeniable that his opinions and accusations were liberally voiced to others who were not reticent about quoting them for publication. Such surrogate allegations were presented to the public not only through the writings of his loyal supporters but by those who were not even Powell admirers. These quotes began with the September 16, 1869, article in the *Chicago Tribune* and continued well into the twentieth century.

Of course, Jack Sumner and George Bradley echoed Powell's opinions about White since they had, after all, endured the perils of Powell's first expedition, but, except for their diaries and a few letters, these men did not pursue the issue. Not so Frederick S. Dellenbaugh, one of the most persistently vocal of James White's attackers.

Dellenbaugh was a distant relative of Powell's brother-in-law, Almon Thompson. He joined the 1871–72 expedition, where, at the tender age of seventeen, he developed an adolescent case of Powell hero worship, from which it is said that he never recovered. In 1902, Dellenbaugh's book *Romance of the Colorado River* was published. In Chapter VII, which he called "James White's Masterful Fabrication," he wrote,

> Had I the space I would give here the whole of White's
> story, for it is one of the best bits of fiction I have ever
> read. He had obtained somehow a general smattering of
> the character of the river, but as there were trappers still
> living, Kit Carson, for example, who possessed a great deal
> of information about it, this was not a difficult matter. The
> many discrepancies brand the whole story as fabrication. I
> doubt if any have been more picturesque than this cham-
> pion prevaricator . . . he had related a splendid yarn.
> What it was intended to obscure would probably be quite
> as interesting as what he told.

It is highly unlikely that Dellenbaugh's virulent opinions were anything other than a reflection of Powell's, fanned and probably exaggerated by his early admiration of the major. It certainly appears that his unsubstantiated suggestion that White was crooked in some way led to the vaguely generalized assumption that White was the villain in the Goodfellow shooting and therefore probably responsible for the deaths of Baker and Strole as well.

Dellenbaugh's obsessive determination to purge White from Grand Canyon history is evident in his view of Powell's "meeting" with James White, contained in a 1917 letter:

> The Major always treated the matter as a joke, and so did
> all of us, and our puzzle merely was to determine the
> man's object in spinning the yarn . . . the Major had never
> seen him—I am sure of that—for I cannot recall a single
> reference that would indicate any sight of the man or any
> serious consideration of his claim.

This may be interpreted as Powell's early dismissal of White, but one should keep in mind that Dellenbaugh was not describing the 1869 expedition but the second one, by which time Powell no longer had any use for White or his raft journey.

Edwin Corle, in his 1946 book *Listen, Bright Angel*, quotes Powell as saying that White was "the biggest liar that ever told a tale about the Colorado." Even Robert Stanton, clearly no admirer of Powell, quoted the major's sentiments in an article in the *Engineering News* of September 21, 1889: "Nobody has ever successfully traversed the Colorado cañon but my parties. The story that a raft once lived to get through is preposterous and was long since exploded." It seems the major could not even bring himself to name the raft's passenger!

It has been said that Powell did not wish to share this magnificent canyon with anyone at all, and although that may have led to the remarkable Grand Canyon arithmetic which counted Powell as number one and Stanton as number two (ignoring their team members), it does not account for his failure even to mention the members of his 1871–72 expedition. Many years later, Almon Thompson wrote a letter on that subject to Frederick Dellenbaugh, revealing an interesting view of his brother-in-law:

> The phase of the Major's character which led him to
> ignore the second expedition is no mystery to me—he
> had no fine sense of justice nor excelled loyalty to a high
> ideal of honor and so far as his subordinates were con-
> cerned did not know the meaning of noblesse oblige.

Major Powell's expeditions showed him to be a man of great physical courage, and his vision for the future of the American Southwest was certainly bold and true, but sadly, even to friends and colleagues, his ethics did not appear to match his many great accomplishments.

CHAPTER 14   ENTER ROBERT BREWSTER STANTON

White put his Grand Canyon journey behind him when he returned to the West. He was apparently able to reduce his experience to a manageable adventure. For two years, he worked at various Barlow and Sanderson jobs throughout the southeastern corner of Colorado Territory. When he decided to settle down, he took the traditional and practical first step.

In 1871, he married a sixteen-year-old girl fresh out of a convent school, Octaviana (Tavvy) Johnson; she was tiny, dark haired, dark eyed, and part Mexican. The marriage took place in Red Rock (Colorado Territory) on November 6, 1871, and Antonio Johnson's name appears on the marriage certificate as a witness. This brother appears to be something of a mystery. Dock Marston hinted that Antonio had committed a crime and was executed. Wherever or from whom Marston gained this information—he never cited a source—it was not from the White family.

For a few more years, White continued with his usual Barlow and Sanderson jobs, although their actual locations remain as vague as most of the family history of that time. In 1872, a son, Edward, was born and died shortly afterward. It was not until the summer of 1875 that a second child arrived; by now there was a family bible to keep track of things—in a way. It lists this newcomer's name as Ven Delas, but in spite of that, some of his siblings insisted that his name was really Benjamin.

White and his family, now enlarged by the arrival of Carrie in 1877, settled for good in the town of Trinidad, Colorado, seven miles north of the Raton Pass from New Mexico and a busy stop on the mountain leg of the Santa Fe Trail. It is a small, quiet town, nestled at six thousand feet against the Sangre de Cristo range of the Rocky Mountains; to the northwest rise the Spanish Peaks, to the east lies the plateau and mesa country. The Purgatoire river runs through it. The air is clear, the snow is delicate and powdery in winter, and the heat dry and bearable in summer.

White started a drayage business and built a house on State Street, combining the only two professions he knew: carpentry (from his father) and horses (courtesy of the U. S. Army). Here Emilia (usually called Emma) was born in 1878 and Flora in 1879. In 1883, he built another house on College Street, finishing it just in time for Bertha, who arrived in October of that year, followed by Bonnie in 1885, and Michaela (or Mitchola or Mick) in 1887. They seem to have had a lot of trouble with their names.

In 1888, White broke his arm and was unable to work for several months. His rich friend, Dan Taylor (later the mayor of Trinidad), held the mortgage on his home, and when White let the payments lapse, Taylor foreclosed. The family stayed on, but the house was no longer theirs. When White recovered, he built a new house, and he and Taylor remained the best of friends. The new house was on Short Street and had a barn for horses and a wagon. Another girl, Esther, came along in the spring of 1890 and finally another son, Arnold, in 1892. Daughter Bonnie died of scarlet fever a few years later. All in all White sired ten children, of which eight survived into old age.

In his prosaic and unexceptional way, White was respected in his community as a hard-working and honest man. He had a great many friends, among them the rich and influential of the town; he used to play poker with them every week at the Bloom mansion. Fame and fortune clearly escaped his grasp; actually, he sought neither one. He related the story of his Grand Canyon adventure to his family, his fellow townsmen, and their children. It was accepted as he was: without

Figure 6.
James White with his wife and children, ca 1906
Back row: Mary Michael, Esther, Em, Bertha, Flora, Carrie
Front row: Arnold, Octaviana, James, Ven
(Photo courtesy of the White family)

question. His listeners said he had to be coaxed into telling the story and never dressed it up.

In 1894, a reminder of his Grand Canyon experience drifted into White's life in the form of a chance meeting with William Hiram Edwards, a boatman on the 1890 expedition led by Robert Stanton. It was brief and seemingly of little significance; however, thirteen years later, it produced the most perplexing of all White's encounters.

In 1889, Robert B. Stanton was chief engineer of an expedition led by Frank Brown, the president of the Denver, Colorado Canyon, and Pacific Railway. After portaging Soap Creek Rapids (a few miles below Lee's Ferry, the traditional start of the Grand Canyon), Brown was washed overboard and drowned at a spot known as Salt Water Wash. At Mile 25 Rapid, two other members of the team also drowned; the survivors thereupon abandoned the railroad survey and the river.

In 1890, Stanton reappeared on the Colorado with new boats (and life vests) and set out to complete the survey; this time he was its leader. As far as the Grand Canyon transit was concerned, it was successful, but the survey backers were unimpressed and dropped the project; Stanton was not able to rekindle their interest. During the late 1890s, he took a huge dredge into Glen Canyon to mine gold from the gravel bars, but his venture, like all similar efforts to capture the Colorado's elusive "floating" gold, failed.

Stanton, however, could not bring himself to abandon altogether the Colorado River or the Grand Canyon. For the rest of his life, he immersed himself in its lore, amassed a boxcar of data, and wrote a prodigious number of words on the subject; it became an obsession with him. He seemed especially driven to point out the errors and foibles of others, emphasizing his own knowledge, expertise, and ability. And, adopting the bizarre chronology of the Grand Canyon initiated by Powell, he declared,

> As early as 1892, I set forth my position in the matter:
> Major Powell's expedition of 1869 was undoubtedly the
> first, and I, having successfully concluded a survey of all
> the canyons of the river in 1889 and 1890, lay claim to
> the distinction of being second down the great river.

When Stanton's boatman, Edwards, read an article in the 1907 *Outing Magazine* which contained Dr. Parry's report and a copy of White's 1867 letter to his brother, he recalled his 1894 meeting with White in Pueblo, Colorado. He immediately wrote to Stanton, advising him of White's whereabouts and recounting their meeting thirteen years earlier.

Stanton, still gathering information on the river and canyon, wrote to James White, asking if he had written the letter and/or the *Outing Magazine* article. White replied (in a letter written, as usual, by one of his daughters), assuring Stanton that there must be some mistake since he had never written anything for publication. The letter ended on a cordial note: "[I] would very much like to see you on your way East, if you will let me know when that will be."

Stanton had summarily dismissed White in his customary manner by calling him a "veritable Munchausen." Now, forty years after White's journey and seventeen years after his own, Stanton was on his way to confront the man whom he considered to be an interloper in Grand Canyon history—surely a severe test of objectivity.

He arrived in Trinidad early on the morning of September 23, 1907, booked a room in the hotel, hired a local stenographer named Roy Lappin, and arranged to interview White. That evening Stanton and Lappin arrived at 401 Short Street. When the amenities had been taken care of, Stanton invited White to tell his story. The notarized transcript of this interview contains five basic points about this story that require close scrutiny:

First, except for getting his years mixed up, White gave a straightforward account of the preliminaries leading up to the river journey. Then, according to the transcript, White said, "We crossed the San Juan River and continued our journey southwest from there until we struck the head of a canyon."

White, according to Parry's report, stated quite clearly in 1868 that his party had prospected for gold *along the San Juan River* and then turned *north* when the San Juan entered a steep canyon. It seems inconceivable that Stanton was unaware of this report, yet he made no effort here to reconcile these conflicting accounts. He noted that he made a sketch in his notebook, showing this southwesterly direction, identified the rivers, and repeated White's statement. White replied, "Yes, sir." No further questions on this subject appear in the transcript.

Second, White's response to Stanton's question about the distance from the San Juan River to the side canyon was "It took us two days to get there." Here, however, according to the transcript, the "two days" is followed by the note "[actually forty-five days]," which suggests an enormous time differential. Any discussion of this surely would have been included as part of the interview, yet the transcript reveals no such discussion. This note could only have been inserted by Stanton after the interview, yet it appears here in the notarized transcript of what Stanton claimed was a verbatim interview.

Third, White related the launching of their raft "on the Grand River." Stanton, who often contended that White was misled by others, surely knew that it was Parry who had identified the Grand River, and, having been down the Colorado himself, also knew that White had not embarked on the Grand. As an engineer, might he not have used a map to demonstrate the northerly direction of the Grand from the San Juan and question the obvious impossibility of going southwest from the San Juan to reach the Grand? But Stanton did not do that; although the Grand was discussed later, the discrepancy itself was not.

Fourth, White described his first three or four days on the river as smooth water, without rapids. Again, Stanton knew that this description did not fit Cataract Canyon, immediately downstream from the Green-Grand confluence. Stanton did not respond at this time to this discrepancy. Later on, however, he berated White for not knowing of these dangerous rapids and went on to describe the smooth waters of Glen Canyon, where, he said, "you might have traveled on your raft with some safety as far as Lee's Ferry." Why did it not strike Stanton that these Glen Canyon waters quite accurately dovetailed with White's description of these first days on the river?

Fifth, White described the first rapid as a "small one." His description of the next rapid was more a recitation of George Strole's death. From then on, he followed his ritual fourteen-day schedule, minimizing the size of the rapids but continuing to speak of "many rapids."

Here Stanton focused on White's comment about "one big rapid" and failed to pursue White's several mentions of "many rapids . . . every day." The investigative portion of the interview ended in a sort of shouting match about rapids, distances, height and color of walls, and the like. Stanton's somewhat pedantic lectures on the USGS surveys apparently weakened White's stubborn resistance and hammered home to him how wrong he was about the Grand, the Green, and especially Cataract Canyon. It ended with White's reluctant admission that maybe he had been lost after all.

Stanton continued with eloquent descriptions of the colors and shapes and heights—"piled up walls and cliffs, brown, red, yellow, green, and flaming scarlet, six thousand feet high"—and scolded White for his paltry descriptions of low walls and white sandstone. He berated him: "Have you never in all these years taken the trouble to look at a government map to find out the truth?" and "Did you never look it up on a map and see that the San Juan empties into the Colorado about 145 miles below the mouth of the Green and figure out the distance you traveled?" He had clearly stopped listening since there is no mention of White's answers to these questions.

Stanton's final revelation was

> I will tell you two more things and these in utmost kindness, I intend to defend you against the charges made, but do you know that most of the people who know anything about the Colorado River think you (and you are so mentioned in several books and pamphlets) the biggest liar

> that ever told a story about the Colorado . . . and further
> it has been believed by some very distinguished men that
> you murdered your two companions and told your story
> in 1867 to cover up your crime.

"I didn't kill them!" White said.

And that is all he said. He was hearing for the first time in his life the accusations of lying and murder that had been made against him, not only verbally but in print, by "very distinguished men." According to the transcript, these four words were his only response. They seem incredibly mild considering the magnitude of the accusations. But, according to the transcript, there followed not a single question from White about them, nor any defense against them, nor further response of any kind on the subject. Stanton's reply was "No, I know you didn't, and . . . I am going to defend you from both charges," and this was apparently so gratifying to White that he begged him, "Don't go. I like you. Stay another day." But Stanton declined the offer. The transcript carries Stanton's final comment: "So we bade each other good-night with a hearty shake of the hand."

After the interview, Lappin returned to his office, where he had only a few hours to type up a rough, eleven-page transcript of his notes. Stanton had brought with him a Santa Fe Railroad book describing the glories of the Grand Canyon; he autographed the fly-leaf and left it with Lappin to give to White. At 2:30 A.M., Stanton boarded the eastbound Santa Fe train.

So, apparently, ended the famous Trinidad interview; however, several letters have come to light which add a somewhat curious post-script to the interview itself and the Stanton-Lappin collaboration. On September 25, Lappin wrote to Stanton: "As per your request, I am herewith sending you the facts of the first part of the story of James White" (who White's employer was, where they quit Barlow and Sanderson, where they stole their horses, etc.). On October 3, Stanton wrote to White asking further questions (the year of his journey, who interviewed him in 1868, Strole's first name, etc.), including, "Do you wish to change any points of the interview?"

On October 12, having received no reply to his letter, Stanton sent a letter to Lappin, telling him he had written to White "to make some inquiries" and then adding, "If you have an opportunity I shall be obliged to you if you could suggest to him a prompt answer to my letter." He also advised Lappin: "In a short time I will send you a copy of the interview for inspection through a friend of mine in Trinidad."

On October 24, White's daughter wrote (for her father) to Stanton with the answers to his questions. Probably in response to the question about changing points in the interview, White did indeed change his point of embarkation to the Green River; his letter states, "It was the mouth of the Green river, instead of the mouth of the Grand river that I passed. Studying the map makes me more certain . . . that I was not lost." In retrospect this statement reveals White's confusion in the wake of the interview: if he had been so sure that he had gone southwest from the San Juan River, as the transcript reports, why was he now discussing an embarkation to the north of the San Juan? It was a question which Stanton apparently did not ask.

On November 1, 1907, Stanton sent the formal transcript of the interview not to Lappin but to William Hiram Edwards in Greeley, Colorado, asking him to "take this document down to Trinidad and get the stenographer . . . to swear to it, in the prepared affidavit on the last page." He explained,

> The reason I ask you to do this, rather than for me to send it to Trinidad is this: I picked up this stenographer, the only one I could get in Trinidad, to take down the interview in shorthand. He proved to be two things: First; a very poor stenographer for such work, and his notes which he wrote out for me afterwards, while being pretty accurate as far as they went, were not verbatim, but were simply a good skeleton of the interview; so, that in writing out this report it is not an exact copy of the words but it is absolutely exact in facts. Now, I fear if I send this to him . . . either he would go to White with it and White would want him to change it or object to his verifying it at all, for the reason that . . . this stenographer, which I did not know when I hired him, was White's next door neighbor, and an old personal acquaintance of the family . . . now if you will go down there and see him, without of course telling him anything I have written you . . .

In 1916, Stanton wrote a letter to Thomas Dawson with a different version:

> years ago, I knew White personally and spent some time with him at his home—heard the story from his own lips;

Figure 7.
James White, age seventy, 1907
(Photo taken at request of R. B. Stanton, courtesy of the White Family)

paid him $25.00 for the telling; hired and took with me a stenographer; took down verbatim every word of White's and mine, spoken in the interview, and had the transcript of the notes sworn to.

The affidavit attached to Stanton's transcript reads as follows:

> I, Roy Lappin, being duly sworn, do depose and say as follows: I am a public stenographer doing business in the City of Trinidad, Colorado. On the 23rd day of September, 1907, I was employed by Robert B. Stanton of the City of New York, to take down in shorthand an interview which he had with James White, residing at No. 401 Short Avenue, in the city of Trinidad, Colorado, and on the evening of said day did go with the said Stanton to the residence of the said White and there took down in shorthand said interview, and furnished the said Stanton a typewritten copy of my notes, and further, the foregoing twenty-three pages contain a true and correct transcript of that said interview, together with the conversation had between the said Stanton and the said White, with certain corrections in grammar and other minor details, which in no way change the meaning or intent of the interview or statements made by the said White.
>
>   [signed] Roy Lappin

Edwards obliged, traveling from Greeley to Trinidad and back, evidently to Stanton's satisfaction, as expressed in his letter of November 13, 1907: "You have won my everlasting gratitude . . . for the prompt and excellent manner in which you succeeded in getting Lappin's affidavit. That incident is closed."

But was it?

When Stanton had told White he had not been in Cataract Canyon, White had asked "Where was I then?" Although Stanton replied that he "would come to that after awhile." he never did respond to the question during the interview. In 1908, however, when he added this encounter to his burgeoning manuscript, that answer emerged loud and clear. When Chalfant's edited version of Stanton's work was finally published in 1932, long after the major players had departed from the fray, it revealed nine distinct references to the Grand Wash Cliffs as White's point of entry to the Colorado river, culminating in Stanton's final, unambiguous conclusion: "[White] did float on a raft or rafts a distance of 60 miles from a point near the Grand Wash Cliffs to Callville, Nevada."

CHAPTER 15 SENATE DOCUMENT NO. 42

Once the Stanton visit faded, life in Trinidad went on much as before; some children left home, White grew older, and his drayage work lightened. He spoke less and less of the Colorado River and his raft journey.

Nine years later, in 1916, Thomas F. Dawson, a former journalist and now an executive clerk in the United States Senate, entered White's life and opened one last chapter on the Grand Canyon of 1867. Dawson wrote to the Honorable Dan Taylor, mayor of Trinidad, inquiring about the possibility of investigating the story of James White. He wished, he said, to refute Major Powell's claim of being the first man through the Grand Canyon and to give the credit to "a Colorado man." Mayor Taylor shared the letter with White who, at seventy-nine, was reluctant to become involved; White's family and friends, however, urged him to think it over. Taylor advised Dawson to contact White directly.

Four months passed without any further word, and the subject was dropped, but a letter from an unexpected quarter changed the picture considerably. It was from a William W. Bass, postmarked Grand Canyon, Arizona, and dated July 11, 1916. After explaining a little about himself and how he had learned about White, he mentioned meeting

Frederick Dellenbaugh, who, he said, "wrote an account of his trip with Powell in which he brands you as a fraud and accomplished liar for claiming you ever made the Raft trip as claimed."

He went on

> Now I am writing my own story of some of my experiences here . . . and I want a good chance to call Dellenbaugh to account for some of his statements, especially the one about you . . . and I want your own story of your trip. . . . I will give you your just dues in all I have to say and also use all the evidence I now have to prove you told the truth.

White was mildly gratified by Bass's opinions but hopping mad about the accusations; when Dawson finally wrote his letter on July 21, he was assured of a ready-made audience for his proposal. Dawson wanted the whole story: Captain Baker, the circumstances of their meeting, where he came from, etc. He wanted to know about Parry (whom he called "Professor Perry"), their meeting and interview, whether this account was accurate, and if he should make it the basis of his pamphlet. He asked about the strength of the raft, the eddy at the mouth of the Little Colorado and whether it could have been somewhere else, about distances and times and what White had to eat: everything.

He ended by saying, "I have no desire to rob Major Powell of any of his deserved fame. He . . . deserves much credit . . . but the fact that he did go through should not be used to rob you of the credit due you." In telling White about the "effort that has been made and is being made to discredit you," Dawson emphasized two points: "I intend to make Professor Perry's . . . article . . . the basis of what I may say unless you pronounce it incorrect," and "it is also pointed out that your estimate of distance from the mouth of the Grand to the mouth of the San Juan is erroneous, as is your estimate of the distance to the mouth of the Little Colorado."

These statements, plus Bass's letter, spurred White's decision to work with Dawson as nothing else could have; he agreed that his daughters, Esther and Em, could take notes of his recollections and put together what details he could remember.

On August 2, 1916, Esther wrote the first of her many letters to Thomas Dawson. After the usual amenities, she said,

> My father is growing old but his memory is fairly good. He
> is busy trying to recall the details and incidents of his trip
> through the Grand Canyon . . . and as soon as he shall be
> able to remember all the things he will be able to tell we
> will prepare a complete statement and forward it.

She explained their confusion over the names of Perry and
Ferry, requested a copy of the "Perry article," and concluded,

> I wish to assure you that we will aid you in every way
> possible, in spite of the fact that our father has always
> been loath to talk about the trip and his experiences
> because of the horrors of the scenes enacted before his
> eyes and because he never sought fame or notoriety.

She forwarded the letter from Bass and one from the Colorado
state highway commissioner, T. J. Ehrhart, written to White in January
1916, about the Goodfellow shooting incident at Brown's Creek.
Dawson had asked "whether after your rescue you wrote any letters
concerning your experience to your folks back in Wisconsin," but
Esther made no mention of White's Callville letter of September 1867.
Of course, the letter itself had never been in White's possession since
he wrote it, and no one in the family had seen the copy published in
the April 1907 issue of *Outing Magazine*. Dawson only learned of its
existence shortly before completing his manuscript; its absence from
Document No. 42 was probably due to the lack of time to locate it or
incorporate it into the text at the last minute. He attempted to reme-
dy the omission by publishing it in an article he wrote for *The Trail*
magazine in 1919.

The next six weeks were filled with considerable and often hec-
tic activity. Esther and Em poked around in White's memory, often a little too insistently; he did not like it, but his girls were no longer children
and refused to be put off or intimidated. He grudgingly gave in (up to
a point), and together they finally produced the promised statement.

These activities, plus Dawson's comments about White's errors
in the distances traveled on the river, created a focus of unusual intensity on his raft journey and forced him to dig further into his memory than he had ever done. In the end, he came to the conclusion that
although his party had been headed for the Grand River, they did not
make it that far. His statement reflected that reevaluation:

> We followed the Mancos down until we struck the San
> Juan. Then we followed the San Juan down as far as we
> could and then swam our horses across and started over to
> the Grand River, but before we got to the Grand River we
> struck a canyon. . . .

The statement was sent to Dawson with a letter in which Esther explained,

> My father was born in 1837 but he is strong for a man of
> his age and his memory of the important incidents of the
> trip is still clear but it fails him when he is called on for
> names and similar data, and what he remembers comes to
> him in a disconnected manner.

In late November, Dawson sent a rough draft of his manuscript, which included Parry's report, Calhoun's article, and a *Rocky Mountain Herald* account dated January 8, 1869. All this was read to White, who kept up a steady stream of corrections. Parry's report was only slightly marked, but the two articles were heavily red-penciled.

The draft was returned with Esther's usual cover letter, but this time her comments hinted that all had not gone as easily as they thought it would.

> Due to father's age he does not remember distances or
> names very well. He is failing rapidly and his memory is
> not the best, but it seems to us that he remembers the
> important events of his journey. In fact he never paid
> much attention to distances and names at the time of his
> perilous voyage. And it must be remembered that when
> he was going through the canyon, all he was thinking
> about was how to get out, and not of the distances
> between streams and the names thereof.

Reading between the lines of this letter (and knowing her), I find evidence of my mother's impatience with her father; she had an almost mathematically precise mind and would have preferred to pin down every last detail of distance and time. My Aunt Em had a more compassionate view and probably reminded her that their father might have had other things on his mind in the canyon. But neither of them recognized the psychological implications of his memory problems; not much progress had been made beyond the attitudes of the 1860s.

All that red-penciling could hardly change the reports, but it gave Dawson some insight into the wide discrepancies in the various accounts. Esther's disclaimers provided a clue to White's apparent state of mind but naturally could shed no light on the cause.

Christmas came and went. The year 1916 became 1917. Then, unexpectedly, a letter dated February 8 arrived from Dawson. He related a meeting he'd had in "Washington City" with "a gentleman who has given much attention to the history of the Grand Canyon." It appeared that White's story had been strongly assailed by this critic, and Dawson was writing

> with a view to impressing upon you the importance of get-
> ting as definite a statement as you can from Mr. White as
> to his being on the Grand River . . . this is the most insidi-
> ous attack that has been made and should be met while
> your father lives and over his signature.

What was this? The statement they had prepared the previous fall had clearly placed the prospecting party in "a canyon before reaching the Grand," so the two women were puzzled, especially by Dawson's next instruction: "Get him to give all the reasons he can for believing he was on the Grand." Even worse they were dismayed by the thought of tackling their father on the subject, but two days later, before they had had time to do anything, a second letter, dated February 10, arrived from Dawson. He was increasingly worried about the "opposition theory," which sent White overland before coming to the Colorado River.

> You will remember that I say in my article that it would
> have been almost as much of a fete [*sic*] to go overland as
> by water. That statement is predicated upon the theory
> that the party was on the Grand when Baker was killed.
> So, bring that fact out as clearly and strongly as possible
> over your father's signature. . . . Our story is going to be
> attacked when printed, and we must make it as invincible
> as possible.

Esther and Em confronted their father with the news. They did not know at the time who this opposition was, but it was clearly someone important to cause Dawson so much anxiety. White's persistent daughters dutifully coaxed their father into yet another discussion of the Grand River. Their session was rather curiously documented by two sketches on the back of Dawson's February 10 letter, both showed the telltale Y that represented the Grand-Green confluence with mysterious downstream squiggles—probably rivers—coming in from the east. Neither sketch was labeled, and all they reveal is a vigorous discussion of the problem.

In spite of (or maybe because of) Dawson's two almost-frantic letters and the subsequent discussions, James White predictably lapsed into his stubborn mode; he refused to change his original statement, and of course he declined to write the letter Dawson had requested.

As if this uproar was not enough that February, yet another letter arrived, this one from a Mr. Robert B. Stanton. Dated February 19, it began, "My dear Miss White: You probably have not forgotten my visit to your father in the fall of 1907."

Esther was puzzled. In 1907, she had been seventeen years old and still in high school; she had no immediate recollection of this Mr. Stanton. She asked Em and her mother about him. Tavvy, who up to now had stayed clear of this Grand Canyon project, remembered the man vaguely, but, as usual with "men's business," she had not been a party to his visit. Em's memory was equally thin, but she had the impression that her father had considered the visit a pleasant one. Scarcely the wiser, Esther read on.

> Recently when in Washington City I heard that he was in poor health and I am writing to give you some information which I hope will please you all.
>
> You will remember that in my interview with your father, I was convinced that everything he told me about his experiences on the Colorado River in 1867, was entirely truthful and in no way, at that time or in his interview with Dr. Parry in January 1868, intended to misrepresent the facts as he knew them, but I was satisfied that the story [Dr. Parry] wrote was distorted and that I intended to write a defense of your father against the untruthful and very unjust charges that has [*sic*] been made against him by others.
>
> That defense was written in 1908, but, for reasons I need not explain, I have not yet been able to publish my book on that and other things connected with the Colorado River.
>
> Only recently I found the original paper on which was written the notes taken by Dr. Parry during his talk with

your father in Arizona in January 1868. These notes prove
positively that at that time he told Dr. Parry the exact
truth and in almost the same words that he used to me in
1907. Showing as I told you that there was not the least
blame attached to your father for any thing Dr. Parry
wrote afterwards. So that in a postscript to my book I have
written the following, based on those original notes:

"It may not be out of place to remard [*sic*] here that
finding at this late day in Dr. Parry's note the record of this
'one big rapid', and <u>only one</u>, just as White wrote in his letter, and also testified to me 40 years afterwards . . . ."

At this point, an aside may be in order: Parry's notes contain the
phrase, "one fall 10 ft?" but also the phrase, "continuous rapids." White's
letter speaks of going over falls from ten to fifteen feet high and of his
raft tipping over three and four times a day. Even in Stanton's interview, White spoke of "many rapids . . . every day," which Stanton then
and in the letter chose to ignore.

"Even after 40 years, all the time being <u>misled</u> by Dr.
Parry's account into believing that he had gone to the
Grand River, and passed through all the great Cañons of
the Colorado, his honesty was not affected in the least
when I gave him positive proof that there were hundreds
of big rapids on the Colorado. He never budged an inch,
but positively re-affirmed that he went over <u>one one</u> [*sic*]
big rapid and that there was only one such on the river—
truthfully qualifying the last statement by, 'Where I went.'
And now after 49 years we find in Dr. Parry's own handwriting (written at the time) the proof that White stated
the same thing to him in January 1868. Truly White is
absolutely vindicated and absolved from the oft repeated
charge that he was the biggest liar that ever told a tale
about the Colorado River."

When my book is published I shall be pleased to send
you a copy.

Won't you write me a few lines and tell me how your
father is. Give him my kindest regards and best wishes for
his health and happiness.

Esther and Em were stunned. They wondered what on earth
this Mr. Stanton was really saying. Could he honestly think it would
please them to hear that he was about to inform the world that their
father had not gone through the Grand Canyon? Did he imagine that

they would be glad to receive this news, to know that Stanton was accusing Parry of misleading their father into believing he had passed through all the great canyons of the Colorado? What did he mean by only one rapid?

It is little wonder that they did not know what to do. They did not want to read this letter to their father, nor did they wish to bother Dawson with it, coming as it did right in the middle of his manuscript preparation. But the letter reminded them of Dawson's "gentleman who has given much attention to the history of the Grand Canyon." Could Stanton and that gentleman possibly be one and the same?

They were rapidly becoming sick and tired of trying to solve the Grand River problem to everyone's satisfaction. They did not look forward to another session with dear papa. For nearly two weeks, they dawdled and did nothing.

The stalemate was broken by the arrival of another letter from Dawson, dated March 8. This letter is not among the White correspondence because it was returned to Dawson a month later at his request. (My mother steadfastly insisted that she could not remember its contents, but her subsequent letters, attitude, and actions during that time period pretty strongly suggest what they were.)

Whatever else the missing letter disclosed, it categorically connected the pieces of the Stanton-Grand River puzzle to form a picture that, to put it mildly, infuriated Esther. At last she and Em knew who the opposition—to them, the enemy—was. They realized that the most basic foundation of their father's story was being undermined, and they now understood Dawson's panic. What they still could not understand was Stanton's letter with its platitudes and the unbelievable suggestion that he was doing White and his family a favor! Still, the letter had to be answered.

We can recognize this opposition theory—that White had never passed through "all the great Cañons of the Colorado"—as arising from Stanton's 1907 interview, but as of 1916 neither the interview nor its conclusions had been published. The transcript of the interview had never been sent to White. Stanton himself had admitted to Edwards that he did not want White to see it. The women were learning of this interview for the first time.

Yet, from what Em said, their father apparently had a good opinion of Stanton; they didn't know why that was, but Esther thought it prudent to avoid identifying its author when they told him about this "south of the San Juan" theory. It was absolutely necessary for her father to make a strong response to it, but they feared any entanglement in personalities, and at this point, White was unpredictable.

It took her nearly a month, but on April 13, Esther finally wrote to Dawson:

> I am enclosing herewith a letter I have written to Mr. Robert B. Stanton, together with a copy of the letter I received from him sometime ago and <u>am returning to you the letter you wrote to me of date of March 8, 1917, as per your request</u>.
> If Mr. Stanton contends that father went over one big rapid there is a mistake some where for when he has related his story to us he has always mentioned going over several rapids both large and small and has also made mention of going over one big rapid near the end of the canyon.
> I have tried to answer Mr. Stanton's letter <u>in accordance with your suggestions and have kept the contents of your letter strictly confidential</u>.
> Answering Mr. Stanton's letter was a hard task as all the way through I wanted to denounce him but refrained from doing so.

Her reply to Stanton of the same date was restrained but included the following:

> I have read your letter carefully to father and he wishes me to correct your statement in regard to the "<u>one big rapid</u>." . . . he said he went over "<u>several rapids</u>" a day, both "big and little," and he also mentions going over one rapid that was larger than the rest, but, as before stated, he went over "several rapids" a day, both "big and little" and not over "<u>only one</u>" big rapid.

Restraint aside, her repetition, quotes, and underlines manage to betray both her anger and her reasons for wanting "to denounce him."

By keeping Stanton's name out of the discussions, she had no trouble preparing her father's final letter to Dawson. Dated April 20,

1917, it was sent over White's own signature and was his last word on the subject:

> Dear Sir: I have come into knowledge of the fact that a charge has been made that I did not reach the Colorado River above the San Juan, but below it. You will notice from the account that I sent you of my trip that when our party started on our prospecting trip we were headed for the Grand River, as Baker said there was gold in that part of the country; but Baker was killed before reaching the Grand River in a canyon between the San Juan and the Grand. . . . Mr. Baker also carried a compass and kept us informed as to the direction we were traveling, and he told us that we were going north to the Grand River.
>
> Baker was killed after we crossed the San Juan River in a canyon between the San Juan and the Grand, being north of the San Juan.
>
> I guess the story will be attacked when printed, but I am willing to talk to anyone and convince them that I entered the Colorado River above the San Juan and not below it.

The underlines are White's, or perhaps they were Esther's only way of conveying her father's sentiments with the necessary emphasis.

Some have thought that the three iterations of the men's positions vis-a-vis the Grand, the Colorado, and the San Juan represent a case of protesting too much, but before this year, White had not given much thought to any outside accounts of his Grand Canyon experience. He had not asked Dr. Parry to interview him in 1868 or General Palmer to meet with him in 1869; he had not sought out Stanton's attention in 1907, nor Dawson's in 1916. White was nearly eighty years old; he was a stubborn old man, who, like anyone who has survived a traumatic event, became confused over details. But this time he had put in his own two cents worth and defended himself. He was certain he had finally set the record straight.

Dawson was not so sure. The manuscript was submitted to the Senate on May 25, 1917 (forty-nine years to the day since that august body had debated helping Major Powell with his Grand Canyon expedition) and was published later that summer. In a final letter, dated September 1, 1917, Dawson confided to "Miss White": "He [Stanton] criticizes the booklet very severely in his letters to me and tells me he is preparing to publish his long-promised book this fall. He will jump all over us, but I don't think we ought to care very much." Just how much Stanton was preparing to "jump" on the booklet, the long-suffering Dawson had only a short wait to discover.

But Dawson, ever the gentleman, did not end his letter on a negative note. He concluded, "I want to tell you . . . how much I appreciate your help . . . without it the work would necessarily have been far less complete. You have been not only a willing worker, but an intelligent one."

He promised to send a dozen copies of Senate Document No. 42 and, as a parting gift for her, one special, bound, and embossed one. Mr. Dawson was as good as his word.

Figure 8.
Esther White's leather-bound copy of Senate Document No. 42, 1917
a gift from Thomas Dawson.
(Photo by R. E. Adams)

Chapter 16   Battle of *The Trail*

Senate Document No. 42 did not resolve the controversy over White's journey; indeed, it merely added fuel to the fire of Robert Stanton's unrelenting opposition to White. In 1919, Thomas Dawson had two articles about White published in *The Trail* magazine. Stanton's response appeared in the September issue.

Before discussing the substance of the article, it seems relevant to examine Stanton's somewhat petulant attitude toward what the magazine's space limitations forced upon his evidentiary references. He complains that: "a hundred or so other reports, diaries, notes, letters and facts considered as one, analyzed and tried by the rules of evidence and the facts of nature and science, are given in full in the manuscript I have written." "All this evidence in the case can not be given here, for it would require perhaps 300 pages of the size of The Trail . . . but, I think I have the right to expect [that] the reader shall accept every quotation I have made and shall make from these documents are [*sic*] correctly quoted, even if in some cases . . . they are paraphrased"; and "the proofs are all given in my larger manuscript." He also included a disclaimer: "It is much to be regretted that space forbids giving you the full notes and my analysis," and a rebuke: "Would that you had the space to publish my full review of the pamphlet." He finally declared, "If I am unable to publish my book, . . . I will have a complete typewritten copy of my manuscript, including my review of [Dawson's] 1917 pamphlet, deposited with the Historical Society of Denver, where anyone can verify each quotation and its bearing by chapter, paragraph and line." Research in Colorado historical archives has not turned up this copy, and the manuscript exists in printed form only as three posthumously edited and published books. None of these contains this review, although his *Colorado River Controversies* may include some of it.

Paraphrasing Stanton's elaborate rhetoric is insufficient to demonstrate the lengths to which his passion and intensity carried him on this subject; his own words are not only relevant, but essential.

Stanton explained why he "consented to write this brief synopsis":

> Everyone who has discussed this story, particularly Mr.
> Thomas F. Dawson, . . . has done so on the basis of the
> possibility and probability of its truth . . . with little knowl-
> edge of the historical facts [and] with extremely little
> knowledge of the true nature of the Colorado and the
> interior of its cañons.

In contrast, he said, "My investigations were made from an entirely different standpoint." Stanton was alluding to his own experiences on the river and claimed, "I had but one idea—to get at the truth or falsity of the tale by gathering facts, not the theories or opinions of men." He cited his finding of original documents and his own 1907 interview with White. As already noted, he made special reference to his own two-volume, unpublished book on the "truth of the Grand Canyon controversy."

He then launched into an evaluation of White's character, prefaced by this statement: "After talking with him so many hours, and corresponding with him for several years. . . ." This misrepresentation seems to be typical of Stanton. Actually he spent one-and-a-half hours with White in 1907, and his correspondence was meager, most of it addressed to either "Miss White" or Roy Lappin, who relayed the messages.

Stanton characterized White as "an honest, truthful and sincere man, as far as his mental abilities would permit him to be . . . on the other hand White is a man of simple mind . . . lacking in *any* logical, reasoning faculty." Stanton found White's story to be made up of personal experiences, clearly and truthfully related but with certain supposed

facts, told to him by others and implicitly believed, which "he embel-
lished with his own faulty memory." White, he said, having "no logical
reasoning faculty whatever . . . had no conception that his embellish-
ments were direct contradictions of the various claims he was making."
These, Stanton continued, were "not untrue in themselves, but were
misplaced as to time and space." Then he stated, "I attempted to separate
the truth from the fiction by extending my cross-examination," a reference of course to his interview. He concluded with "his personal experiences on the river, and his real knowledge of what he saw, the truth of
which does not depend upon time and place, is [*sic*] shown to be
absolutely correct." Stanton, in arguing that White's description of the
sixty-mile stretch between Grand Wash Cliffs and Callville was absolutely correct, revealed the driving force of the entire article.

Stanton next evaluated the men who, at one time or another,
had written in support of White. He denigrated all statements made
by Dr. Parry, Major Calhoun, Dr. William Bell, General Palmer, and
especially Thomas Dawson. The evaluation included such terms as
"palpably misleading assertions," "unsupported opinions," "dogmatic
assertions," "bad memory, inattention to valuable information . . . and
want of careful observation." Most of these were reserved for Dawson
and used examples from his letters to impugn his motives and imply
that he had willfully distorted the truth. Stanton devoted six-and-a-
half pages to this subject.

On the sixteenth page of the article, Stanton returned to the
lynchpin of White's point of entry: the 1907 interview into which he
had inserted the notation, "[actually forty-five days]," after White's
answer of "two days" (to reach the side canyon from the San Juan).
Having already defined the stupidity and ignorance that he said had
led to this enormous mistake, Stanton now focused on two of White's
descriptions—the canyon walls and the river and its rapids—and
argued that

> White, even with his limited abilities, was capable of
> observing the general nature and character of the cañon
> walls and the character of the river . . . and he was and is
> perfectly capable of remembering them, and describing
> them in such a manner that his description can be readily
> and clearly recognized by anyone acquainted with the con-
> ditions that . . . exist in the cañons and on the river . . . .

Stanton hinted of White's spiritual qualities—or lack thereof:

> he is even more capable of remembering clearly and distinctly to his dying day his personal physical experiences on his trip, such as come to every man going down the Colorado, and such as are so often and so suddenly driven deep into one's brain, and which chill one to the very marrow . . . all we of the cañons have experienced them.

And he defined the workings of White's memory:

> such personal experiences become fastened on the memory *indelibly*, and remain clear and distinct ever afterward. . . . White is no exception to the rule . . . he had and has an abundance of intelligence to see such things and to *feel* and note his personal experiences in the rapids and clearly and accurately to remember them to this day, and more correctly and distinctly to describe them.

But why did Stanton insist that White was capable of remembering details of the river accurately and distinctly yet consider his estimates of time and distance on land so grossly inaccurate? Even if he was unaware of White's six years of travel across the West, common sense would suggest that his land descriptions would be far more accurate because he was well clothed, well fed, and under no particular strain rather than any observations he might make while he was near starvation, severely battered by the hostile environment of an unknown river, and in mortal fear for his life. This entire evaluation of White's mental abilities seems to have less to do with logic than obsession.

In this article, Stanton also stated that he gave White a twenty-five-dollar check in 1907, maintaining that he "demanded" money to tell his story. (Roy Lappin, in a 1953 letter to *Deseret Magazine*, said that Stanton "pressed a $20 gold piece into his hand.") Stanton's canceled check, in fact, still exists, and no one denies that he gave White the money, but White's version of the transaction will never be heard. One clue argues for a different interpretation: the undeniable fact that White invited Stanton to come to Trinidad to discuss the canyon.

Stanton went to his grave certain that he had prevailed, and he was not far from wrong. His arguments and conclusions were believed by a great many people. Many consider them to this day the final word on the journey of James White.

CHAPTER 17   THE WHITE FAMILY AND DOCK MARSTON

Before 1917, the White family knew nothing about the articles and books about White, except for the *Kenosha Telegraph* account which White had seen when he went home in 1869. They were totally unaware of the fifty-year-old controversy over his voyage. Dawson opened the door on these facts of life during preparation of his Senate document, and the discovery was a mixed blessing. When Dawson's pamphlet was finally published, the family gave a collective sigh of relief and closed the Grand Canyon door that he had opened.

The post-1917 explorations of the Colorado River and the Grand Canyon held no interest for them. They were ignorant of Stanton's feud with Dawson conducted in the pages of *The Trail*. Dr. William Bell, who had published Major Calhoun's account in 1869–70 and defended and believed White's journey, came to Trinidad on October 24, 1917. It was a brief visit, and although it pleased the family, it had little significance. In 1922, Ellsworth Kolb also came to Trinidad. He was a dedicated Colorado River runner about whom no one in the family had ever heard. This visit had less significance than Bell's.

In 1920, White had one eye removed due to glaucoma but continued to work. Then, in 1926, he broke his hip; this injury made work impossible. He died on January 14, 1927, at his home in Trinidad and was buried with all due honors in the Elks' Cemetery. His headstone includes the remarkable notation, "Co. E, Fifth California Volunteers."

White's children were by then widely scattered across the country. Some corresponded with one another; some never did. Some paid visits to each other or, rarely, Trinidad. Ven lived in Salt Lake City and never married. Carrie married a dispatcher for the Santa Fe Railroad, lived in Needles, California, and had no children. Em married a local man and lived in Trinidad all her life; she took care of her father and mother until they died. It also seemed she took care of everyone's children at one time or another but had none of her own. Bertha married a railroad man in Hawaii and had one child, Esther Catherine. Mick married a telephone man, lived in Portland, Oregon, and had two sons, Palmer and Arnold. Flora married a construction worker; they lived all over the country, following the hazardous job assignments that were his specialty; I only recall Nebraska and Florida. They had no children. Arnold served in World War I; he then worked for and later owned Levi's Department Store in Bisbee, Arizona. He and his wife had one son, Jimmy. Later, he owned a store in Long Beach, California.

Esther went to business college and worked in Denver. She married my father there; I was their only child. We moved to New York City when I was a year old and lived there until the stock market crash of 1929. I had extended visits to Aunt Em in Trinidad. After the crash, we, like thousands of others, drove across the country to Los Angeles, stopping to stay briefly with all the aunts along the way. We moved to Portland, Oregon, in 1932, and my father died shortly after. I moved to Seattle, Washington, in 1943, where, with a few breaks, I have lived ever since. My mother moved to Seattle when she retired and remained there until her death.

I offer this brief history to illustrate the disconnected nature of James White's family. There were some strong sibling attachments but sadly, some equally strong, often overriding, antagonisms as well. Because these relationships were fragmented, White's children never maintained his Grand Canyon journey as a vital and energetic family tradition. My mother and Aunt Em knew more about their father's raft journey, thanks largely to involvement in Thomas Dawson's 1917 investigation for his Senate document. But forty years would pass before either of them gave further thought to the subject.

In 1959, my mother received a letter from an Otis Marston. Marston was, he explained, a Grand Canyon historian who was interested in researching James White and his disputed raft journey. Eventually we learned that Marston had been an engineer, naval officer, stockbroker, lecturer, and writer, but it was as a researcher that he made his appearance in our lives.

He had tracked down Arnold in Long Beach, California, Bertha in Los Angeles, and Em, who still lived in the family home in Trinidad. He interviewed and corresponded with them, but they all pointed him toward my mother. Marston's primary interest was the behind-the-scenes work she had done in 1916–17 to help Thomas Dawson prepare Senate Document No. 42.

Marston's not-so-subtle suggestion that she dig into the family past held little appeal for my mother. In fact his letter struck an oddly familiar chord with her: history about to repeat itself. It was a siren song she had heard before, and she was not sure she wanted an encore. Besides, she was slightly suspicious of Marston.

Although I had made that childishly spirited defense of my grandfather in the sixth grade, I'm not sure that I literally believed in his journey; I certainly made no effort to investigate it. When Marston came along, I still knew little about Grand Canyon history beyond Dawson's pamphlet, but his letter intrigued me, and I urged my mother to respond. With more letters came more information. Marston turned out to be quite a remarkable gentleman.

He first ran the Colorado in 1942 as a passenger in a commercial boat and emerged as a dedicated Colorado River runner who was, as David Lavender observed, "wedded to the river." He boated the Colorado in a variety of craft, ran a powerboat and a jet boat upriver, was the advisor on the Disney film, *Ten Who Dared*, and either knew more or (depending on your point of view) claimed to know more about the river and the canyon than anyone, alive or dead. He was better known by his nickname of "Dock."

In an eerie replay of 1917, I inherited my mother's role as inquisitor, digging into her memory as she had so relentlessly done with her father. Reluctant or not, she supplied me with most of the White family history. She had a phenomenal memory; she had kept letters and carbon copies of replies, as well as some official documents—all of which came as a complete surprise to me, especially the materials she had retained from preparing Dawson's pamphlet. Later, I was able to talk to my Aunt Em; she was considerably older than my mother and had a softer and more tolerant perspective on her father. These two were gold mines of information.

My relationship with Dock Marston had a quid pro quo: I supplied him with everything I learned about the family history, and he sent me a flood of letters and articles, even galley proofs of not-yet-published books on the Colorado River, the Grand Canyon, and all the players thereon and therein. From this snowstorm of data, I learned what the outside world, especially Colorado River runners, thought of James White and his raft journey; I began to see the shape of the controversy that eddied around both. I was shocked by the depth of the animosity aimed at White and astonished that these people's opinions were considered gospel by so many and widely echoed in later attacks.

At some point, Dock suggested that I write a book about the man he called my grandpappy. Great idea, but in the face of so much negative data, it seemed as if there was little chance of successfully rehabilitating James White and his voyage.

Then, surprisingly sandwiched among all that negative stuff, Dock sent me the galley proofs of *First Through the Grand Canyon* by Richard E. Lingenfelter, published in 1958. Although the author, following Stanton's lead, had assigned White a point of embarkation south of the San Juan River, he nevertheless set him firmly within the Grand Canyon. Dock himself had written the book's foreword but warned me sternly not to believe in Lingenfelter's conclusions. But of course I welcomed them and wondered, as I did more and more often, just which direction Dock was going.

Soon I received another small glimmer of light: a review of Lingenfelter's book by Dr. Harold A. Bulger, published in 1961 by the Missouri Historical Society. He agreed that White had been in the Grand Canyon but proposed a point of embarkation north of the San Juan.

Then in 1969, after nearly a decade of reading, discussing, questioning, and arguing, I received a very significant letter from Dock:

About a week past at Omaha was the opportunity to
talk with Robert C. Euler, Prescott College, Arizona, and
the discussion went along the lines of a book about your
grandpappy. Bob reviewed the Lingenfelter book. He has
made water transits of the Grand Canyon several times
and has choppered over and into much of it. . . . a copy of
his review is enclosed.

The review had been written in 1959. Dr. Euler and his coauthor,
Dr. Henry F. Dobyns, like Bulger, argued for a northern route from the
San Juan River. This news was so exciting that I did not even stop to
wonder why it had taken Dock ten years to send the review to me.

Within a few weeks, Euler himself wrote to me, declaring that he
was looking forward to working with us on a book. With Dock I had
easily accepted the role of acolyte, student, and/or water carrier. Now I
had to become accustomed to associating with a scholar trailing a lumi-
nous string of accomplishments in the fields of anthropology, archaeology, and American Indian ethnohistory. I felt like a frog in a crocodile
pond, but his letter convinced me that the crocodiles were friendly.

Dock, Euler, and I did indeed work together—sort of. In retrospect it seems like a slightly humorous and confusing collaboration.
Dock continued to write letters (I never caught up with them) and
send a multitude of articles, mostly by people with varying degrees of
disbelief in White (but with the occasional pearl). Euler was always
encouraging and, even better, was engaging in a series of aerial recon-
naissances of the area northwest of the San Juan River at Comb Wash
and pursuing some vital physical evidence.

Beyond the family investigation, I was doing some modest
research of my own. Spurred by the Euler-Dobyns suggestions of
stress, I started to dig into its effects on survivors of similar traumatic
situations, mostly via various books on the subject, and finally enlisted
the help of a psychiatrist who had done studies for the air force on survival in the Arizona desert.

By the autumn of 1972, I had completed a manuscript. It had
some reasonably good research in it, but Dock tore it to shreds with
an eleven-page, typewritten, single-spaced critique that curled my
ego. Still, I have to admit that the kindest comment anyone could
have made about the manuscript would have been "so-so." Euler had
written an excellent scholarly manuscript, and Dock had gathered

together a compilation of some of his earlier monographs on White, but it contained nothing new.

By 1976, Dock was drifting farther and farther away from our original concept. He may have felt overwhelmed by some of the evidence that was turning up in White's favor, or he may just have been growing weary. In any case, we were unable to create a cohesive book. We continued to keep in touch, and we all remained friends, but it became obvious that this collaboration was not going to work. On August 30, 1979, Dock "ran his last rapid," much to our sorrow.

Bob Euler and I tried to revive the book as a two-way project, but although we completely agreed with each other's views, we seemed unable to come up with the magic formula for integrating them. Yet it is no exaggeration to say that this book could not have been written without his enormous contribution.

In 1992, my husband and I moved to Arizona. I wanted the experience of living on the Colorado River. Although we remained there—some seventy miles south of old Hardyville—for only three years, it was a remarkably enlightening experience. The Mojave Desert, the heat, the now-subdued but still-powerful Colorado River, even the grotesque remnants of the Hardyville cemetery and the drowned stone warehouse under Callville Bay—the ghosts of 1867 worked a kind of magic that produced two unexpected results: I got angry, and I actually began to consider going solo on a book.

The idea that this chapter of western American history should remain exclusively defined by men who portrayed White as either a villain or a joke was not acceptable. Many of us had worked hard over the years on what often seemed like a quixotic pursuit; now it seemed a betrayal to allow our research to go to waste. So thirty-plus years after Dock Marston jokingly suggested that I write a book about my "grandpappy," I put away the excuses and set out to take his advice.

Chapter 18 Grand Canyon History: Discoveries and Rediscoveries

My first step was an attempt to learn more about Grand Canyon history. From Marston's copious data and my own extracurricular reading, I began to assemble the scattered pieces.

The most ancient history of the Grand Canyon and its aboriginal inhabitants lies in the sporadic discoveries of archaeological ruins and resultant speculations. The old legends impart an aura of mystery and myth, but they are not part of this discussion. I have great regard for the American Indian tribes, and I do not doubt that these people, especially the Anasazi, long ago preceded the white man onto the Colorado River and into the Grand Canyon; however, the white man's history is more relevant to the present purpose.

In the beginning were Francisco Vásquez de Coronado and his 1540 expedition seeking the fabled Seven Cities of Cibola; García López de Cárdenas, the so-called discoverer of the Grand Canyon; Francisco Tomas Garcés, the Franciscan missionary who "rediscovered" the canyon in 1776; Fray Silvestre Vélez de Escalante and Francisco Atanasio Domínguez, who discovered the famous Crossing of the

Fathers in Glen Canyon. Representing the Spanish heritage of the Colorado River and Grand Canyon, these explorers looked into the canyon from its rim. If they found a way down to the river, it was simply to cross it in their anxiety to get out of there as fast as they could. There was, after all, no gold in it to steal, no souls in it to save; they had no interest in it—except perhaps for a brief admiration of the awesome landscape.

Those curious Yankees who came later explored the United States from top to bottom and side to side by way of the soldier, trapper, prospector, settler, just plain adventurer, and ultimately, the scientist. In spite of their efforts, they were remarkably slow in getting around to the Colorado River's Big Cañon. Lieutenant Ives and his steamboat *Explorer* tiptoed up the Colorado River as far as Black Canyon in 1857, and a few Mormon boatmen floated sixty miles downriver from Grand Wash Cliffs to Callville in the spring of 1867. Many others were sniffing around the edges; they were creeping up on it, but these forays did not reveal the estimated five hundred to seven hundred mile mystery of the Grand Canyon.

Then, on September 7, 1867, James White appeared on his raft at Callville and started a new and contentious chapter in Colorado River and Grand Canyon history. The three newspaper accounts of White's journey appeared before the month was out, two in California and one in Prescott, Arizona Territory; Dr. Parry's report was read in the St. Louis Academy of Science in February of 1868 and published shortly thereafter in its *Transactions*. Front-page accounts of White's journey appeared across the country in the midwestern and eastern press. The stage was set for controversy.

Less than two years after the White story appeared, Major John Wesley Powell embarked on the Green River in May 1869. He claimed that he had contemplated and prepared for his expedition for years before launching his boats. His statements that White's journey had not happened and that he, Powell, was first through the Grand Canyon successfully discredited White's earlier acclaim. The United States government and the majority of published books gave official credit to the major, endorsing his journey as a discovery.

From his first expedition in 1869 through his second in 1871–72, Powell was in sole possession of the canyon. Stories have been advanced that he believed himself to be not only the first to make the journey but the last. It even looked that way after Frank Brown's 1889 disastrous attempt failed and killed three men, including himself. Of course such exclusivity was never possible; where one man went, another was bound to follow. Seventeen years after Powell, the strong-willed and determined Robert Stanton succeeded with his 1890 voyage, proclaiming for himself the title of second through the Grand Canyon.

By the time Stanton and Dawson had their verbal shootout in *The Trail* in 1919, thirty years had passed since Stanton's expedition. Only a handful of adventurous men had followed him down the river and through the canyon: Flavell and Montez in 1896, Galloway and Richard in 1896, Wooley in 1903, Russell in 1906, Stone (with Galloway) in 1909, the Kolb brothers in 1911, and Russell again in 1914. David Lavender, in his book *River Runners of the Grand Canyon*, defines this group as freelancers who pursued no grand design.

Seven years later, the USGS began trolling for dam sites. William Darrah, writing Powell's biography in 1951, states, "[Brown's] proposed railroad, if authorized and constructed, would interfere with the reservation of the canyons as a potential source of irrigation waters, and the major envisioned great storage dams in the Colorado River." Darrah also relates that "[Powell's] vision of harnessing the Colorado River is becoming reality. Hoover Dam in the Boulder project was erected a few miles north of a site which the major had long ago considered feasible."

Between 1921 and 1923, the USGS made several exploratory trips to locate potential dam sites. These early explorations eventually led to Boulder Dam and Glen Canyon Dam. There were even proposals for dams within Grand Canyon itself, but Major Powell would probably have had no enthusiasm for these. The Colorado River runners of this period included Freeman, Dodge, Lint, Kolb, Blake, Moore, and Birdseye.

A typically 1920s era of Grand Canyon exploration now began. Pathé-Bray set out to make the big Grand Canyon moving picture. Clyde Eddy raced to beat them to it, introducing a bear and a dog into the now fascinating realm of firsts. He need not have hurried; the Pathé-Bray film was never released. Eddy returned for another go, but his competition gave up. Although these pioneers did not exactly set the world on fire, they awakened greater interest in the Colorado and the canyon with their press coverage and deliberate publicity.

In 1928, newlyweds Glen and Bessie Hyde appeared in the canyon and disappeared there forever; they were something of an enigma and their fate has only recently been explored and explained in Brad Dimock's excellent book *Sunk Without a Sound*. But their disappearance at the time attracted the press and fed the lure of the mystery and romance of this place. It could hardly be long before the boating entrepreneurs discovered the commercial possibilities. The Great Depression probably slowed development, but Boulder Dam may have given it a boost.

In 1937, however, before the tours arrived, Buzz Holmstrom made his lonely voyage from Green River to Boulder Dam. He did not fit into any of the existing categories. He was a brave young man with an agenda more spiritual than practical, another enigma of the river. His trip was heralded by "Believe-It-or-Not" Ripley as the first solo voyage through the Grand Canyon. In 1938, Norm Nevills and his guided tours became the new pioneers. One of their early passengers was Barry Goldwater—a great endorsement for this exciting new pastime.

But before the tour business got off the ground, river travelers were few and far between. By 1940, nearly three-quarters of a century after James White's journey, only a hundred brave men (depending on your arithmetic) had run the Colorado through the Grand Canyon, not to mention two women, one bear, and a dog. The men kept diaries and logs and wrote lots of letters; a few wrote books. These few, however, established a river-runner tradition. The opinions of most later boatmen reflected their own experiences, but they were influenced by the declarations of Powell, Dellenbaugh, and Stanton. Keeping faith with the tradition, most of them echoed to some degree the defamation of White's character and a strong disbelief in his journey.

Darrah, Powell's biographer, reports in *Powell of the Colorado* that "there were others who, with loud fanfare, challenged [Powell's] priority," implying that James White had legions of champions, whereas in reality that "loud fanfare" barely rose above a whisper. Indeed, it was hard to find anyone in Powell's lifetime, except General Palmer, who was willing to come to White's unqualified defense. But Darrah still complained that "even though White . . . has been discredited, the shadow of doubt, the ever present question, remains in documented history. The underdogs have had their defenders even against uncontested truth and fact."

A remarkable example of this gospel occurs in Edwin Corle's book *Listen, Bright Angel* in the suggestively Biblical declaration: "Stanton's book concludes the argument. It leaves no room for doubt. It answers every question. It is final."

To be fair to river runners, neither Darrah nor Corle ran the Colorado River, but their books championed their heroes and reflected their biases without the leavening of personal experience and promoted the denigration of James White just as much, if not more, because they gave the appearance of objectivity.

Along the way, an occasional article surfaced that fell outside the traditional view. In 1922, a piece by J. Cecil Alter appeared in "Tribune Travelogs," a regular feature of the *Salt Lake Tribune*. Alter was for a time director of the Utah State Historical Society and a solid historian. He adopted the premise of Senate Document No. 42 and took White's opponents to task. He accused Dellenbaugh of jealousy, scolding him for denouncing Ives and Wheeler for taking government backing when, as a member of Powell's second expedition, he knew that the major had also been financed by the U. S. government. He also scolded George Wharton James, another writer with limited experience on the Colorado, for a criticism of White that he had borrowed from earlier detractors. Forty years later, Alter wrote in a letter to Dock Marston, "I didn't get much of a 'hand' for the White narrative," but he maintained, "I have not changed my mind; White COULD have done, just what he said he did."

Amid all the denunciations, an occasional glimmer crept into a criticism that actually strengthened White's cause. Lewis Freeman, one of the post–World War I river runners who were investigating the dam sites, pointed out in 1923 what he thought was surefire proof of the impossibility of White's voyage:

> Riding a loosely-bound bunch of logs in really rough
> water—I can think of no more certain preliminary to

inevitable suicide than such an action. . . . On a make-shift raft like White's by letting go and getting completely away from the floundering logs when they were drawn under, a man *might* come up himself with enough wind to last him until he struck the next eddy. But tied to the logs, the only question would be as to whether drowning would precede or follow a rap on the head from his wallowing if not dissolving raft.

Freeman, however, was actually describing a method of survival which White had reported to Stanton in 1907 when he described his lariat rope as "50 feet long tied to the raft and tied around my waist" and his method of retrieval as "I took hold of the rope and jumped into the river and pulled myself to the raft and climbed on."

Another interesting critic was Virginia McConnell. Her specialty was Captain Baker, the slain leader of White's party. She believed it "highly probable" that White had killed Baker. Back in 1861, Baker had led a party of gold seekers into the San Juan Mountains, but when these intrepid prospectors found horrendous weather, terrible hardships, hostile Utes, and no gold, they blamed Baker and were ready to kill him. Her reasoning went like this: since Captain Baker was eminently killable in 1861, it should be assumed that White killed him in 1867. Although her opinion was certainly anti-White, her research had one redeeming factor: the well-documented fact that Baker knew the San Juan Mountains, the Dolores and San Miguel Rivers, and points north extremely well, too well in fact for him to be as lost as some of White's other critics claimed.

Barry Goldwater, after running the river through the canyon with Nevills, wrote his book *Delightful Journey down the Green and Colorado Rivers*, which persuasively stated this 1946 opinion:

> To those who say that such a voyage could not be made on a raft, I answer that men in desperate circumstances have accomplished more dangerous feats than running Colorado River rapids on a raft, although I would never, in my weakest moments, venture such a trip. To those who say that White is wrong on certain points, I say to imagine yourself starved, cold, and scared as hell in the middle of the Colorado River on a raft, and then ask yourself whether you would give a tinker's damn about the scenery or details of it. I repeat that nothing yet has been

brought forward to make me accept anyone other than
White as the first through here.

In 1948, he was still of that opinion, but twenty-one years later
the senator wrote a letter to Dock Marston which revealed some
ambivalence on the subject:

> I don't know where you get the information that I
> hoped that White was the first man through Canyon. . . .
> All I have ever hoped was that somebody would someday
> conclusively prove that he wasn't. I frankly have my
> doubts, but I also recognize that a man could do what he
> reports that he did and clarification in this field . . . is
> needed as in any other connected with our favorite river.

Yet in 1994, Goldwater wrote a generous letter to me: "I understand you are writing a book about James White's journey. I can't tell
you how pleased I am. I'm sure you are doing all you can to finish this
in time for all us old timers to be able to read it." I think Goldwater,
like many Colorado River runners, may have had doubts about the raft
journey but believed it deserved further investigation.

In 1955, Bill Beer and John Dagget swam the Colorado through
the Grand Canyon. They started on Easter Sunday, April 10, with provisions stowed in waterproof boxes which they used as underarm
floatation devices through the rapids. They emerged on May 5 with
some nasty cuts, scrapes, and bruises but quite alive. Their adventure
caused some mellowing on the subject of White's journey and the
appearance of a few new tentative believers, but no one was truly
going out on a limb.

An interesting video, *Call of the Canyon*, chronicles the 1988
experience of Manfred Kraus, who swam the entire length of the
Grand Canyon in two weeks. It was suggested that Kraus's trip lent
credence to the White voyage of 1867; indeed the entire video was
pro-White. It even included a clip of Bob Euler explaining why there
was good reason to consider White's voyage viable.

What is possibly more intriguing is one remarkable metamor-
phosis in White's story; his voyage was still denied, of course, but a trans-
formation of magical proportions seems to have occurred. In a 1982
article in *The American West* magazine, David Lavender resurrected the

accusation that White had murdered his two companions, citing the shooting of Joe Goodfellow as proof that White was capable of "passions." But only three years later, when Lavender's book *River Runners of the Grand Canyon* appeared, White and his raft had turned into a rather benign twentieth-century legend, a "modern folk story" somewhat akin to George Washington and the cherry tree but without the noble sentiment. Lavender neatly transformed White and the controversy over him into an irrelevant footnote.

These discoveries and rediscoveries are as many and varied as the layers of spectacular walls that flare from river to sky within this magnificent chasm. Our investigation into the validity of James White's 1867 Grand Canyon journey is but the latest layer of rediscovery.

CHAPTER 19   BOB EULER AND SQUARE ONE

It was clear from the start that determining what really happened to White in 1867 required an investigation into a very cold case; all the players were dead and could not be questioned; corroborating eyewitnesses were lacking; even circumstantial evidence was somewhere between thin and nonexistent.

Bob Euler started with two undisputed facts: one, White, Baker, and Strole were prospecting for gold in the San Juan Mountains of Colorado Territory in the summer of 1867, and, two, White was rescued from a makeshift log raft on the Colorado River at Callville, Nevada, on September 7 of the same year. A beginning and an ending. But, the crucial question was what happened in between and, especially, where did White and Strole enter the river? It is important to understand that—for the Colorado River boatmen who denied White's raft journey—this "point of embarkation" defined the only true transit of the Grand Canyon. But in 1867, there were no Colorado River boatmen, and this definition did not yet exist. While no one at that time, least of all these hapless prospectors, could possibly have known how to identify such a point, speculation on the subject was not slow to follow White's rescue and has been ubiquitous ever since.

The rescuers, old-timers in the river and desert community, observed White's physical and mental condition and compared it to that of Jacob Hamblin and his fellow Mormons who had boated the sixty miles downriver from Grand Wash Cliffs to Callville in April of that year. They reckoned that White must have entered the river upstream of that wash—ergo, inside Big Cañon. From White's description of his experience, and from the well-known and undeniable fact that Big Cañon was a mysterious, largely unknown area into which few, if any, white men had ever ventured, they further concluded that he had very likely started somewhere upstream of the start of the cañon and, as Senator Sherman had so succinctly stated in May 1868, "went in at one end and came through at the other."

Parry, a scientist who seems to have had at once too much and too little knowledge, came up with the first specific point of embarkation: thirty miles up the Grand River. Unfortunately, he was wrong. The experience of the Powell expedition in Cataract Canyon (below the junction of the Green and the Grand) allowed Powell to discredit that point of entry. By implying "false in one, false in all," he was able to deny White's journey altogether, without bothering to offer an alternative point other than some vaguely implied spot at the very end of the canyon. This opinion was amplified by similar observations made during Powell's 1871-72 trip and Stanton's expedition of 1890. In 1907, Stanton claimed outright that White's point of entry was Grand Wash Cliffs, placing him definitively outside the Grand Canyon. This assessment has been the one largely accepted by Colorado River boatmen and historians.

Did the problem lie in the purely physical question of where the Grand Canyon began and ended? Today's alpha and omega are a sort of "first commandment": Lee's Ferry is considered the official alpha, and Grand Wash Cliffs the official omega of the canyon, but where did this commandment come from? In 1922, when the historic Colorado River Compact divided the river's water between the upper and lower Colorado basins, a gauging station for measuring stream flow was located at Lee's Ferry and became mile zero for all distances upstream and down. As for Grand Wash, I have been told that a factor associated with a Paleozoic rock sequence emerging from the north and plunging back beneath the surface at Grand Wash Cliffs actually defines the geological end of the canyon. While these facts are politically and scientifically interesting, they are irrelevant to river transits of the Grand Canyon. It is an article of faith for all Colorado River boatmen that these boundaries were set in 1869 by John Wesley Powell. Anyone who failed to cover this stretch of the Colorado could not claim a Grand Canyon transit—witness the sad fact that the Howland brothers and Bill Dunn were denied a Grand Canyon run because they left the river at Separation Rapid.

Thomas Dawson in 1917 sought to confirm Parry's point of entry in the face of Stanton's opposition, but White's insistence that he had entered "a canyon before reaching the Grand" merely added to the confusion.

As more people ventured onto the Colorado River, various books and articles about the Grand Canyon were written, advancing different theories about White; most were serious, many were self-serving, but none offered bona fide supporting evidence. Eventually, articles of a more frivolous nature began to appear in Sunday supplements, outdoor magazines, and adventure thrillers; some were casual fillers or whimsical tales, a few offered wild fantasies involving secret caves, Indian treasures, or Egyptian gold.

In 1958, Lingenfelter's book brought a refreshing glimmer of sanity into the controversy. He had no personal agenda and his theory accepted the premise (which first appeared in Stanton's interview) that the party had gone southwest from the San Juan River. He gave credence, however, to the "two days" White said it took them to reach the side canyon, and placed White and Strole in Navajo Canyon, fairly close to present-day Page, Arizona; this was above the Grand Canyon boundary at Lee's Ferry. If, as Dock Marston later claimed, this was incorrect, Lingenfelter's blunt opinion of Stanton's conclusion was right on target when he said, "It is one thing to say that White did not make a trip from the Grand River to Callville, but it is vengeance to draw the line so thin that his voyage begins just where the Grand Canyon ends."

Bulger's review of this book praised its author, but suggested an entry point farther north—in White Canyon:

> Not having much success in their search for gold they
> moved down the San Juan River. Where canyons begin
> they left the river. This would be in the area a little below
> the present-day settlement of Bluff, Utah . . . they went
> north, aiming to get to the Grand River. The party proba-
> bly went north by way of either Butler Wash or Comb

> Wash, more likely the latter . . . they did not veer much to
> the west because of the many canyons associated with
> Grand Gulch . . . As they went north to northwest, they
> passed over a mountain ridge . . . This would be Elk Ridge
> or its western extension toward White Canyon.

He, too, took aim at White's accusers:

> It seems unfortunate that there was in the past so
> much irrational endeavor to discredit White, and so little
> thoughtful effort to analyze the reports. It is difficult to
> think that White or those around him knew enough of the
> geography of the Colorado River to fabricate such a story.
> His simple narrative is easier to believe than alternate fan-
> tastic suggestion.

The Euler-Dobyns review of Lingenfelter's book was probably
the first step toward Bob Euler's later detective work; it pointed out for
the first time the major flaw in Stanton's proposed cross-country route
from the San Juan River to the Grand Wash Cliffs:

> White could not have entered the river via Peach
> Springs or Diamond Creek Canyons further west. These
> south rim tributaries . . . would have been barred to White
> in 1867 by *Pai* [the Walapai and Havasupai Indians] bands
> which lived in their bottoms, and were then at war with
> United States troops. White's party was attacked by Indians
> and retreated through an uninhabited canyon; had it been
> in *Pai* country, the prospectors would have had to fight
> *through* the Indians to reach the river. This applies to almost
> all south rim canyons west of the Little Colorado River.

Many issues of the *Arizona Miner* of 1867 carried evidence of
this, describing in gruesome detail the many terrifying "Walapai raids"
on soldiers and civilians alike in that area. In fact, it was probably this
factor that convinced editor John Marion of the validity of White's
journey through the canyon; like Euler and Dobyns, he would have
rejected an entry point at Grand Wash Cliffs.

Omitting the trivial or fantastic accounts in the popular press,
there were at least sixteen different points of embarkation earnestly
proposed over the years: on rivers like the Green, the Grand, the
Colorado, the San Juan, the Little Colorado, the Dirty Devil, the
Escalante, and the Virgin, as well as in side canyons like White, Dark,

Elephant, Navajo, Lake, Robbers' Crossing, Gunnison Crossing, and Diamond and Spencer Creeks. But there must be even more than sixteen places in this vast river system where one might emerge from a side canyon or stream and launch a raft. The problem was the wild and desolate land that surrounded and jealously guarded such places. It is astonishing how many points of entry were suggested with casual disregard for the possibility of getting to them.

Bob Euler was president of Prescott College and head of an archeological dig on Black Mesa when he began what was the first, and only serious and intensive, field investigation of White's point of entry. His subsequent appointment by the U.S. Department of the Interior as the Grand Canyon anthropologist placed him fortuitously close to his area of research. He was eminently qualified for the task.

Discarding the earlier points of embarkation that were rooted in guesswork, interpretation, and prejudice, Euler chose to start with a clean slate. He began by studying White's own statements, descriptions, and estimates about the disputed land journey leading to the river:

1. the San Juan River entered a canyon without bottomland (Parry's survey report)
2. the party traveled north from the San Juan (Parry's survey report)
3. the men crossed a mountain or mountainlike ridge (Parry's survey report)
4. their horses' feet were sore (James White's 1867 letter)
5. they traveled 50 miles from the San Juan to a side canyon (Parry's survey report)
6. they had access into the side canyon from the south, but no exit from it to the north (White's 1917 statement)
7. there was water in the side canyon, but no running stream (White's 1917 letter to Dawson)
8. they walked twelve to fifteen miles from the point of Baker's death to the river (Parry's survey report)

The study reinforced his and Dobyn's earlier theory. Although the area south of the south rim of the Grand Canyon was Euler's backyard, he was less familiar with that desolate triangle of land bounded by the San Juan River, the Colorado River, and the Utah-Colorado border. This territory covers hundreds of square miles, it is rugged and difficult of access, and it abounds in side canyons. As he explained, his preliminary reconnaissance was "by fixed wing aircraft in order to obtain a general understanding of land forms and patterns." Following that, he said, "more specific sections were flown by helicopter with landings made at selected points." The search was on.

The San Juan canyon (point 1) was not in question; this is an unmistakable barrier to further continuous travel along the river except by boat. The main objective of his aerial reconnaissance, Euler said, was

> to locate practical routes over which horsemen might have traveled. It might be argued that the best way to have accomplished this would have been by horseback, but the advantage of being able to view larger segments of country from the vantage of a few hundred feet in the air gave a perspective of the region that could not have been perceived from the ground.

Near the San Juan entrenchment, Comb Wash runs roughly north–south along the western flank of the elegant and spectacular Comb Ridge. This huge wash had been proposed by Bulger as part of White's route; Euler agreed that it was definitely the best way north, but suggested that White Canyon was not compatible with White's estimated fifty miles from the San Juan River to the unknown side canyon (point 5):

> Had they gone all the way up Comb Wash to its head near Elk Ridge, they would have had to ride a distance of at least twice what White claimed since they still would have had to turn back or southwesterly, toward White Canyon.

As for access to the side canyon with horses (point 6), and the twelve to fifteen miles to the river (point 8), Euler observed,

> As one heads the Grand Gulch network and flanks Elk Ridge, the prominent drainage of White Canyon lies invitingly dead ahead . . . (but) because of the cliffs it is not possible to get horses into the inner gorge of White Canyon at its upper extremity . . . [also] a glance at the map will show that had White been in upper White Canyon, he would have had a hike of much greater distance before finding the Colorado.

After exploring Bulger's suggested route, Euler began a search for a shorter one. A few miles up Comb Wash, Lime Ridge appears to the west. Considering the descriptions of a mountain ridge and horses' sore feet (points 3 and 4), this avenue looked promising:

it would be possible to effect a horseback traverse over
Lime Ridge and then up one of the westerly forks of Lime
Creek to the Grand Gulch Plateau . . . [where] they would
probably have headed toward The Bears Ears, a prominent landmark just south of Elk Ridge. A more westerly
route would have been prevented by the sharp walled,
branching course of Grand Gulch.

Once they had circumnavigated Grand Gulch, they
probably saw Indian trails heading southwesterly along the
Red House Cliffs. This region was occupied by Ute
Indians and they undoubtedly traveled from spring to
spring—waterhole to waterhole—through it frequently.

It is my contention that the prospectors, not finding a
plausible route into White Canyon, rode down along the
east flank of the Red House Cliffs looking for a break
through them to the Colorado. The first break in these
imposing cliffs, well known to later Mormon travelers, is
Clay Hills Pass . . . a relatively easy horseback route up to
Greenwater Spring from which the entire broad plateau
between there and the Colorado would have been visible.

This route would have brought the prospecting party onto the
plateau that overlooks Bullfrog Creek and Hall's Crossing. Here,
White's description of backtracking to the side canyon pointed strongly to Moqui Canyon, just north and east of those two streams. Euler
believed that once having arrived on this plateau, they would have
inevitably struck this side canyon.

But was this a viable solution? Or were there more questions?

Point 5, the fifty-mile distance was satisfied; but that alone was
not enough. If Moqui was the right canyon, points 6,7,and 8 (access to
the side canyon from the south, but not from the north; water in the
side canyon, but not a running stream; and distance from the point of
Baker's death to the river) had to be satisfied as well. It was all or nothing. He and his pilot took off for another exploratory look.

Euler explained what they found:

Approximately 12 miles up Moqui Canyon from its junc-
ture with the Colorado there are several stabilized sand
dunes, the only break in an otherwise sheer-walled canyon,
down which horses could be taken. In the Moqui Canyon
channel near the base of these dunes there is some running surface water today. Below this point, the stream sinks
beneath the surface and the channel is usually dry.

One other factor leads me to believe that White,
Baker and Strole rode their horses down the sand dunes
into Moqui Canyon at this point on the afternoon in
August, 1867. In White's account to Dawson . . . he
remarked that, upon leaving the side canyon "We could
not get out of the canyon on the opposite side; so we had
to go out of the canyon the same way we went down." The
location of the falling sand dunes in Moqui Canyon is the
only point for many, many miles where the geography
makes White's statement ring true; directly opposite the
sand dunes the cliffs of Moqui are sheer and unscalable.

The reader may wonder, as I did, what these "stabilized sand dunes" were, whether they had been there in White's time, and whether they would really have provided adequate access into the canyon. In basic terms (as it was explained to me), the dunes are the result of the prevailing southwesterly winds which continually blow sand into the eroded crevasses or steps in the rocky canyon walls. Weather and the settling process consolidate the sand over time into strong ramplike dunes, which in most areas reach only partway to the plateau above, but in this case go clear to the top. Spreading desert vegetation, however sparse it may appear, has far-reaching and tough horizontal roots intended to capture the meager rainfall; in its growing process, it further stabilizes the dunes into a permanent hill, steep but firm. Geologists state that these dunes were indeed there in 1967 and are, in fact, phenomena of very long standing in geologic time. It seems clear from recent reports of unwanted incursions into Moqui Canyon that they are still supporting an astonishing amount of rough activity.

Euler's conclusions from this evidence were considered with the customary degree of scientific reserve; critics are always waiting in the wings with questions. But he had exhaustively examined White's descriptions and estimates before he began his search; he did not allow his findings to stray beyond the limits of possibility. His fieldwork was impeccable, and his conclusions were then, and are now, the result of scientifically objective reasoning.

Moqui Canyon represented a key piece in the James White puzzle; this, and the results of our other research, provided the means to refute the allegations and accusations made against White during this century-old controversy.

CHAPTER 20   IN JAMES WHITE'S FOOTSTEPS

By 1975, my husband, Bob, and I had been long and seriously involved with my grandfather and his odyssey. We were ready to
attempt a firsthand field trip. This was the best kind of research—neither scientific nor scholarly but certainly the most rewarding. Armed
with a decade and a half of Dock-oriented lore, mountains of data,
research into stress, survivals, and lunar ephemera, and, best of all, the
possibilities of Bob Euler's Moqui Canyon, we planned a "JW vacation." Our intention was to get as close as possible by airplane and car
to the land of White's preriver prospecting journey.

Sightseeing through Utah ended at Page, Arizona, where we
chartered a small airplane. From Page we flew east/northeast as far as
Cortez, Colorado, taking pictures all the way. Our desire to go farther,
all the way to Silverton (or Baker's Park), was foiled by its 9,300-foot
altitude; it was too high for our Cessna Cardinal. So we flew on toward
the Dolores River, then turned south to fly along the Mancos River,
enjoying the birds-eye view of the awesome beauty of Mesa Verde.

Where the Mancos enters the San Juan River, we circled to
study the north embankment. There is no question that this feature
would have forced Baker's party to cross to the south side of the San
Juan, but as we continued to follow the course of that river, it became

clear that progress along only one side of the river was impeded by the distribution of sandbanks and bottomland. It looked very much as though the party would have had to cross and recross the river several times to do any prospecting.

We found the high vertical cliffs which capture and entrench the San Juan River and which in 1867 made further bottomland passage impossible for the party. We found Comb Wash with its companion Comb Ridge; its spectacular formation and color were, like so much of this magnificent land, incredible. We had asked our pilot, Jeff Murphy, to follow along the Red House Cliffs south of the Bear's Ears and turn west at Clay Hills Pass. We had the sky to ourselves and the land below as well, so when Jeff wanted to get his bearings, he merely swooped down to read the road signs. I was too busy taking pictures to notice, and Bob is a pilot so it didn't bother him, although he did remark later that he was glad Jeff wasn't nearsighted.

He took us, as requested, to Lake Powell where Bullfrog Creek and Hall's Creek meet and then flew north to the entrance to Moqui Canyon. We asked him to fly up the canyon for about twelve miles and find some stabilized sand dunes on the south side, with sheer walls to the north. He seemed skeptical but flew on, and, at just about the twelve-mile point, he exclaimed, "There they are!" as though we had just discovered the New World. And in a way, we had. There had never been any doubt about Bob Euler's research, but actually seeing the dunes made us feel like partners in the discovery.

We had now seen everything possible for this flight, so we returned to Page via Lake Powell, with a short detour over the Glen Canyon Dam and downstream to Lee's Ferry. It was rewarding to discover that this flight had taught us much that we had missed in all the years of reading books and maps. White's journey now took on a reality that it had lacked before.

The next step was to cover on land what we had seen from the air. Starting at Durango, Colorado, we rode General Palmer's Denver and Rio Grande narrow-gauge steam train along the Animas River to Silverton. In Durango, we stayed at the General Palmer House (and imagined we were staying with a friend of the family). We found tempting maps of jeep trails across to the Dolores River; although our car wasn't up to them, they proved that horses had no trouble, now or in 1867.

We followed the Mancos River as far as the boundary of the Ute Reservation but did not have enough time to seek permission to go farther down the valley. Later on, coming to the Four Corners, we stopped just to admire this land; it is all so magnificent in its spectacular grandeur and unearthly silence—so desolate, so harsh, so forbiddingly empty, and so beautiful.

We followed the San Juan River, sometimes near, sometimes far, and actually ventured into Comb Wash, where we stood in dry quicksand, a sensation close to standing on glare ice, and hoped our car would make it back up to the road. We located and literally begged local guides to take us all the way down Comb Wash to the San Juan, but they looked at the sky to the north and declined; flash floods, they said, turn Comb Wash into a roaring nightmare, and they were unwilling to chance it that day. Northwest of Mexican Hat, we encountered Cedar Mesa and enjoyed (!) the terrifying ride up twenty-six hundred feet of switchback red dirt road, without guard rails—happily without any traffic.

Along the Red House Cliffs, State Route 276 runs straight and lonely. At many points, it appeared that there might be a way through, but the first opening was indeed Clay Hills Pass. We paused at Greenwater Spring, admired the lizards, and from there headed west over the harsh stony plateau leading to Lake Powell and Hall's Crossing. To the north lay Moqui Canyon, but we did not see it; to our earthbound eyes, the plateau seemed unbroken.

At Hall's Crossing, we rented a twentieth-century motorboat and went north to Moqui Canyon. Buoyed at the mouth was a sign that read "Moki Canyon." Since then I have found both spellings on various maps, and I have no idea which one is correct. Later in my research, I learned that there are two spellings for Pierces Ferry, or Pearces Ferry, near the end of Grand Canyon, so maybe James White was not the only one with spelling problems.

We went up the canyon as far as the flooding waters of Lake Powell would take us, seeing a vista of caves, redrock cliffs, drowned treetops, hidden coves, desert scrub and saltbush, and the remarkable sand dunes. Some bore the unmistakable footprints of a few hardy souls who had earlier climbed around them. When we ran out of lake, we left the boat and climbed up and over a small hill; within four hundred yards, it seemed that we had stepped clear out of the twentieth century and into the 1867 world of James White. The remoteness and silence were complete; Bullfrog Marina, its motorboats, even Lake Powell seemed like alien intrusions.

At Lee's Ferry, we rented a small boat with an outboard motor and putted almost up to Glen Canyon Dam. Having read over and over the river runners' insistence that White's raft would have inevitably gotten hung up on the many sandbars in the river that make smooth sailing impossible, we cut the motor and let our boat drift back downstream without human interference. For miles, floating along in the silence, we found sandbars aplenty, but we did not touch a single one. Of course, we were aware that river contours change, more today than in White's time, so the only conclusion we drew from our unimpeded travel was that one shouldn't draw conclusions. We were gratified nonetheless, for it meant that getting hung up on sandbars was not a constant factor.

On our way home along U. S. 93, we came within fifty miles of Grand Wash Cliffs, that tantalizing point of entry favored by Stanton. We knew there were many things we had not had sufficient time to cover, but this trip had certainly brought James White to life.

Years later, living in Arizona added another dimension: the implacable heat, the arid landscape, the unearthly silence, the deep night with nearly impenetrable blackness at one's feet and a scintillant sky overhead, a moon to read by, flash floods through the arroyos. No book or map or film could match that experience.

In a hesitant footnote to the conclusions proposed by Robert Stanton, we visited—at last—the Grand Wash Cliffs. Once off U. S. 93, we saw not a single car. Through unending scrub and an unexpected Joshua tree forest, keeping station with the forbidding cliffs to the east, we were physically unaware of the river to the north, although we knew it was there. A bare two hundred yards from where the Colorado, still a river, meets the Lake Mead reservoir, we saw the water.

This presented us with a puzzle of sorts. Had we been prospectors heading west or southwest across Arizona Territory at the approximate latitude of present day Interstate 40, we would not have seen any clear sign or physical landmark to lead us unerringly to the Colorado River by this northerly route. We searched for such signs, but could not find even one.

At Lee's Ferry, where some White critics claimed he and Strole could easily have escaped the river through Paria Canyon, we had paused and considered that possibility. The riffles at this point seemed insignificant compared to Badger Creek and Soap Creek Rapids several miles downriver. The water seemed as benign as it must have been in Glen Canyon in 1867, but the bleak and dusty hills did not present an obvious escape route. Even in 1869, according to George Bradley, Powell had missed the Paria, and he was looking for it. In 1867, two things must have appeared almost painfully certain to White and Strole: this was an arid and forbidding land, and it still belonged to the Indians. It struck us that these two men had made a reasonable choice: weighing unknown land against unknown river, they decided to stay with the means by which they could reach downstream white settlements.

James White knew something about these settlements. He could not have helped but observe the Colorado as a north/south river at Fort Yuma in 1862. As the prospecting party moved west along the San Juan River, Captain Baker and his compass had told them that the Colorado ran north to the Grand and the Green. White and Strole had clearly traveled south on their raft. That ninety-degree turn to the west within the depths of the Grand Canyon was unknown to Captain Baker, and had the men gone south/southwest across the Arizona desert, they would have expected to intercept a north-south river, not search for an east-west one.

From the maps and the history and geography books to the evidence of Lee's Ferry and this foray into the Grand Wash, we became convinced that James White's footsteps were not here at Pierces Ferry. Always the souvenir hunter, I picked up a little clam shell and put it in my pocket. We took one last, long look at the place where Lake Mead intrudes its placid waters upon the mighty Colorado River and turned away.

That trip and the three years spent living in the desert Southwest were more than just pleasant experiences; they expanded our knowledge. Our only regret is that we were never able to follow James White onto the Colorado River and through Big Cañon.

CHAPTER 21 SUMMARY AND CONCLUSIONS: PART A

D iscrediting James White's journey by attacking his character or denigrating his mental capacity seems particularly egregious. These allegations will be considered first.

White was a liar who told his story to make himself important.

The nineteenth-century American West was a fertile field for storytellers. They included novelists, journalists, painters, Wild West show entrepreneurs, explorers, prospectors, engineers, and just plain adventurers. The symptoms included high levels of exaggeration and pure hyperbole. They thought fast, possessed glib tongues, and shared a threadbare partnership with the truth.

Evidence is lacking to cast James White in this role. He was, in fact, self-effacing, taciturn, secretive, practical, and prosaic, basically incapable of convoluted invention or fantasy, unable even to talk his way out of the army's stolen coffee charge or make himself a hero in the shooting of Joe Goodfellow. He lacked the imagination to create a tall tale or the chutzpah for a bravura display of his experiences.

By 1871, White had turned his back on the years of rough-and-tumble existence on the trail and reverted to a reflection of his formative years in Wisconsin. He took modest pride in supporting his family, being a good citizen, and providing a good education for his children. He insisted on good linen and china on his table, proper behavior from the family, good manners, and piano lessons for his daughters, all symptoms of a nineteenth-century middle-class lifestyle.

White's western adventure stories never exhibited the imagination required to invent such physical characteristics as rivers going into canyons, mountain ridges, side canyons, or continuous rapids, nor was he capable of embellishment of any sort. If anything, his stories—including the Grand Canyon journey—became increasingly milder over the years. He made no attempt at self-aggrandizement and, except for that twenty-five-dollar check from Stanton, never made a dime off his raft trip. He was profoundly unaware of whatever fame he had been accorded. It was just as well, for it came from Colorado River runners and was entirely negative.

The accusations of lying were largely due to the exaggerated account written by Major Calhoun. He claimed to have the story straight from White's "own lips," but the evidence points much more strongly to the colorful Calhoun himself as the true candidate for Grand Canyon yarn spinner.

White was a thief, and/or he murdered his companions, then lied to cover his crime.

White was attacked in the early days following Powell's expedition as some kind of thief who rafted down a stretch of river to save his hide. Just a hint of this by Frederick Dellenbaugh was considered a viable argument against his voyage. But the most bizarre accusation was that he murdered his partners and used an imaginary Colorado River-Grand Canyon raft trip as an alibi.

Of course, the nineteenth-century West was a violent land, peopled by a great many lawless white men. Indians were fighting throughout the territory: Ute and southern Paiute around the San Juan territory; Yavapai, Walapai, and Havasupai along the southern rim of the Grand Canyon, to name but a few. Along the Arkansas River and the Santa Fe Trail, the Arapaho, Comanche, and other powerful tribes made whites nervous and kept a "shotgun" riding on their stagecoaches. There was indeed a lot of killing going on, but in those years murder seemed to rank a poor second to cattle or horse stealing (unless, of course, the target was an Indian horse—always considered fair game).

In this setting, might murder be a reasonable possibility? Consider this hypothetical case: White, Strole, and Baker leave Baker's Park and head for the San Juan River. Somewhere along the way, White kills Baker and Strole. What are his options? Unfamiliar with the area where he commits this crime, he can head either north or south into unknown and forbidding territory, where neither horses and supplies nor Baker's notes and compass can offer, let alone guarantee, a chance for survival. Or, wise to the facts of western life he has acquired in his six years of experience, he can turn around and retrace his steps to Baker's Park.

There is only one smart choice: Baker's Park and points east. If Baker's party were the sole residents of Eureka Gulch and Baker's Park at the time of their departure, our murderer has nothing to explain to anyone. Or, if there were other gold seekers in that area who still happen to be around, he can hide the horses and supplies and stagger bravely into camp, in which case his Indian ambush story makes him the local hero. Or, in a more practical scenario, he can walk in boldly with his ill-gotten possessions. "What happened to your buddies?" asks a curious Eureka Gulch prospector. "Indians," replies White. If the prospector believes his story, he is properly sympathetic; if not, he mutters, "Right!" and goes back to his diggings.

Either way, there is no sheriff to go out into that unfamiliar and dangerous land to retrieve the victims, no posse to track the hostiles, and no deputies to make an arrest. Like roads and signposts, law enforcement at this time was conspicuous by its absence. It is far more likely that any prospector still in residence would merely shrug his shoulders and make damned sure his pistol was loaded.

But hypothetical scenarios aside, this idea that concocting a complicated Ute ambush, embarking on an uncharted river, and weaving a fantasy about rafts and rapids could constitute an alibi for a crime is ludicrous in the extreme. More to the point, such an accusation becomes a smokescreen since it must be patently obvious that liars, thieves, and murderers have as much ability to ride a raft down a river as upstanding and God-fearing mortals. White's moral character has no bearing on his journey.

White was so mentally deficient that he had no concept of time or distance.

It has been well established that James White spent the years between 1861 and 1867 covering hundreds of miles throughout the West and Southwest, sometimes alone, often in company. If he had not by then learned the basics of estimating time and distance, he would hardly have made it as far as he did since these skills were absolute requirements for survival in that territory.

Stanton's premise that White went overland from Four Corners to embark on the Colorado at Grand Wash Cliffs, floated sixty miles to Callville, but was so abysmally ignorant that he mistook this journey for a raft voyage on the Colorado River through the Grand Canyon seems hard to swallow. Still, it must be examined because so many believe it.

The questions, "Why leave the San Juan River?" and "Why cross totally unknown territory?" are relevant since it is obvious that Baker's party did leave the San Juan at some point and cross unknown territory either to the north or south. But which way was it?

White's 1867–68 statement indicated that the party's goal after Baker's Park was the San Juan River, that they spent some time prospecting along that river, and that they then traveled north. In 1907, according to Stanton's interview transcript, White said they left the river immediately after coming to the mouth of the Mancos and traveled southwest, a gross contradiction. We can accept this as a benign product of White's advanced age or blame it—as Stanton did—on White's ignorance. However, we cannot forget that Stanton's premise required that White (alone or with companions) make this overland journey to the southwest.

Any point where the prospectors might have left the San Juan River would have presented essentially the same choices: along the flank of the southerly continuation of Comb Ridge, down to Monument Valley, thence to the area of present-day Tuba City, south to Gray Mountain to miss the impassable gorge of the Little Colorado, west across the waterless Coconino Plateau, skirting the Aubrey Cliffs, then northwest along the Grand Wash Cliffs to Pierces Ferry. This route could have been physically possible had they had help from friendly Navajos, but most of these tortured people were absent from their lands at that time, under detention by Kit Carson at Bosque Redondo in eastern New Mexico Territory; those who had escaped the Long Walk were in hiding, did not trust white men, and were unlikely to emerge to offer their services as guides.

This Comb Ridge route adds up to approximately three hundred miles, with no food except an occasional jackrabbit, an uncertain water supply, and a rate of travel gradually reduced because of the men's decreasing strength. No matter how far east along the river they started, the difficulties would have been just as great; the routes would have converged in any case, and the distances overland would have increased. It would have been an incredibly tough journey, one whose physical features were entirely opposite to those White described. The canyon system that characterizes this area is mind boggling, and finding a way around it equally so. In 1867, constant experimental probing was far more likely than any straight-line travel, adding miles and time to the route.

It is important to note that it was Stanton's interview which spawned the contention that White had gone overland and entered the Colorado at Grand Wash Cliffs. According to the transcript, White said the party crossed the San Juan River at the mouth of the Mancos and traveled southwest from there. An examination of this point clearly shows that there is no bottomland for several miles on the north side along which men or horses can travel; crossing the San Juan here was a necessity, not a choice (see figure 9). During the remainder of the interview, White spoke only of the Grand River—in a northerly rather than a southwesterly direction—certainly a matter of some confusion.

The accusations of mental deficiency in White were not supported by anything more than the diagnosis put forth by Stanton in his *Trail* article; however, that and the interview were remarkably effective in promoting the theory of an overland journey and a Grand Wash Cliffs point of entry.

If Stanton's premise is correct, the most glaring question of all remains: Such a long and arduous land journey bears absolutely no resemblance to a sixty-mile river voyage through Boulder Canyon; no

Figure 9.
The Mancos River at its confluence with the San Juan
(Photo by R. E. Adams)

mental deficiency can explain the substitution. And if not because of
mental deficiency, why should White deny a land journey and make
up such a complicated river story instead? It seems more and more
likely that Stanton's insistence that White went overland was wishful
thinking, based solely on a desire to place him outside the Grand
Canyon.

Chapter 22   Summary and Conclusions: Part B

A raft journey through the Grand Canyon was impossible.

> In any one of a hundred different instances death awaited
> a wrong decision, when we had neither the knowledge nor
> experience for our choice; [it was] partly the marvelous
> chain of coincidences—or "miracles"—that led us through
> forty-seven days and nights, into and out of another world
> and back to civilization again.

These are the words of a pilot forced down over the notorious
Hump in the Himalayas during World War II. He and his copilot, both
with broken ankles, walked through an uncharted and formidable
wilderness after their plane crashed into a mountain. Impossible! But
it happened.

"Help, I can't swim," a sailor kept shouting as he knifed through
the oil-slicked waters of Pearl Harbor on December 7, 1941, stroking
like an Olympic champ. Impossible! But it happened.

Impossible feats of strength and endurance, courage and heroism, are commonplace in wars and disasters, natural or otherwise. Most
so-called survivals are in the final analysis nothing more than beating

the odds in a thousand unique ways. In that sense, James White's survival of his Grand Canyon journey was no more or less impossible than a thousand others.

The Grand Canyon was an unknown wilderness 134 years ago. Major Powell and his men in 1869 suffered through the dangerous rapids and menacing walls, the isolation and fear, the threat of injury and eroding food supplies. Their perception that a lone man trapped in its depths had no hope of rescue and no chance of survival under the conditions described by White led irrevocably to the initial cries of impossible. The Grand Canyon today is no longer an unknown wilderness. Those who ride the rapids—whether in kayaks, prams, expedition boats, "baloneys," inner tubes, or wet suits—contemplate these depths with more excitement than fear. They marvel at the canyon's grandeur and the awesome forces that created it and enjoy the experience. The idea that surviving on a log raft within its depths is impossible is no longer as compelling as it once was.

It is claimed that a log raft voyage through the Grand Canyon has never been repeated, although several attempts have been made. Some see this as proof that the first one didn't happen, but given the recent addition of inner-tube and swimming transits of the canyon, discrediting White's raft trip now appears to rest less on its impossibility than on a lack of eyewitness confirmation.

Simply saying that something is impossible is not enough; alternatives are required. And indeed several were offered to explain how White got from the San Juan River to Callville, but they were far more improbable than White's own explanation. Here was a man who lacked a self-defeating imagination; he possessed not only exceptional physical strength but a frontiersman's mental toughness. He also had two vital advantages: the benign face of the Colorado during August and September of 1867 and his fortuitous arrival at Callville in daylight and in the presence of Captain Wilburn's barge and crew. Viewed objectively, White's journey emerges as a classic case of survival.

White's distance estimates were inaccurate.

Two specific distance estimates have been repeatedly cited as proof that White did not go where he said he did. The first one derives from Dr. Parry's report:

they reached the Animas branch of the San Juan River.
Here their prospecting for gold commenced, and being
only partially successful, they continued still farther to the
west, passing the Dolores, and reaching the Mancos,
which latter stream was followed down to the main valley
of the San Juan. Crossing the San Juan at this point, they
continued down the valley in a westerly direction for
about 200 miles, when the river entered a cañon.

The notes backing up this portion of the report read "came to Colorado
City—left 20th May—for San Juan—struck Animas—Dolores—
Mancos Canon followed to San Juan down that 200 miles crossed to
north side."

Following the pattern of Parry's punctuation in these notes, it
appears that he lumped together 1) the party's arrival at the Animas, 2)
gold seeking at Eureka Gulch and Baker's Park, 3) travel to the Dolores,
the Mancos, and the San Juan Rivers, and 4) travel along the San Juan
until it went into a canyon. This gives the strong impression that the
entire prospecting section of the trip was one continuous experience.

When he wrote his formal report, Parry separated and expanded this group of events into discrete segments but applied the two
hundred miles only to the distance along the San Juan River.
Considering that there was at the time no way to check it out, it seems
just as reasonable to attribute the two hundred miles in Parry's report
to an error caused by the lack of detail in his notes than to condemn
White for inaccuracy.

White, in his own letter, says,

i Went prospeCted with Captin Baker and gorge strole in
the San Won montin Wee found vry god prospeCk but
noth that Wold pay. then Wee stare Down the San Won
river wee travel down a bout 200 miles then Wee Cross
over on Coloreado and Camp.

He, too, jumped from the San Juan mountains to the San Juan
River valley, using as a segue only the words "stare down" (started
down). Given the vagueness and lack of detail in White's letter, it seems
just as reasonable to interpret his two hundred miles this way:

I went prospecting with Captain Baker and George Strole
in the San Juan Mountains. We found very good prospects,
but nothing that would pay. Then we started down [to] the

> San Juan River. We traveled down about 200 miles, then we
> crossed over on [to the] Colorado and camped.

The distance from the Silverton area across to the Dolores and down the Mancos and then down the San Juan River to Comb Wash is about 200 to 230 miles. This distance matches up far more logically to White's 200-mile estimate than the obviously shorter distance from the mouth of the Mancos River to Comb Wash and deserves to be considered at least as valid as that proposed by White's detractors.

The other disputed estimate is the fifty miles White said they traveled from where the San Juan River becomes entrenched to the side canyon where the Indian ambush occurred. Objection to this figure arose primarily from Stanton's insistence upon the Grand Wash Cliffs point of entry, discussed in chapter 21.

The following map and inset (figures 10 and 11) are from Samuel Bowles's book *Our New West*, published in 1869, and they graphically illustrate the state of nineteenth-century knowledge about the huge territory surrounding "the Great Cañon." Any reliance on distances either shown or implied on Bowles's map must be faulty; comparison with a present-day map (figure 12) may explain part of the early confusion.

White could not have gone through the Grand Canyon in fourteen days.

It was Parry who assigned the date of August 24 to White and Strole's embarkation on the Colorado River, based solely on White's vague schedule and the known date of his arrival in Callville. No one questioned it then, and few have questioned it since. Most of White's detractors did not believe that he could have traveled that distance through the canyon in so short a time, while Stanton struggled to rationalize two weeks of travel to cover the sixty miles from Grand Wash Cliffs to Callville that Jacob Hamblin managed in two days. Actually, without any real evidence to anchor elapsed time, the time factor should have been considered a variable because it was unknown.

There may be a clue to this elapsed time in White's letter to his brother. In reading it, I was struck by the possible significance of the words he had crossed out. He could hardly have done this for any language refinement; there must have been other reasons. Some corrections

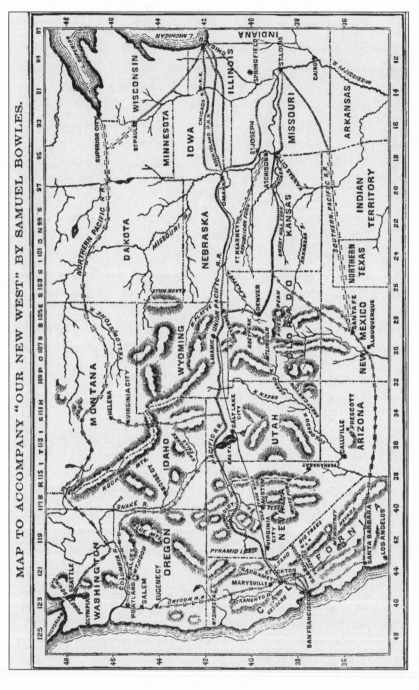

Figure 10. Map of western United States, 1869 (from Samuel Bowles, *Our New West*)

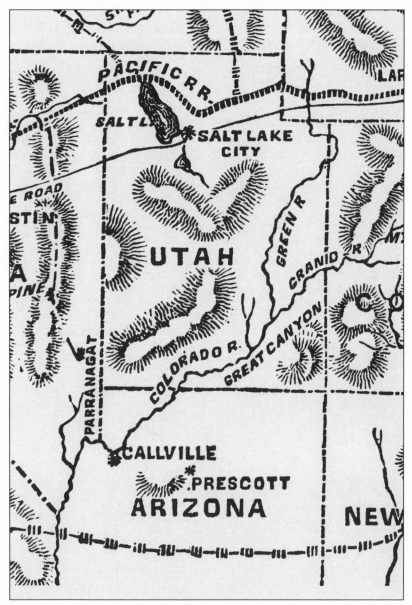

Figure 11. Inset from western United States map, 1869.

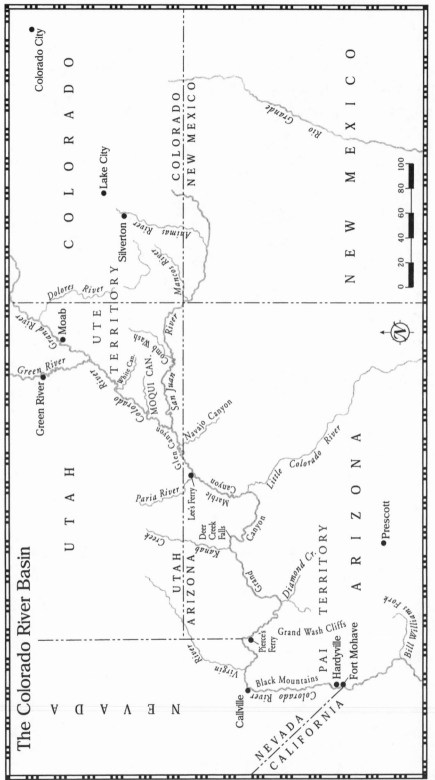

Figure 12.

were obviously due to confusion over how many days had passed, but I believe that one word was definitely replaced to clarify a fact.

In his description of escaping down the side canyon, he wrote that they arrived at the river "just at dalk [dark]," then crossed it out and wrote "night." There were so many errors that it is highly unlikely he would make a change to correct the spelling. What possible significance could this replacement have? Dark and night both convey the fact that the sun has set, but it is possible for it to be night without being dark. There is no darkness quite like night in an uninhabited landscape deep within a canyon; that darkness is truly black. And a night that is not dark must be one illuminated by light from some source; in that country at that time it had to be by moonlight. And that moonlight must indeed have been significant for White and Strole.

Consider their activities upon arriving at the river after fleeing down Moqui Canyon. To continue their escape by river, they had to collect driftwood logs and lash them together with lariat ropes to make a raft. They could not take a chance of attracting the Indians' attention by lighting a fire, but neither could they perform these tasks in the blackness of this remote area. Without some kind of light, they would have had to hide and wait for daylight, which, by White's account, they did not do.

White, describing their Mulberry Creek raid for the Indian horses, specifically recalled waiting for the moon to rise because they needed its light; they faced a similar situation in Moqui Canyon. That crossed-out word "dark" only makes sense if when they reached the river, it was after sunset, and the moon was already shining. This would make a significant difference in the timetable.

In the summer, the full moon gives light from about sunset to sunrise, shining all night long. A waxing moon is progressing toward full and rises before sunset; a waning moon is moving away from full and rises progressively later, leaving an increasingly longer period of darkness between sunset and moonrise. The lunar month is roughly twenty-eight days.

According to the almanac for 1867, full moon occurred on August 15. At fourteen days past full moon (August 29), it would be new moon or effectively no moon at all. During the two weeks between August 15 and 29, the moon was waning, rising later and later in the night until by August 24, it was coming up quite close to dawn. White stated that they built and launched the raft between sunset and midnight and embarked on the river about midnight, which requires the presence of moonlight for that period and, I think, implies moonlight for some time after they set out. August 24 does not correlate with these activities. The waxing August moon rose well before sunset from August 1 to August 7 or 8 but did not shine through midnight or beyond, so these dates do not meet the requirement, either. But closer to the full moon of August 15, moonrise occurred before sunset, and moonlight would have extended through the later hours of the night.

Guessing when and how much moonlight was available to White and Strole is pure speculation, but it is possible to eliminate certain dates, and August 24 as the date of embarkation is one. There is no way to pinpoint an exact date since one guess is as good as another, but one may choose between several possible dates—perhaps August 13 through August 16; any one of these four days would fit the bill. Since the date of White's appearance in Callville is not disputed, this would allow roughly twenty-one to twenty-four days to make the journey from Moqui Canyon to Callville, a more likely time period than White's "14 days."

One of White's recollections was awakening in the belief that it was daylight but discovering that it was really about three o'clock in the morning. On August 27 and 28, the moon rose between 3:00 A.M. and 4:00 A.M., but it is highly unlikely that this event occurred only three or four days after White and Strole embarked on the river. White implies being alone when this happened, and it seems related to a later period when White was struggling to survive the rapids. If they embarked between August 13 and 16, then moonrise on August 27 or 28 (thirteen or fourteen days later) would make more sense. This memory of White's is neither bizarre nor sinister; I and many others have experienced this same phenomenon in Arizona.

In any case, the lunar evidence seems to expand those fourteen days of travel on the river, which in turn suggests that White's rigid schedule was the result not of careful timekeeping but of some form of stress. This possibility is discussed in chapter 23.

CHAPTER 23   SUMMARY AND CONCLUSIONS: PART C

Those parts of White's story which described the land over which he traveled in 1867 and the Grand Canyon landscape, as well as that suspect fourteen-day timetable of events on the river, were major stumbling blocks to later acceptance of his journey. Rather than outright dismissal of White's journey based on these apparent inaccuracies, however, some alternative factors should be considered.

White's descriptions of the Grand Canyon and the river were inaccurate.

In their 1959 review of Lingenfelter's book, Euler and Dobyns observed,

> the psychological state [White] was in, after one of his
> companions was killed by Indians and the other drowned,
> would have inhibited scientific study by even the most
> habitual intellectual. A pilot forced down near the river in
> July 1959, who built a log raft and started floating down to
> Page, was suffering from shock and emotional upset more
> than from exposure when rescued only three days later;
> and he had watched no one die and had only aid to
> expect from any Indian he might have met.

Although stress is now considered a major factor in many areas of our lives, this was the first mention of its likely role in the journey of James White. In general stress varies widely and must be measured against a baseline—in White's case, the arduous physical conditions of the trail, his relationship to this environment, and, especially, his particular character and personality.

In the nineteenth century, the people who left established homes and went west to seek their fortunes were hardy and courageous, not only willing to accept but determined to overcome hardships and setbacks. White was no different. Over a period of six years, he traveled the West on horseback, foot, and stagecoach. After his army stint, he went back to Colorado and Kansas, then over the Continental Divide to Silverton and the San Juan Valley. He lived in minimal army barracks and stagecoach stops, in tents, or, even more primitively, in bedrolls on the ground. There were no maps or signposts to guide him. After so many years, this environment would have seemed commonplace to him.

White was active, tough, down-to-earth, and courageous, but he was a man of limited imagination. Probably the only events between 1861 and 1867 that could be called stressful were the court martial, the Mulberry Creek horse raid, and the Goodfellow shooting episode, and these had little lasting impact on his life.

He had no battlefield experience while in the army, and whatever forays he may have had against hostiles were either at a distance or without violent conclusion. It seems safe to assume that watching Captain Baker die in a hail of bullets during a Ute ambush in the middle of unknown territory was the most traumatic event in his life up to that point. Despite this, White (and Strole) reacted with considerable coolness and courage and managed to escape. The death of George Strole obviously represented a quantum jump in his stress level, for it was then that the odds turned against him and the river became no longer simply a means of escape but an active menace.

Dr. Eddy, my helpful psychiatrist, had made a study of stress during his U.S. Air Force stint in Arizona and emphasized that, in addition to the element of fear, the purely physical stress of submersion, concussion from the rock-strewn river, increasing starvation, and pain would have affected White's cognitive processes to a high degree. Add to that the unfamiliar and spectacular nature of the land surrounding him:

mile-high cliffs with their constantly changing colors and tortured shapes, the menacing roar of the rapids echoing against the confining walls, the chaotic, turbulent waters and deep holes of a rampaging river. Eddy thought it would have been medically exceptional for White not to have suffered from both physical and psychological trauma.

This type of stress produces, along with other unpleasant things, hallucinations. Did White hallucinate? It is a virtual certainty; too many others have experienced these phenomena under similar conditions to dismiss the probability. Did he talk about them? Of course not. He would not even have known what they were. All the evidence points to his having suppressed his perceptions or replaced them with a commonplace explanation. Anything so far out of the realm of normal experience carried the taint of insanity, a terrible fear—even in our enlightened world.

White's descriptions distressed the river runners who came after him. In 1906, the Passenger Department of the Santa Fe Railway published an anthology titled *The Grand Canyon of Arizona*. It is filled with the most glorious prose, describing this most spectacular of Nature's wonders. In C. A. Higgins's essay, "The Titan of Chasms," phrases like "an inferno, swathed in soft celestial fires" and "a whole chaotic underworld" abound. Even Major Powell waxed poetic with "from black buttress below to alabaster tower above . . . these elements weather in different forms and painted in different colors; . . . a facade of seven systems of rock has its sublimity multiplied sevenfold." And the engineer, Robert Stanton, rhapsodized, "Those terrifying, frowning walls *are moving, are changing!* A new light is . . . creeping over them . . . coming out from their very shadows; . . . they are *being colored* in gorgeous stripes of . . . yellow, brown, white, green and purple." And further, "The Grand Canyon . . . is a living moving pulsating being, ever changing in form and color."

These walls were described by others as "constantly changing" in the varied sunlight and shade with "colors bleached to alabaster in the blinding sun" and "walls blanched of their color." All these observations were made by perfectly normal river runners. It seems fair to suggest that fact and stress could have combined to produce the "white sand stone rock" White's detractors found so outrageously inaccurate.

As for White's rigid schedule on the river, we have presented physical evidence that it was several days longer than the fourteen days he claimed. White's arrangement of his experiences on the river produced a two-week schedule of utterly mundane events, one for each day, until he ran out of them, and he then forged this pattern into an unshakable memory. His stubborn recitation of events like a mantra, even fifty years later, suggests that he was exhibiting a typical symptom of time compression, combined with a haphazard recollection of events—a natural result, according to Eddy, of stress and isolation.

One cannot entirely fault White's attackers for not recognizing the effects of stress during their era. What should be clear today, however, is that James White was alone on a flimsy raft on a river moving relentlessly over a course unknown to him; he saw primarily water and rock and more water. He was not a sightseer; that extravagant riot of color, light, form, movement, and sound which so enchant the present-day visitor would have been overwhelming for a man struggling to hold onto reality. Under those conditions, would it not be reasonable to find that White's memory was little more than a fragmented chronicle of the events that followed Strole's death?

Whatever knowledge White had of the land and river were obtained from other sources.

Today almost no part of our planet remains unexplored. Data on nearly every square mile have been recorded and stored and are readily available for instant recall to anyone with a computer. One of the few remaining mysteries is how to turn back the clock and imagine what it must have been like before science and technology gave us all this knowledge. Still, any attempt to assess nineteenth-century circumstantial physical evidence requires us to do exactly that. We need to examine White's route in the light of nineteenth-century realities and recognize that he had knowledge about that part of the country which no one has satisfactorily explained how he came to possess (see figure 13).

Dellenbaugh argued that White got his information about the canyon and the surrounding territory from Kit Carson but made no attempt to explain how Carson, serving at Fort Sumner in New Mexico Territory in the fall of 1867, conveyed these details to White, let alone how Carson obtained them himself. The idea that White learned about the Colorado River and the Grand Canyon from a source other than from firsthand experience gained credence despite the fact that in 1867 that region was untraveled and unknown.

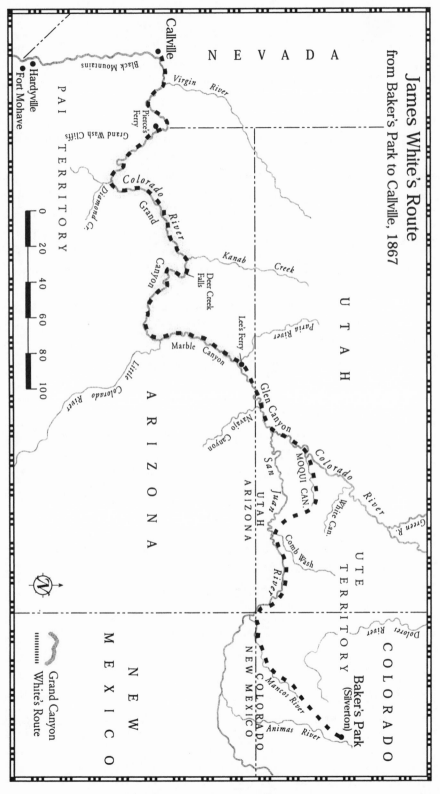

Figure 13

Later on, when the earlier accounts about White were discarded in favor of the opinions of those who had run the Colorado River, it was suggested that he obtained his impressions of the canyon as late as 1917 from sources which were by that time readily available. The only evidence to support these suggestions was that such sources existed, a hopelessly circular argument.

One possible source was the photograph. The art of photography was in its infancy in the 1860s; the first photographs of the Grand Canyon and environs were not taken until 1871, when Timothy O'Sullivan, part of Wheeler's upriver trip, covered the area from Fort Mohave to Diamond Creek. Powell's second expedition of 1871–72 produced many wonderful photographs by E. O. Beaman, J. Fennemore, and J. K. Hillers; more than excellent, they were incredible, given that the wet collodion process required that camera, glass plates, darkroom tent, and all the necessary processing chemicals—altogether about a ton of equipment—be carried to the point from which the pictures were taken. But these photographs were not published until 1902, long after White's descriptions had been well documented.

As for any written words about the Grand Canyon, all articles published prior to the writings of Powell, Dellenbaugh, or Stanton were accounts of White's own trip, and even if he had read them, they could not possibly have given him any information he didn't already know.

The most important thing is to discover whether or not White's recollections square with facts known today but unknown to anyone else at that time.

A) White's 1917 statement of what he saw as he traveled down Mancos Canyon:

> a large lookout house about 100 feet high, which was built out of cobblestones. Farther down the canyon we saw houses built of cobblestones, and also noticed small houses about 2 feet square that were built up about 50 feet on the side of the canyon and seemed to be houses of some kind of bird that was worshiped.

This is a spare, but unmistakable, description of the Anasazi ruins in the Mancos Valley, as easily visible to White in 1867 as they were to the Hayden Survey in 1874 (see figure 14).

Figure 14
Ruins of Anasazi tower, Mancos Canyon
(Drawing by Wm. H. Jackson for the Hayden Survey, 1874-75; lithograph by
Thomas Sinclair & Son, in Wm. H. Holmes, "Report on the Ancient Ruins of
Southwestern Colorado," *Ninth Annual Report of the United States Geological
and Geographical Survey of the Territories*, plate xxxiv)

Figure 15
San Juan River at the point where it enters a canyon
(Photo by E. Adams)

> *B) White's assertion that the party could no longer continue along the
> San Juan River because it entered a canyon with no bottomland:*

This landmark does exist; it lies between Bluff and Mexican Hat in
Utah (see figure 15).

> *C) White's combined mention of a northerly direction from the
> San Juan, a mountain ridge, and their horses' sore feet:*

This combination of details prompted Euler, Dobyns, and Bulger to
point unerringly to Comb Ridge, then Lime Ridge or Elk Ridge
respectively, adding somewhat parenthetically that either route could
cause "sore fite" (see figures 16 and 17).

> *D) White's description of the side canyon where Baker was killed:*

This description covered several physical features which had to be
assessed as a whole before it could be considered truly representative
of any real side canyon. These were 1) fifty miles from the San Juan; 2)
accessible on the south side; 3) no egress from the north side; 4) water

Figure 16
Comb Ridge and the mouth of Comb Wash.
(Photo by R. C. Euler)

Figure 17
Lower Lime Creek forks
(Photo by R. C. Euler)

Figure 18
Moqui Canyon. Note the stabilized sand dunes, *lower left*, and the sheer walls, *lower right*
(Photo by R. C. Euler)

for horses and men but no running stream down to the river; and 5) the twelve- to fifteen-mile distance from the point of Baker's death to the river.

Euler made an exhaustive search to determine whether such a combination of factors pointed to any real location in that area. There were several sites which matched one or another point, but the unique combination did indeed occur in a single place—Moqui Canyon (see figure 18).

> *E) White's assertion that he and Strole floated downstream on smooth water for (at least) three days, followed by severe rapids in which Strole was drowned.*

Is there any place on the Colorado where this combination of features exists? Yes. Even Stanton allowed this possibility when he told White in 1907, "You would have had . . . 185 miles of comparatively smooth water in Glen Canyon; . . . over this stretch you might have traveled on your raft with some safety as far as Lee's Ferry." There is no other description of features along the Colorado that so closely matches Glen Canyon from Moqui Canyon to the formidable rapids known as Badger Creek at Mile 8 and Soap Creek at Mile 11.5. The sixty-mile stretch from Grand Wash Cliffs through Boulder Canyon to Callville does not offer such a match.

After Strole's death, most of what White was able to recall was so deeply affected by physical and psychological stress that it was close to meaningless; however, there is one exception which can be considered. White, in his 1917 statement, described an unusual sight:

> I stopped and looked at a stream of water about as large
> as my body that was running through the solid rocks of
> the canyon about 75 feet above my head, and the clinging
> moss to the rocks made a beautiful sight. The beauty of it
> can not be described.

Does such a waterfall—not cascading over the top of a cliff, as most conventional falls do, but running through a hole in solid rock— exist in the Grand Canyon? It does; it is at mile 136 and is called Deer Creek Falls (see figure 19). Powell described it, too, but with a more poetic twist: "we pass a stream on the right, which leaps into the Colorado by a direct fall of more than 100 feet, forming a beautiful cascade. On the rocks in the cavelike chamber are ferns, with delicate fronds and enameled stalks."

There are other waterfalls in the Grand Canyon, such as Vasey's Paradise, but the juxtaposition of bad rapid and waterfall, as well as distance into the canyon, suggests Deer Creek. More to the point is whether a waterfall like the one described by White exists, not which one of several he saw.

The descriptions offered by White detailed definitive features and landmarks which were unknown to anyone else in 1867. The fact that these descriptions were linked in somewhat intricate relationships with his time and distance estimates belies the possibility that they could have come from an outside source. It is therefore difficult to escape the conclusion that James White did see and experience what he described and that he could not have done so had he not actually traversed the Grand Canyon.

Figure 19
Deer Creek Falls, Grand Canyon
(Photo by R. C. Euler)

Chapter 24 Resolution

In the year 1917, the United States Congress authorized a bronze plaque to be placed at the Grand Canyon to honor Major Powell. The United States Senate, pursuant to Senate Resolution No. 79, also authorized the Government Printing Office to publish the manuscript entitled *The Grand Canyon*, written by Thomas F. Dawson and sponsored by Senator Shafroth of Colorado. The prestigious approval of Senate Document No. 42 gave hope to James White's small band of supporters that such official recognition of his journey might effectively counter the negative rhetoric which had, for fifty years, denied him any place in Grand Canyon history.

It was with this hope that White's hometown newspaper, the Trinidad *Chronicle News,* carried a report from the nation's capital, stating that U. S. Representative Edward Keating of Colorado had proposed that "a monument in honor of James White" be erected in a "suitable" location overlooking the Grand Canyon. It was not Keating's intention, the report noted, to replace the monument soon to be erected there in Powell's honor but to give proper recognition to the "first man through the Grand Canyon."

Keating's proposal languished for six fruitless years. Frederick Dellenbaugh, still carrying the Powell banner, protested, "I hear that there is a proposition . . . to put up a monument to . . . White. This would be a foolish thing under the circumstances for while we may not be able to prove he did not go through the canyons, it has not been proved that he did." He need not have worried; no recognition, official or otherwise, was forthcoming, and the controversy over White's journey continued; in short, nothing changed.

This book has endeavored to answer an entrenched opposition with new evidence: to expose the biases of White's detractors, to defend White's reputation, and to demonstrate the validity of his raft journey beyond a reasonable doubt. The bare facts substantiate Dellenbaugh's statement that "we may not be able to prove he [White] did not go through the canyons"; indeed, it is clear that Dellenbaugh and company could not and did not offer proof of any kind. His assertion that "it has not been proved that he did" relied exclusively on the absence of an eyewitness. The implication, however, that White's journey *could never be proved* is disingenuous; physical evidence can and does offer proof as powerful as an eyewitness account.

At some point in the making of this book, when we were certain that our evidence was compelling enough to overturn the opposition's contentions, the old idea of Keating's monument surfaced once more. It was recently suggested that if this evidence is truly valid, someone, someday will come along and erect a plaque to honor White. While I am sure it would be satisfying to find my readers demanding—en masse—the tribute sought by the honorable representative from Colorado eighty-three years ago, I'm afraid that such an event has about as much chance of happening as my persuading Miss Smith to award me that sixth-grade A.

Still, if the evidence warrants, should recognition be withheld? A plaque is a fair and tangible way to acknowledge that James White's voyage actually happened and, further, that his survival provided a catalyst for the ultimate exploration of the Grand Canyon. It would in no way denigrate Major Powell or his accomplishments, and it would certainly vindicate the belief in White exhibited by Dr. Parry, General Palmer, Dr. Bell, Thomas Dawson, Senator Shafroth, Representative Keating, and the supporters who followed them. To that end, then, we have commissioned the following graphic expression of our own modest tribute to James White.

IN RECOGNITION OF

JAMES WHITE

[1837-1927]

A COLORADO GOLD PROSPECTOR WHO

IN AUGUST/SEPTEMBER, 1867,

TRAVERSED THE UNEXPLORED

GRAND CANYON OF THE COLORADO

WHITE'S ESCAPE FROM AN INDIAN AMBUSH ON

A RAFT DOWN THE COLORADO RIVER BECAME A

REMARKABLE VOYAGE OF DISCOVERY, PROVING

THAT A WATER TRANSIT OF THE GRAND CANYON

WAS POSSIBLE AND OPENING THE WAY FOR ALL

GRAND CANYON VENTURES - AND ADVENTURES -

FROM POWELL TO THE PRESENT

Appendix A: James White's 1867 Letter

This is a copy of James White's letter to Joshua White, September 1867, as edited by the author:

> Navigation of the Big Canyon
>   A Terrible Voyage
> Callville   September 26, 1867
> Dear Brother,
>   It has been some time since I have heard from you. I got no answer from the last letter that I wrote, for I left soon after I wrote. I went prospecting with Captain Baker and George Strole in the San Juan Mountains. We found very good prospects, but nothing that would pay. Then we started down [to]* the San Juan River. We traveled down about two hundred miles. Then we crossed over on [to the]* Colorado and camped. We laid over one day. We found out that we could not travel down the river, and our horses had sore feet, and we had made up our minds to turn back when we were attacked by fifteen or twenty Ute Indians. They killed Baker, and George Strole and myself took four ropes from our horses and an ax, ten pounds of flour, and our guns. We had fifteen miles to walk to the Colorado. We got to the river just at ~~dark~~** night. We built a raft that night. We got it built about ten o'clock. We sailed all that night.

We had good sailing for three days, and the ~~third~~** fourth day George Strole was washed off the raft and drowned. That left me alone. I thought it would be my time next. I then pulled off my boots and pants. I then tied a rope to my waist. I went over falls from ten to fifteen feet high. My raft would tip over three and four times a day. The third day we lost our flour, and ~~days~~** seven days I had nothing to eat [but my] rawhide knife cover. The eighth [and/or]** ninth day I got some mesquite beans. On the thirteenth day, [I met] a party of friendly Indians. They would not give me [anything] to eat, so I gave my pistols for the hind parts of a dog. I ate one for supper and the other for breakfast. On the fourteenth day, I arrived at Callville, where I was taken care of by James Ferry.

I was ten days without pants or boots or hat. I was sunburnt so I could hardly walk. The Indians took seven head of horses from us. Josh, I can't write you half I underwent. I saw the hardest time that any man ever did in the world, but thank God, I got through safely. I am well again, and I hope these lines will find you all well. I send my best respects to all.

Josh, answer this when you get it.

Direct your letter to Callville, Arizona.

James White

*   These sentences are crucial in assessing the accusations of inaccuracy made against White. In *Colorado River Controversies*, Stanton also edited this letter, but my additions are, I believe, more consistent with the actual geography of the region.

**   These crossed-out words are significant because either they are clarifications by White or indicate his confusion at the time about the timetable.

APPENDIX B: JAMES WHITE'S 1917 STATEMENT

The following statement was dictated by James White to his daughters in 1916, at the request of Thomas Dawson. It was published in Senate Document No. 42 in 1917.

I was born in Rome, N.Y., November 19, 1837, but was reared in Kenosha, Wis. At the age of 23 I left for Denver, Colo., later drifting to California, and there enlisted in the Army at Camp Union, Sacramento, in Company H, California Infantry, Gen. Carleton (some doubt as to the correct spelling of his name) being general of the regiment, and the company being under Capt. Stratton. I served in the Army three and one-half years, being honorably discharged at Franklin, Tex., on May 31, 1865. From there I went to Santa Fe, N. Mex., and then to Denver. In the fall of that year I went from Denver to Atchison, Kans., with Capt. Turnley (some doubt as to the correct spelling of this name) and his family, and from Atchison I went to Fort Dodge, Kans., where I drove stage for Barlow & Sanderson, and there I got acquainted with Capt. Baker, also George Stroll [sic] and Goodfellow. This was in the spring of 1867, and the circumstances under which I met them were as follows: Capt. Baker was a trapper at the time I met him there, and the Indians had stolen his horses, and he asked me to go with him to get his horses, and I went with him, George Stroll, and Goodfellow. We could

not get his horses, so we took 14 head of horses from the
Indians. The Indians followed us all night and all day, and
we crossed the river at a place called Cimarron in Kansas,
and we traveled across the prairies to Colorado City, Colo.

Before going further with my story I would like to
relate here what I know of Capt. Baker's history. He had
been in the San Juan country in 1860 and was driven out
by the Indians. He showed me lumber that he had sawed
by hand to make sluice boxes. I was only with him about
three months, and he spoke very little of his personal
affairs. When we were together in Colorado City he met
several of his former friends that he had been prospecting
with in the early sixties. I can not remember their names.
The only thing I know is that he mentioned coming from
St. Louis, but never spoke of himself as being a soldier,
and I thought "Captain" was just a nickname for him. He
was a man that spoke little of his past or personal affairs,
but I remember of him keeping a memorandum book of
his travels from the time we left Colorado City.

After reaching Colorado City, Colo., Baker proposed a
prospecting trip to the San Juan. There we got our outfit,
and that spring the four of us started on the trip and went
over to the Rio Grande. At the Rio Grande, Goodfellow
was shot in the foot, and we left him at a farmhouse, and
the three of us proceeded on our trip. From the Rio
Grande we went over to the head of it, down on the
Animas, up the Eureka Gulch. There we prospected one
month. We dug a ditch 150 feet long and 15 feet deep. We
did not find anything, so we went down the Animas about
5 miles, crossed over into the Mancos. At the head of the
Mancos we saw a large lookout house about 100 feet high,
which was built out of cobblestones. Farther down the
canyon we saw houses built of cobblestones, and also
noticed small houses about 2 feet square that were built
up about 50 feet on the side of the canyon and seemed to
be houses of some kind of a bird that was worshiped. We
followed the Mancos down until we struck the San Juan.
Then we followed the San Juan as far as we could and
then swam our horses across and started over to the
Grand River, but before we got to the Grand River we
struck a canyon; so we went down that canyon and campt-
ed there three days. We could not get out of the canyon
on the opposite side; so we had to go out of the canyon
the same way we went down. There we were attacked by
Indians and Baker was killed. We did not know there were
any Indians about until Baker was shot. Baker, falling to
the ground, said, "I am killed." The Indians were hiding

behind the rocks overlooking the canyon. Baker expired
shortly after the fatal shot, and, much to our grief, we had
to leave his remains, as the Indians were close upon us;
and George Stroll and I had to make our escape as soon
as possible, going back down in the canyon. We left our
horses in the brush and we took our overcoats, lariats,
guns, ammunition, and 1 quart of flour, and I also had a
knife scabbard made out of rawhide, and I also had a
knife, and we started afoot down the canyon.

We traveled all day until about 5 o'clock, when we
struck the head of the Grand Canyon of the Colorado
River. There we picked up some logs and built us a raft.
We had 200 feet of rope when we first built the raft, which
was about 6 feet wide and 8 feet long, just big enough to
hold us up. The logs were securely tied together with the
ropes. We got on our raft at night, working it with a pole.
We traveled all night, and the next day, at 10 o'clock, we
passed the mouth of the San Juan River. We had smooth
floating for three days. The third day, about 5 o'clock, we
went over a rapid and George was washed off, but I caught
hold of him and got him on the raft again.

From the time we started the walls of the Canyon were
from two to three thousand feet high, as far as I could estimate at the time, and some days we could not see the sun
for an hour, possibly two hours. Each day we would mix a
little of the flour in a cup and drink it. The third day the
flour got wet, so we scraped it off of the sack and ate it.
That was the last of the flour and all we had to eat.

On the fourth day we rebuilt our raft, finding cedar
logs along the bank from 12 to 14 feet long and about 8 or
10 inches through. We made it larger than the first one.
The second raft was about 8 feet wide and 12 feet long. We
started down the river again, and about 8 o'clock in the
morning (as to our time, we were going by the sun) we
got into a whirlpool and George was washed off. I
hollered to him to swim ashore, but he went down and I
never saw him again.

After George was drowned I removed my trousers,
tying them to the raft, so I would be able to swim in case I
was washed off. I then tied a long rope to my waist, which
was fastened to the raft, and I kept the rope around my
waist until the twelfth day.

About noon I passed the mouth of the Little
Colorado River, where the water came into the canyon as
red as could be, and just below that I struck a large
whirlpool, and I was in the whirlpool about two hours or
more before I got out.

I floated on all that day, going over several rapids, and when night came I tied my raft to the rocks and climbed upon the rocks of the walls of the canyon to rest. I had nothing to eat on the fourth day.

On the fifth day I started down the river again, going over four or five rapids, and when night came I rested on the walls again and still nothing to eat.

On the sixth day I started down the river again, and I came to a little island in the middle of the river. There was a bush of mesquite beans on this island, and I got a handful of these beans and ate them. When night came I rested on the walls again.

The seventh, eighth, ninth, and tenth days were uneventful, but still going continuously over rapids, and still nothing to eat. So I cut my knife scabbard into small pieces and swallowed them. During the entire trip I saw no fish or game of any kind.

On the eleventh day I went over the big rapid. I saw it before I came to it, and laid down on my stomach and hung to the raft and let the raft go over the rapid, and after getting about 200 yards below the rapid I stopped and looked at a stream of water about as large as my body that was running through the solid rocks of the canyon about 75 feet above my head, and the clinging moss to the rocks made a beautiful sight. The beauty of it can not be described.

On the twelfth day my raft got on some rocks and I could not get it off; so I waded onto a small island in the middle of the river. On this island there was an immense tree that had been lodged there. The sun was so hot I could not work, so I dug the earth out from under this tree and laid under it until the sun disappeared behind the cliffs. This was about noon. After resting there I got up and found five sticks about as big as my leg and took them down to the edge of the island below my raft. I then untied the rope from my raft and took the loose rope I had around my waist and tied these sticks together. I slept on this island all night.

On the thirteenth day I started out again on my newly made raft (leaving the old raft on the rocks), thinking it was daylight; but it was moonlight, and I continued down the river until daylight. While floating in the moonlight I saw a pole sticking up between two large rocks, which I afterwards learned the Government had placed there some years before as the end of its journey.

When daylight came I heard some one talking, and I hollered "hello," and they hollered "hello" back. I discovered then that they were Indians. Some of them came out to the raft and pulled me ashore. There were a lot on the bank, and I asked them if they were friendly, and they said they were, and I then asked them to give me something to eat, when they gave me a piece of mesquite bread. While I was talking to some of the Indians the others stole my half-ax and one of my revolvers, which were roped to the raft. They also tore my coat trying to take it from me.

After eating the bread I got on my raft and floated until about 3 o'clock in the afternoon, when I came upon another band of Indians, and I went ashore and went into their camp. They did not have anything for me to eat, so I traded my other revolver and vest for a dog. They skinned the dog and gave me the two hind quarters and I ate one for supper, roasting it on the coals. The Indians being afraid of me, drove me out of their camp, and I rested on the bank of the river that night, and the next morning, the fourteenth day after I got on my raft, I started to eat the other quarter, but I dropped it in the water. I floated that day until 3 o'clock and landed at Callville, and a man came out and pulled me ashore.

Jim Ferry or Perry (not sure as to the first letter of this name) was a mail agent at that place. He was also a correspondent for some newspaper in San Francisco. He took me in and fed me. When I landed all the clothing I had on my body was a coat and a shirt, and my flesh was all lacerated on my legs from my terrible experience and of getting on and off the raft and climbing on the rocks. My beard and hair were long and faded from the sun. I was so pale that even the Indians were afraid of me. I was nothing but skin and bones and so weak that I could hardly walk. Jim Ferry or Perry cared for me for three days, and the soldiers around there gave me clothing enough to cover my body.

I was at Callville about four weeks, and a boat was there getting a load of salt, and I got on that boat and went to Fort Mojave. There I met Gen. Palmer and told him my story.

From Fort Mojave I went to Callville again and there worked for Jim Ferry (or Perry), carrying the mail for three months between Callville and Fort Mojave. Then he sold out to Jim Hinton, and I carried mail for him for a month. He sold out, and we each bought a horse and pack animal and we started from Callville, going to Salt Lake in the spring of 1868. From Salt Lake City we went to Bear River. There we took a contract of getting out ties. Then I hired out as wagon boss. Then I quit and run a saloon. I sold out and then went to Omaha, Nebr. From there I went to Chicago, and from there to Kenosha, Wis., to visit my old home. That was in 1869.

From Kenosha I went to Chicago, and from there to Leavenworth, Kans., and later to Kansas City, Kans. From there I went to Junction city, Kans., and then to Goose Creek. I drove stage in and out of Goose Creek for Barlow and Sanderson, for whom I had worked in Fort Dodge. I was transferred from Goose Creek to Fort Lyon or Five Mile Point. From there I went to Bent Canyon, Colo., and kept home station. From there I went to Las Animas, Colo., and minor places, later drifting to Trinidad, where I have lived since 1878.

These are the plain facts. There are many minor points that could be mentioned, but did not think it would be necessary to mention here. I have never been through that country since my experience, but have had a great desire to go over the same country again, but have never been financially able to take the trip.

[signed] James White.

"These are the plain facts," said James White in 1916 as he was nearing the age of eighty. Even a cursory examination of this statement and a brief comparison with his 1867 letter, the early accounts (by Parry, Grandin, Kipp, and Beggs), and the meeting with General Palmer reveal that his "plain facts" for the time spent on the Colorado River were, in fact, a jumble of odd anecdotes, mistaken persons and places, wrong times, and, quite possibly, hallucinatory events. His fourteen-day schedule remained as rigid and incredible as it had been from the day he first articulated it.

But these are minor and peripheral faults, and it would be a mistake to discount the core of his recollections. Too much of what he said over the years remained constant and consistent with a voyage through the Grand Canyon, however impossible anyone might have thought it.

CHAPTER NOTES

These abbreviations refer the reader to appropriate sections of the bibliography:

(B) Book

(D) Documentary

(G) Government document

(L) Letter

(M) Manuscript

(N) Newspaper article

(P) Periodical article

CHAPTER 1   CALLVILLE

Page

11–12   *Callville.* McClintock, *Mormon Settlement in Arizona.* (B)
          This book provides an excellent description of the area, Callville's relationship with Hardy and Hardyville, and the town's demise in 1869.

12   *followed suit with Callville.* Paher, *Callville—Head of Navigation.* (B)

12   *For many years, steamboats.* Lingenfelter, *Steamboats on the Colorado River.* (B)
          This is a marvelous history not only of the steamboats but the entire region during the years from 1852 to 1916.

12   *Lieutenant Ives.* Ives, *Report on the Colorado River.* (G)

CHAPTER 2   WHO WAS JAMES WHITE?
15   *Connecticut Yankees.* James White's statement in appendix B.
          This is essentially an autobiographical sketch requested by
          Thomas Dawson for Senate Document No. 42. White dictated it
          to his daughters, and it is the only complete statement he made
          on his personal history.
15–16   *James's father, Daniel, [and] James's mother, Mary.* This biographical
          information comes from the White family Bible. The flyleaf lists
          births from Daniel White (1796) through James White's children
          (1892), along with some deaths.
17   *Denver! It had everything.* Dallas, *Gold and Gothic.* (B)
17–18   *Virginia City, Nevada.* Twain, *Mark Twain in Virginia City.* (B)
          This reprint of chapters from *Roughing It* is a captivating look
          into the time period which coincided with White's miserable
          mining experience and desperate entry into the Union Army.

CHAPTER 3   WHITE'S WAR
19   *"Ht: 5' 7""* U.S. Army, Service Records. (G)
21–23   *The transcript.* U.S. Army, "Further Proceedings of a General
          Court Martial . . . Trial of Private James White." (G)

CHAPTER 4   THE ROAD TO GOLD
24–25   *White continued along the Santa Fe Trail.* James White's statement in
          appendix B.
25–27   *Captain Charles Baker.* McConnell, "Charles Baker and the San
          Juan Humbug." (P)
          A galley proof of this article published in *The Colorado
          Magazine,* was lent to me by Dock Marston in 1970. At that time,
          Dock proposed McConnell as a fourth contributor to a book by
          himself, Robert Euler, and me.
27–28   *Indians . . . had stolen his horses.* James White's statement in
          appendix B.
28   *shooting match between Joe Goodfellow and White.* Ehrhart, Letter to
          Thomas F. Dawson. (L)
          This letter corroborates White's statement about where he,
          Baker, and Strole were in the period just prior to White's raft voy-
          age. The letter was written fifty years after the fact, but there is no
          evidence that their presence in the San Juan area had ever been
          called into doubt before then.

CHAPTER 5   THE RESCUE
32   *"Haiko, haiko."* Tillman, Letter to George Davidson, 16
          September 1897. (L)

Tillman explains, "This word 'hico' is a Mexican word for white man." However, the consensus of Indian experts is that the word is Paiute for "white man" and is spelled in several ways. The Paiute language is related to other Uto-Aztecan languages, and variations are found in various parts of Mexico, so maybe both interpretations are right. I chose *haiko* for its phonetic value.

32–34   *White's rescue.* Grandin, Letter to Frank Alling, *Alta California*, and Kipp, Letter to Simon Wolff, *Los Angeles News*; also see Beggs, "Navigation of the Big Cañon," *Arizona Miner.* (N)

33   *"By God, he's some loco'd."* Tillman, Letter to George Davidson, 16 September 1897. (L)

Tillman's recollection of White's rescue is essentially the same as Wilburn's and Ferry's as reflected in the writings of Grandin, Kipp, and Beggs; he also recalls the Indians calling White Ya-Na, which means "loco" or "crazy."

34   *a supper he remembered.* James White's statement in appendix B.

CHAPTER 6   DOWNRIVER CRIER

36   *Jacob Hamblin and a couple of other Mormon men.* Miller, *The Deseret News.* (N)

This article is a firsthand description of a voyage in a sixteen-foot skiff from one to one-and-a-half miles upstream of Grand Wash to Callville: "We calculated the distance . . . to be about 65 miles, 45 miles of which, from the mouth of the Grand Wash to the mouth of the Virgen [*sic*], it is presumed a white man has never passed down before." To get to their starting point, the men launched their boat at the mouth of the Virgin, rowed upstream, then turned around and rowed downstream. The voyage took less than two days; they started on April 15 and reached Callville on April 16.

37   *Indians had taken his gun.* Tillman, Letter to George Davidson, 23 June 1897. (L)

Tillman clarifies the Paiutes' meeting with White at the mouth of the Virgin River.

37–38   *E. B. Grandin.* Grandin, Letter to Frank Alling, *Alta California.* (N)

39–40   *J. B. Kipp.* Kipp, Letter to Simon Wolff, *Los Angeles News.* The letter also appeared in the *San Bernardino Guardian* and the *San Francisco Bulletin.* (N)

CHAPTER 7   THE NEWS SPREADS EAST

42–43   *Hardyville.* Lingenfelter, *Steamboats on the Colorado River.* (B)

43   *he had a finger in every pie.* Hardy, Letter to George Davidson, 5 August 1897. (L)

Hardy displayed a faulty memory about White's rescue: "Mr. Tillman, Wilber [*sic*] and eight other men . . . brought back with them Mr. White." This implies either that Hardy was at Callville (which he was not) or that the men brought White to Hardyville (which they did not). Marston's comment in a letter to "Canyoneer Bob" (Dr. Robert C. Euler) was "Hardy was selling . . . a bill of goods as he does not appear with those who pulled White from the river."

44   *John Marion.* Lyon, "Gentlemen of the Editorial Fraternity." (P)

John Marion's reputation as a cantankerous, opinionated editor strongly suggests that he would never have published the story of James White in his paper if he had not supported its validity. He obviously believed that the Walapai would have been far more likely to kill White, had he traveled overland, than the Colorado River, however dangerous.

44   *Now he was both owner and editor.* Meacham, "To the Public," *Arizona Miner.* (N)

This article contains the announcement of John Marion as the new proprietor and editor of the *Miner*, "the leading journal of the Territory."

45   *Marion was more than ready to accept.* Ibid.

The Sharlot Hall Museum in Prescott, Arizona, was generous with its help on the history of both the paper and Marion, especially in allowing me to read the *actual* newspapers; it was impossible to restrict my reading to Beggs's article.

45–47   *"Navigation of the Big Cañon."* Beggs, *Arizona Miner.* (N)

A reprint of this article in the *Deseret Evening News* of 27 January 1868 adds this comment: "Honorable Erastus Snow, who has perused the account, says it is true that such a man did come down the river. He was seen by Brother Andrew S. Gibbons of St. Thomas and described the trip to him. Brother Gibbons is an Indian interpreter and had opportunities of knowing that he told the truth." Such allusions to sources confirming White's story abound throughout the literature and correspondence of the period without, for the most part, revealing specifically the identity of these sources. Erastus Snow, however, was a prominent Mormon apostle and one of the leaders in charge of settlements in the Virgin River basin; Andrew Gibbons was a Mormon leader at St. Thomas who had accompanied Jacob Hamblin on many of his explorations; these men were knowledgeable witnesses.

48   *"Dear Brother."* For an edited copy of White's letter, see appendix A.

CHAPTER 8   GENERAL PALMER AND THE RAILROAD SURVEY

53–54   *General William Jackson Palmer.* Fisher, *A Builder of the West.* (B)
54   *Palmer led extensive surveys.* Palmer, *Report of Surveys across the Continent.* (B)
56   *"James—White—Kenosha Wisconsin."* Parry, notes from an interview, Bancroft Library. (M)
These notes were published first in Stanton's book *Colorado River Controversies* and again in Lingenfelter's book *First Through the Grand Canyon.* The notes and White's original letter of 1867 were given to Lingenfelter by Parry's heirs, and he donated them to the Bancroft.

CHAPTER 9   DR. PARRY'S REPORT

59–66   *Parry's report.* This report is included in its entirety as it appeared in the *Transactions of the St. Louis Academy of Natural Science,* 2(1868). (P)

CHAPTER 10   MAJOR CALHOUN'S VERSION

68–75   *"Twenty years ago."* Calhoun, "Passage of the Great Canyon of the Colorado River," *Wonderful Adventures.* (B)
75   *William Bell . . . included Calhoun's account.* Calhoun "Passage of the Great Canyon of the Colorado River," *New Tracks in North America.* (B)
Later, probably inspired by the White voyage, Calhoun wrote a novel entitled *Lost in the Canyon* about a white man, a faithful Negro servant, a faithful Ute Indian guide, and a faithful dog, all of whom rafted down the Colorado River together. It is an exciting western adventure, complete with extravagant rhetoric, that bears a remarkable resemblance to his two accounts of James White.

CHAPTER 11   MAJOR POWELL

77–79   *The second army official.* Darrah, *Powell of the Colorado.* (B)
79   *Byers's newspaper published the major's plans.* Rocky Mountain News, 6 November 1867. (N)
79–80   *"GENERAL: A party of naturalists."* Powell, Letter to General Grant. (L)
This letter was included in the *Congressional Globe* for 25 May 1868.
80   *Powell dusted off his lobbying skills.* Darrah, *Powell of the Colorado.* (B)
81–82   *The Powell resolution. Congressional Globe,* 40th Cong., 2d sess., 1868. (G)

83   *"before even this experience was known."* Bowles, *The Switzerland of America.* (B)

83   *Jack Sumner's idea.* Sumner, Letter to Frederick Dellenbaugh, 7 February 1904. (L)

This letter gave notice that Sumner had started to write his version of the "so-called Powell exploring expedition which will differ some from Powell's report." Thirty-five years is a long time to carry a grudge, but it's not surprising if he believed that he, not Powell, had conceived the idea of exploring the Grand Canyon. Sumner was equally unlikely to credit James White's voyage as the catalyst for the 1869 expedition.

CHAPTER 12   ON THE ROAD AGAIN

84   *Rumors of gold strikes up north.* Simon, Letter to James White. (L)

Simon wrote to White in 1917 recollecting their friendship and experiences in Utah during 1867–68.

84   *Along the way, they heard about the Union Pacific.* James White's statement in appendix B.

85   *"Interesting Narrative."* Kenosha Telegraph. (N)

87   *The first was written . . . by . . . Parry.* Parry, "The Great Colorado of the West," *Weekly Gazette.* (N)

The following excerpt was copied from the original newspaper at the State Historical Society of Iowa in Iowa City. It was written in Hardyville on 10 January 1868: "Judge then of my satisfaction in accidentally meeting on the banks of this very same river, a living man, who had made the passage through the entire length of this great cañon, alone—seeing the sole companion of his voyage sink into the whirlpool before his eyes; fleeing from the fearful fate of Indian warfare, trusted himself on a few frail timbers, and after a journey of over 500 miles, shooting over the rapids, submerged in a whirlpool, and entangled in eddies, was finally rescued and reached the settlement at the head of navigation at Callville. I, of course, eagerly drew from the man, his strange narrative, and have penned it down, an official report to the railroad company, in whose employ I now am, the results of which will of course be duly made accessible to the public." This seems to indicate that Dr. Parry was a true believer.

87   *others then cropped up sporadically . . .* Lippincott's Magazine. [Beggs], "A Terrible Voyage." (P)

I have seen this article referred to many times but have never seen the article. The author is listed as John Clerke but is actually William Beggs. Its title, *A Terrible Voyage,* should have been a dead giveaway.

87   *Rocky Mountain Herald.* Beggs, "A Thrilling Adventure." (N)

Our old friend Beggs was at it again. He dressed this article up by adding, "He was scarcely alive, and one of the first persons who saw him exclaimed, 'My God, that man is a hundred years old!'" Beggs made more money out of White's voyage than White ever did.

87   *Chicago Tribune.* "A Romantic Voyage" in "The Round Table." (N)

It was claimed that this account sired the one in the *Daily Pantagraph* (see the next entry), but if so, the Bloomington author should be drummed out of the corps, for this version is totally different. The article is a paraphrased version of Parry's report and was given to the *Tribune* by Samuel Bowles.

87   *Daily Pantagraph.* 24 May 1869. (N)

This account of White's trip is highly inaccurate, and although the writer first says it was furnished by the *Tribune,* he later claims *Lippincott's Magazine as* its source. The *Pantagraph* author identifies White's point of embarkation as the San Juan River and quotes General Palmer (also incorrectly) as having conducted White's interview in Hardyville and Fort Mohave. That's enough evidence to convince us that whatever the source, the nineteenth-century media were worthy forerunners of today's lot.

87   *Rocky Mountain News.* 23 June 1869. (N)

This article carrying another account of White and speculation about Powell appeared while Major Powell was in Cataract Canyon.

87   *New York Sun.* "Half-Mile Below Ground." (N)

Possibly the most exaggerated account, this article purported to be an actual interview with White in Callville, complete with an old priest, "clay pipes and glasses." The story is doubtless a spinoff from Calhoun, with variations, and adds an account of Powell's expedition, including detailed descriptions of his boats.

87   *Whatever the scenario.* James White, Letter to Joshua White. (L)

Copies of this letter found their way into the *Outing Magazine* and the files of Robert Stanton; the original was lent in 1958 to Dr. Richard E. Lingenfelter, who, with the blessings of the Parry heirs, gave it to the Bancroft Library.

88–89   *"On the coach."* Palmer, Letter to Queen Mellen. (L)

89   *An account of the shooting.* Ehrhart, Letter to Thomas F. Dawson. (L)

90   *White stated only that Goodfellow had been shot.* James White's statement in appendix B.

90   *"White said that Professor Powell."* Palmer, Letter to Queen Mellen. (L)

90   *"was the very opposite."* Palmer, Letter to Robert C. Clowry. (L)

CHAPTER 13   POWELL'S CONQUEST OF THE GRAND CANYON

92   *"How anyone can ride that on a raft."* Darrah, "J. C. Sumner's Journal." (P)

92   *"This point has not been determined."* Darrah, "George Y. Bradley's Journal." (P)

92   *"The major sought out James White."* Darrah, *Powell of the Colorado.* (B)

93   *Powell's . . . expedition began.* Darrah, *Powell of the Colorado.* (B)

94   *a visit recalled by Bill Hardy.* Hardy, Letter to George Davidson, 12 August 1897. (L)

94   *Two of the men left the river at Yuma.* Darrah, *Powell of the Colorado.* (B) See also Sumner, Letter to Frederick Dellenbaugh, 15 February 1904. (L)

Darrah stated that Sumner left the river at Yuma, but Sumner maintained that he continued to the head of the Gulf of California—one of the many instances of the different stories and interpretations which emerged from this expedition.

94   *"Colonel [sic] Powell pronounces the reported adventures." Chicago Tribune,* 16 September 1869. (N)

94–96   *"It gives me great pleasure."* Palmer, Letter to Robert C. Clowry (L)

97   *he published his account of his expeditions.* Powell, *Exploration of the Colorado River.* (B)

98   *"Had I the Space."* Dellenbaugh, *Romance of the Colorado River.* (B)

99   *"The Major always treated the matter as a joke."* Dellenbaugh, Letter to Robert B. Stanton. (L)

This reference to Powell's "meeting" with White continued, "We simply thought it preposterous. And I think so still." Of course, Dellenbaugh was not on the first but the second expedition, and by then, Major Powell was singing an entirely different song.

99   *"the biggest liar that ever told a tale."* Corle, *Listen, Bright Angel.* (B)

99   *"Nobody has ever successfully traversed the Colorado."* Stanton, *Engineering News,* 21 September 1889. (P)

99   *"The phase of the Major's character,"* Thompson, Letter to Frederick Dellenbaugh, 23 October 1902. (L)

CHAPTER 14   ENTER ROBERT BREWSTER STANTON

Robert Stanton was a prodigious writer on the Colorado River and the Grand Canyon. Nevertheless, his two books, *Colorado River Controversies* (1932) and *Down the Colorado* (1965), were published posthumously, edited from a large, two-volume manuscript. This manuscript, plus a voluminous number of letters written by and to him, are in a collection in the New York Public

Library. All the Stanton letters here were researched by Dock Marston, and his original copies are in his collection in the Huntington Library. I received copies directly from Dock, except for the correspondence between Stanton and Edwards after the September interview; these letters were confirmed in the Huntington by Michael Clemans in 1995. References to the Marston Collection letters are asterisked.

101–3   *White put his Grand Canyon journey behind him.* White family documents, personal family interviews.

103   *In 1890, Stanton reappeared on the Colorado.* Stanton, *Colorado River Controversies.* (B)

104   *"As early as 1892, I set forth my position."* Ibid.

104   *Stanton's boatman, Edwards, read an article.* "The Story of James White," *Outing Magazine.* (P)

104   *He . . . wrote to Stanton.* Edwards, Letter to Robert B. Stanton, 1 April 1907. (L)★

104   *Stanton . . . wrote to James White.* Stanton, Letter to James White, 16 May 1907. (L)

104   *"[I] would very much like to see you."* White, Letter to Robert B. Stanton, May 1907. (L)★

104   *"veritable Munchausen."* Source unknown.

I cannot pinpoint this exact quote, although it probably came via one of Dock's letters. It is a remark that carries Stanton's literary flavor. There is a clue in *Colorado River Controversies*: Julius Stone's foreword states, "The utter impossibility of such a journey as White claimed he had made at once convinced [Stanton] that White . . . was another Munchausen."

104   *He arrived in Trinidad.* Lappin, Letter, *Deseret Magazine.* (P)

After reading an earlier article in *Deseret Magazine*, Lappin wrote a letter to the editor to claim acquaintance with White and Stanton: "I introduced [White] to Stanton who asked him if he was the James White who had been the first white man to run the Grand Canyon of the Colorado. Old Jim, dubious of Stanton, answered 'Yep.' He remained dubious until Stanton pressed a $20 gold piece into his hand. . . . I heard the old man relate his harrowing experience riding a raft down the Colorado. Believe me, it would be a thriller in today's movies!"

105–7   *The notarized transcript of this interview.* Stanton, *Colorado River Controversies.* (B)

106   *"you might have traveled on your raft."* Ibid.

In a letter written to Stanton on 22 September 1907,★ Hiram Edwards discusses his own theory of White's trip: "he [may have] crossed from below Bluff somewhere on the San Juan and struck the Colorado somewhere between Hite and the San Juan as he makes no mention of Cataract Canyon at all and if he passed through there he would surely know it." There is no evidence that Stanton paid any attention to Edwards's opinions.

107   *After the interview.* Lappin, Letter, *Deseret Magazine.* (P)

Lappin states, "The interview took about an hour and a half, after which Stanton and I returned to my office, where I typed the story on 11 single-spaced pages. At 2:30 a.m. Stanton was on a Santa Fe limited headed for New York."

107   *a Santa Fe Railroad book."* Black, *The Grand Canyon of Arizona.* (B)

Seventeen men and one woman penned a series of essays on the beauties of the Grand Canyon; among them were such luminaries as Joaquin Miller, William Allen White, Thomas Moran, and, of course, Major Powell. Stanton signed the flyleaf with large, bold strokes: "To Mr. James White. Compliments of Robt. B. Stanton. Trinidad. Sept. 23rd '07." Two flourished pen strokes, one above, one below, emphasized a slanted directive: "See Page 43," which was Stanton's own contribution.

107   *"As per your request."* Lappin, Letter to Robert B. Stanton. (L)★

107   *wrote to White asking further questions.* Stanton, Letter to James White, 3 October 1907. (L)★

107–8   *having received no reply to his letter.* Stanton, Letter to Roy Lappin, 12 October 1907. (L)★

On the same date, Stanton wrote a letter to Mr. Gibson★ regarding Lappin and the White interview: "Took a stenographer with me and had a very extended and most interesting interview with him and got even a more wonderful story in regard to the impossible journey, which he never took by the way, than has ever been published before. I am writing this up with my personal information and comments on the same and it will form an *amusing, if not wonderful, chapter* in my forthcoming book" [italics added].

108   *"It was the mouth of the Green."* White, Letter to Robert B. Stanton, 24 October 1907. (L)

108   *"The reason I ask you to do this."* Stanton, Letter to Hiram Edwards, 1 November 1907. (L)★

On the same date, Stanton also wrote to Roy Lappin,★ introducing Edwards as his messenger and asking, "Please be kind enough to comply with the request on the last page of this interview by properly certifying to the same."

108–10   *"years ago, I knew White."* Stanton, Letter to Thomas F. Dawson. (L)★

110   *"I, Roy Lappin, being duly sworn."* Stanton, *Colorado River Controversies.* (B)

110   *"You have won my everlasting gratitude."* Stanton, Letter to Hiram
Edwards, 13 November 1907. (L)★

110   *But was it?* Bell, Letter to Robert B. Stanton, 7 December 1907. (L)★
In response to a letter from Stanton attacking Calhoun's story,
Bell states, "I shall be interested to hear what you gleaned from
White himself, for it will give me some idea as to how much of
Major Calhoun's story is to be relied upon." Bell had a stake in
the accuracy of his publication; the 9th edition of the *Encyclopedia
Britannica*, published in 1892 (pp.163–64), appears to echo Bell's
book: "The mysteries of the Great Cañon were first invaded by
an unlucky 'prospector' James White, who along with a compan-
ion thought it safer to trust himself to the river than to the
Indians." Later letters were not so generous.

110   *Chalant's edited version.* Stanton, *Colorado River Contoversies.* (B)

CHAPTER 15   SENATE DOCUMENT NO. 42
All letters written to and carbon copies of those written by the
White family that are quoted in this chapter were originally in
my mother's possession. They were given to Dock Marston and
are now in his collection at the Huntington Library. All the
other letter citations were provided directly to me by Dock
Marston.

111   *Dawson wrote to the Honorable Dan Taylor.* Dawson, Letter to Mayor
Daniel Taylor. (L)

111   *Taylor advised Dawson to contact White.* Taylor, Letter to Thomas F.
Dawson. (L)

111–12   *letter from an unexpected quarter.* Bass, Letter to James White. (L)

112   *Dawson finally wrote his letter.* Dawson, Letter to James White. (L)

113   *"My father is growing old."* Esther White, Letter to Thomas F.
Dawson, 2 August 1916. (L)
White obviously did tell his story to his children and friends, but
my mother often said that he refused to go into the details of Baker's
and Strole's deaths or anything associated with the rapids because it
"upset" him; he would simply become silent if pressed. Not until
the project for Dawson did my mother and aunt actually force their
father into many recollections they had never heard before.

113   *no mention of White's Callville letter.* Stanton, Letter to Thomas F.
Dawson. (L)
Stanton told Dawson, "I have had in my possession White's
original letter written in 1867, the only statement on the subject
White ever wrote." Dawson's receipt of this letter coincided with
his sending his manuscript to Esther.

114   *"We followed the Mancos."* James White's statement in appendix B.

114	*"My father was born in 1837."* Esther White, Letter to Thomas F. Dawson, September 1916. (L)
114	*Dawson sent a rough draft.* Dawson, Letter to Miss [Esther] White, 28 November 1916. (L)
114	*"Due to father's age he does not remember."* Esther White, Letter to Thomas F. Dawson, December 1916. (L)
115	*"a gentleman who has given much attention."* Dawson, Letter to Miss [Esther] White, 8 February 1917. (L)
115	*"You will remember."* Dawson, Letter to Miss [Esther] White, 10 February 1917. (L)
116–17	*"Recently when in Washington."* Stanton, Letter to Esther White, 19 February 1917. (L)
118	*The stalemate was broken.* Dawson, Letter to Esther White, 8 March 1917. (L)

118   This letter was returned to Dawson and is missing from all files. Despite efforts to jog her memory, my mother either could not or would not recall its contents.

119	*"I am enclosing . . . a letter."* Esther White, Letter to Thomas F. Dawson, 13 April 1917. (L)
119	*"I have read your letter."* Esther White, Letter to Robert B. Stanton. (L)
120	*"Dear Sir: I have come into knowledge."* James White, Letter to Thomas F. Dawson. (L)
120	*Dawson was not so sure.* Dawson, Letter to Robert B. Stanton. (L)

The tense and almost sinister atmosphere surrounding the Dawson-Stanton feud over White is illustrated by a couple of phrases in this letter: "While I engage in the confessions which you seem to require of me" and "for some reason unknown to me you seem to want to put me in the 'hole' with White."

120–22   *"He [Stanton] criticizes the booklet."* Dawson, Letter to Esther White, 1 September 1917. (L)

CHAPTER 16   BATTLE OF *The Trail*

123   *Senate Document No. 42.* Bell, Letter to Robert B. Stanton, 2 October 1917. (L)

Stanton, still in pursuit of Dawson, wrote to Bell on 28 November 1917, asking questions about White, Calhoun, Parry, Palmer, and Powell. Bell responded, "I read Mr. Dawson's pamphlet with great interest. It seems to remove every doubt, if any existed, as to whether White did pass through the Canyon or not." Then he added, "It seems to me odd that some of Major Powell's friends should think that the passage of a prospector unwillingly through the Grand Canyon previous to the Powell expedition, could in any way detract from the great merit of the work done by him in its exploration."

123   *it merely added fuel to the fire.* Dellenbaugh, Letter to Robert B. Stanton. (L)

Dellenbaugh tells Stanton, "We have not done [White] an injustice."

123   *Stanton's unrelenting opposition.* Stanton, Letter to Frederick Dellenbaugh. (L)

Stanton confides to Dellenbaugh that Dawson's pamphlet is "pure trash—nothing more or less."

Also see Bell, Letter to Robert B. Stanton, 21 February 1918. (L) Still pursued by Stanton's letters, Bell states, "The serious fact remains—so far as I can judge—that none of the local folks in 1867–70, seem to have even suggested that Baker was killed less than a hundred miles from Callville, and that White took to the water only 60 miles above it—your starting point." Bell appears to be wavering under Stanton's insistence on Grand Wash Cliffs as White's starting point, but he is not about to give in and is clearly annoyed: "Palmer's acquiescence is criticized very unjustly in my opinion. So are my own suggestions; . . . the tone of your criticism generally is much to be regretted. These endless criticisms blur the outstanding facts which you wish your readers to grasp." The tone of this letter is in considerable contrast to his letter of 7 December 1907.

123   *two articles about White.* Dawson, *The Trail.* (P)

I have not seen these articles, but Keplinger refers to one of them in a letter which appears under Correspondence in *The Trail,* December 1920. (P)

123–26   *Stanton's response.* Stanton, "The Alleged Journey." (P)

125   *denigrated all statements made by . . . Dr. William Bell.* Dawson, Letter to W. W. Bass. (L)

Marston made a copy of this letter on 7 December 1961 from an unknown source. In it Dawson discusses William Bell's interesting opinion that White "embarked upon the Colorado at a point much below the mouth of the Grand . . . that White struck the river near Dandy, or Robbers' Crossing," another name for Hite.

All the correspondence and articles that continued for years after the publication of Senate Document No. 42 reveal the most explosive and ugliest aspects of the White-Powell controversy.

126   *certain that he had prevailed.* Keplinger, Correspondence. (P)

Describing Dawson's article as "containing a copy of a letter by Mr. White, dated September 26, 1867," Keplinger trashes every point that Dawson made and espouses Stanton's views. This gentleman had been with Major Powell on his climb of Long's Peak in 1868, which might explain his "expertise" on this subject. After Stanton's article and this letter, Dawson must have wished heartily that he had never heard of James White.

126   *the final word on the journey of James White.* Stanton, *Colorado River Controversies.* (B)

The final word was evangelized in 1932 by James Chalfant, who edited portions of Stanton's manuscript, beginning with the dedication: "To All Truthful Colorado River Voyagers." A foreword by Julius Stone, the preface by Chalfant, and the introduction by Stanton (adapted from his manuscript) alluded sixteen times to the truths presented by the author and twenty-four times to the lies, inaccuracies, distortions, nonsense, and falsifications of history reported by other Grand Canyon travelers and historians. It is not surprising then that this book became something of a Bible for almost all the early Colorado River runners; it is even more impressive that it was reprinted as late as 1982 and still finds wide acceptance. The ultimate irony, however, is that a few months before his death in 1979, Dock Marston wrote a commentary for this edition and, despite having sparked and nourished my book, finally embraced Stanton and banished White to a river entry below Grand Canyon.

CHAPTER 17   THE WHITE FAMILY AND DOCK MARSTON

Sources for this chapter are, as expected, mostly family documents and personal recollections; connections with outsiders are documented where possible by listed source material.

127   *Dr. William Bell . . . came to Trinidad.* Bell, Letter to James White. (L)

127   *although it pleased the family.* Emilia White, Letter to Thomas F. Dawson. (L)

127   *Ellsworth Kolb also came to Trinidad.* Kolb, Letter to L. R. Freeman. (L)

Kolb tells Freeman, "I would like to know the truth about White. I talked to him a few years before he died, but he was so childish it was impossible to make head or tail of his story." Kolb does not say when he met White, but just five years before this letter, White was working with Dawson to produce Senate Document No. 42, and he was compos mentis then. Kolb's statement, therefore, remains more confusing than enlightening.

128   *He died on January 14, 1927.* Chronicle News, 14 January and 30 January 1927. (N)

129   *"wedded to the river."* Lavender, *River Runners of the Grand Canyon.* (B)

130   *had assigned White a point of embarkation.* Lingenfelter, *First Through the Grand Canyon.* (B)

130   *a review of Lingenfelter's book.* Bulger, "First Man through the Grand Canyon." (P)

131   *The review had been written in 1959.* Euler and Dobyns, Review of *First Through the Grand Canyon.* (P)

CHAPTER 18   GRAND CANYON HISTORY: DISCOVERIES AND REDISCOVERIES

133   *The most ancient history.* Euler, *The Grand Canyon Up Close and Personal.* (B)

133   *In the beginning.* Hughes, *The Story of Man at Grand Canyon.* (B)

134   *Lieutenant Ives and his steamboat* Explorer. Ives, *Report on the Colorado River.* (G)

134   *a few Mormon boatmen.* Miller, *The Deseret News.* (N)

134   *He claimed that he had . . . prepared.* Thompson, Letter to Frederick Dellenbaugh, 21 October 1902. (L)

Thompson, who was Powell's brother-in-law, confided to Dellenbaugh, "So far as I know the Major never had any idea of exploring the Colorado before 1868–69. . . . I think the idea grew up with him in 1868." The *Rocky Mountain News* article of 6 November 1867 bears this out.

135   *Only a handful of adventurous men.* Lavender, *River Runners of the Grand Canyon.* (B)

135   *"[Brown's] proposed railroad."* Darrah, *Powell of the Colorado.* (B)

136   *In 1928, newlyweds Glen and Bessie Hyde.* Dimock, *Sunk Without a Sound.* (B)

136   *In 1937, however, . . . Buzz Holmstrom.* Welch, Conley, and Dimock, *The Doing of the Thing.* (B)

137   *"Stanton's book concludes the argument."* Corle, *Listen, Bright Angel.* (B)

137   *In 1922, a piece by J. Cecil Alter.* Alter, "Tribune Travelogs." (N)

137   *Ives and Wheeler for taking government backing.* Wheeler, *Geographical Report.* (G)

137   *He also scolded George Wharton James.* James, *The Grand Canyon of Arizona.* (B)

137   *"I didn't get much of a 'hand.'"* Alter, Letter to Otis Marston. (L)

137–38   *"Riding a loosely-bound bunch of logs."* Freeman, *The Colorado River, Yesterday, Today and Tomorrow.* (B)

138   *Another interesting critic.* McConnell, "Captain Baker and the San Juan Humbug." (P)

138–39   *"To those who say that such a voyage."* Goldwater, *Delightful Journey down the Green and Colorado Rivers.* (B)

139   *In 1948, he was still of that opinion.* Goldwater, Letter to Harry
        Aleson. (L)
            Goldwater told Aleson, "The matter of Jim White is getting to
        be like arguing religion. . . . I still say it could be done and with
        that I let the matter drop."

139   *"I don't know where you get the information."* Goldwater, Letter to
        Otis Marston. (L)

139   *"I understand you."* Goldwater, Letter to Eilean Adams. (L)

139   *swam the Colorado.* Beer, *We Swam the Grand Canyon.* (B)

139   *experience of Manfred Kraus. Call of the Canyon* (videotape). (D)

139   *resurrected the accusation.* Lavender, "James White: First through the
        Grand Canyon." (P)

140   *But only three years later.* Lavender, *River Runners of the Grand
        Canyon.* (B)

CHAPTER 19   BOB EULER AND SQUARE ONE

142   *first specific point of embarkation.* Parry, "Account of the Passage
        through the Great Canyon." (P)

142   *White's point of entry was Grand Wash Cliffs.* Stanton, *Colorado
        River Controversies.* (B)

143   *Howland brothers and Bill Dunn.* Powell, *Exploration of the Colorado.*
        (B)

143   *"It is one thing to say."* Lingenfelter, *First Through the Grand
        Canyon.* (B)

143–44 *"Not having much success."* Bulger, "First Man through the Grand
        Canyon." (P)

144   *"toward White Canyon."* Ibid.
            "In this general location there are two canyons through which
        they might have descended to the Colorado, Dark Canyon . . . and
        White Canyon. . . . Dark Canyon descends as a series of steps into
        which waterfalls have cut irregular grooves, so that it is quite diffi-
        cult to traverse. At the mouth of Dark Canyon is a dangerous rapids,
        and there are a half dozen more . . . down stream . . . . Since White
        and his party encountered no rapids in the first three days of the
        voyage, we can rule out Dark Canyon as the one they descended.
        In fact, because of the complicated interlocking canyons between
        Dark Canyon and White Canyon they must not have wandered
        onto the Dark Canyon Plateau." Bulger settled on White Canyon;
        Euler and Dobyns disagreed with this point of embarkation.

144   *"White could not have entered the river."* Euler and Dobyns, Review
        of *First Through the Grand Canyon.* (P)

144   *many terrifying "Walapai raids."* U.S. Congress, *Walapai Papers,* 74th
        Cong., Doc. 273. (G)

In October 1866, George W. Leihy, superintendent of Indian affairs for Arizona Territory, wrote that the Walapai tribe "occupies the country back of the Colorado river bottom, to and beyond the meridian of Prescott, ranging north to the Nevada line, and south nearly to the right bank of the Williams Fork. They have been considered as in a state of war with the whites for more than a year past." Dr. Robert Euler, a preeminent expert on the Pai, assessed the situation this way: "From then until the Indians were finally defeated in 1869, no white man was safe in their territory. None would have been allowed to travel unmolested nor, do I believe, undetected through it."

145   *The area south of the south rim.* Euler, personal communications from 1969 to the present; meetings from 1975 through 1992.

146–48   *"to locate practical routes."* Euler, unpublished manuscript. (M)

CHAPTER 21   SUMMARY AND CONCLUSIONS: PART A

157   *Stanton's premise that White went overland.* Stanton, *Colorado River Controversies.* (B)

CHAPTER 22   SUMMARY AND CONCLUSIONS: PART B

160   *"In any one of a hundred."* "Only God Knew the Way." (P)

160   *"Help, I can't swim."* Lord, *Day of Infamy.* (B)

162   *"they reached the Animas."* Parry, "Account of the Passage through the Great Canyon." (P)

167   *Mulberry Creek raid.* James White's statement in appendix B.

CHAPTER 23   SUMMARY AND CONCLUSIONS: PART C

171   *the most glorious prose.* Black, *The Grand Canyon of Arizona.* (B)

179   *"we pass a stream."* Powell, *Exploration of the Colorado River.* (B)

CHAPTER 24   RESOLUTION

181   *Edward Keating of Colorado. Chronicle News,* 24 January 1917. (N)

181–82   *"I hear that there is a proposition."* Dellenbaugh, Letter to Lewis R. Freeman. (L)

References, Sources, and Related Subjects

From my sixth-grade impersonation of Don Quixote until meeting Dock Marston in 1959, I knew little about the Grand Canyon. From 1959 until 1972, in addition to quizzing my mother for answers to Dock's questions, I was the recipient of a kaleidoscopic blizzard of disparate letters, newspaper and magazine articles, excerpts from obscure books, government documents, and unpublished manuscripts—all accompanied by three- and four-page letters from Dock, brimming with curious facts, vacillating opinions, and wry humor.

When Dock orchestrated a three-way collaboration on a book, he naturally assigned the roles of river and land gurus to himself and Bob Euler; to me he allotted the task of chronicling the personal minutiae of James White's life. He felt this was the proper chore for a granddaughter who didn't know much about writing historical treatises. The assignment carried two corollaries: opinions and ideas which impinged upon Dock's expertise were irrelevant, and I had no need to know the sources of the research he shared with me.

After Dock's death, I tried to locate the sources of the unidentified references—with limited success. Dock was right—I am no historical scholar, but with some help from those who are, I have done my best.

LETTERS

Letters were generally the most important primary source for this book. Originals of those written to the White family and carbon copies of those written by them during my mother's assistance in preparing Thomas Dawson's Senate Document No. 42 were in my possession until I gave them to Dock in 1972. Sources for the remaining correspondence given to me by Dock are noted where known. All items provided by Dock may be found in the Marston Collection in the Huntington Library in California.

I have tried to track down the copyright owners of these letters. Where the author had sufficient fame to merit an institutional collection, permission to publish was granted; in some cases verification of claimants was not possible. With the others, I was unable to trace any heirs. If it turns out that I have infringed any rights, I offer my sincere apologies.

Most of these letters have never been published before; they are critical in understanding the behind-the-scenes events surrounding James White, his supporters and detractors, and the controversy that developed over his journey.

The correspondence originally in possession of the White family is identified by [W].

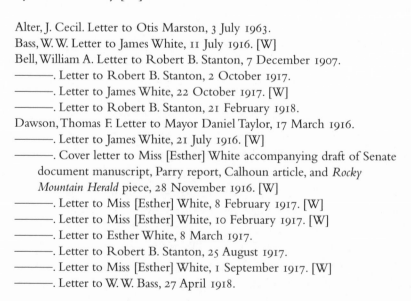

Alter, J. Cecil. Letter to Otis Marston, 3 July 1963.

Bass, W. W. Letter to James White, 11 July 1916. [W]

Bell, William A. Letter to Robert B. Stanton, 7 December 1907.

———. Letter to Robert B. Stanton, 2 October 1917.

———. Letter to James White, 22 October 1917. [W]

———. Letter to Robert B. Stanton, 21 February 1918.

Dawson, Thomas F. Letter to Mayor Daniel Taylor, 17 March 1916.

———. Letter to James White, 21 July 1916. [W]

———. Cover letter to Miss [Esther] White accompanying draft of Senate document manuscript, Parry report, Calhoun article, and *Rocky Mountain Herald* piece, 28 November 1916. [W]

———. Letter to Miss [Esther] White, 8 February 1917. [W]

———. Letter to Miss [Esther] White, 10 February 1917. [W]

———. Letter to Esther White, 8 March 1917.

———. Letter to Robert B. Stanton, 25 August 1917.

———. Letter to Miss [Esther] White, 1 September 1917. [W]

———. Letter to W. W. Bass, 27 April 1918.

Dellenbaugh, Frederick. Letter to Robert B. Stanton, 9 August 1917.

———. Letter to W. W. Bass, 19 August 1920.

———. Letter to Lewis R. Freeman, 7 February 1923.

Edwards, William Hiram. Letter to Robert B. Stanton, 1 April 1907.

———. Letter to Robert B. Stanton, 22 September 1907.

Ehrhart, T. J. Letter to Thomas F. Dawson, 22 November 1916. In *The Grand Canyon,* Senate Document No. 42. Washington, D.C.: GPO, 1917.

Goldwater, Barry M. Letter to Harry Aleson, 29 January 1948.

———. Letter to Otis Marston, 18 December 1961. Barry M. Goldwater Personal and Political Papers. Arizona Historical Foundation, Tempe.

———. Letter to Eilean Adams, September 1994. Barry M. Goldwater Personal and Political Papers. Arizona Historical Foundation, Tempe.

Hardy, William H. Letter to George Davidson, 5 August 1897 (in response to Davidson's letter of 17 July 1897). Robert B. Stanton manuscript, Marston Collection. Huntington Library, Pasadena, California.

———. Letter to George Davidson, 12 August 1897. Robert B. Stanton manuscript, Marston Collection. Huntington Library, Pasadena, California.

Keating, Edward, U. S. Representative. Letter to Esther White, 27 February 1917. [W]

Kolb, Ellsworth. Letter to L. R. Freeman, 27 December 1922 (copy of handwritten letter).

Lappin, Roy. Letter to Robert B. Stanton, 25 September 1907.

Palmer, William Jackson. Letter to Queen Mellen, 9 August 1869, William Palmer Collection, Division of State Archives, Colorado Historical Society, Denver.

———. Letter to Robert C. Clowry, 4 December 1906, Collections of the Manuscript Division. Library of Congress, Washington, D.C.

Powell, J. W. Letter to General U. S. Grant, 2 April 1868. *Congressional Globe,* 25 May 1868.

Simon, Adam. Letter to James White, 29 August 1917. [W]

Stanton, Robert B. Letter to James White, 16 May 1907. [W]

———. Letter to James White, June 1907. [W]

———. Letter to James White, 3 October 1907. [W]

———. Letter to Roy Lappin, 12 October 1907.

———. Letter to Mr. Gibson, 12 October 1907.

———. Letter to Hiram Edwards, 1 November 1907.

———. Letter to Roy Lappin, 1 November 1907.

———. Letter to Hiram Edwards, 13 November 1907.

———. Letter to Hiram Edwards, 11 December 1907.

———. Letter to Hiram Edwards, 7 January 1908.

———. Letter to Thomas F. Dawson, 22 November 1916.

————, Letter to Esther White, 19 February 1917. [W]

————. Letter to Frederick Dellenbaugh, 30 August 1917. Manuscript Collection. University of Arizona Library, Tucson.

Sumner, Jack. Letter to Frederick Dellenbaugh, 7 February 1904. Manuscript Collection. University of Arizona Library, Tucson.

————. Letter to Frederick Dellenbaugh, 15 February 1904. Manuscript Collection. University of Arizona Library, Tucson.

Taylor, Mayor Daniel. Letter to Thomas F. Dawson, 7 April 1916.

Thompson, Almon H. Letter to Frederick Dellenbaugh, 21 October 1902. Manuscript Collection. University of Arizona Library, Tucson.

————. Letter to Frederick Dellenbaugh, 23 October 1902. Manuscript Collection. University of Arizona Library, Tucson.

Tillman, John. Letter to George Davidson, 23 June 1897 (in response to Davidson's letter of 17 June 1897). Robert B. Stanton manuscript. Marston Collection. Huntington Library, Pasadena, California.

————. Letter to George Davidson, 16 September 1897. Robert B. Stanton manuscript. Marston Collection. Huntington Library, Pasadena, California.

White, Emilia. Letter to Thomas F. Dawson, 24 October 1917. [W]

White, Esther. Letter to Thomas F. Dawson, 2 August 1916. [W]

————. Cover letter to Thomas F. Dawson accompanying James White's statement, September 1916. [W]

————. Letter to Thomas F. Dawson, 24 November 1916. [W]

————. Cover letter to Thomas F. Dawson accompanying return of Senate document manuscript, December 1916. [W]

————. Cover letter to Thomas F. Dawson accompanying his returned March 8 letter, a copy of Robert B. Stanton's February 19 letter, and her reply to Stanton, 13 April 1917. [W]

————. Letter to Robert B. Stanton, 13 April 1917. [W]

White, James. Letter to Joshua White, 26 September 1867. Bancroft Library, University of California, Berkeley.

———— (written by Emilia White). Letter to Robert B. Stanton, May 1907. [W]

———— (written by Emilia White). Letter to Robert B. Stanton, 24 October 1907. [W]

———— (written by Esther White). Letter to Thomas F. Dawson, 20 April 1917. [W]

MANUSCRIPTS

Euler, Robert C. Unpublished manuscript, 1972–75.

Parry, Charles Christopher. Notes from an interview with James White conducted on 2 January 1868. Bancroft Library, University of California, Berkeley.

BOOKS

Once again, excerpts from many of the books listed here came to me via the ubiquitous Marston express and suffered from a lack of precise documentation. Some were incomplete galley proofs which were promptly returned. Some of the references came from public libraries long before this book in its present form was started; only a small percentage of the listed books actually belong to me.

Ambler, J. Richard. *The Anasazi.* Flagstaff, Ariz.: Museum of Northern Arizona, 1977.

Bass, William Wallace. *Adventures in the Canyons of the Colorado. By two of its earliest explorers, James White and W. W. Hawkins, with Introduction and Notes.* Grand Canyon, Ariz.: Author, 1920.

Beer, Bill. *We Swam the Grand Canyon.* Seattle: The Mountaineers, 1988. Reprint, 15-minute Press, 1999.

Black, W. J., ed. *The Grand Canyon of Arizona.* N.p.: Passenger Department of the Santa Fe Railroad, 1906.

Bowles, Samuel. *Our New West.* Hartford, Conn.: Hartford Publishing Co., 1869.

———. *The Switzerland of America; A Summer Vacation in the Parks and Mountains of Colorado.* Springfield, Mass.: S. Bowles & Co., 1869.

Calhoun, A. R. "Passage of the Great Canyon of the Colorado River by James White, the Prospector." In *New Tracks in North America,* compiled by William A. Bell. London and New York: William A. Bell, 1870.

———. "Passage of the Great Canyon of the Colorado River by James White, the Prospector." In *Wonderful Adventures,* 2d ed. Philadelphia: J. B. Lippincott & Co., 1874.

———. *Lost in the Canyon.* New York: A. L. Burt, 1888.

Cooley, John. *The Great Unknown.* Flagstaff, Ariz.: Northland Press, 1988.

Corle, Edwin. *Listen, Bright Angel.* New York: Duell, Sloan & Pearce, 1946.

———. *The Story of the Grand Canyon.* New York: Duell, Sloan & Pearce, 1951.

Dallas, Sandra. *Gold and Gothic. The Story of Latimer Square.* Denver: Lick Skillet Press, 1967.

Darrah, William Culp. *Powell of the Colorado.* Princeton: Princeton University Press, 1951.

Dellenbaugh, Frederick Samuel. *Romance of the Colorado River.* New York: Putnam's Pub. Co., 1902.

———. *A Canyon Voyage.* New York: Putnam's Pub. Co., 1908.

Dimock, Brad. *Sunk Without a Sound.* Flagstaff, Ariz.: Fretwater Press, 2001.

Dobyns, Henry F. and Robert C. Euler. *The Havasupai People.* Phoenix: Indian Tribal Series, 1971.

————. *The Walapai People.* Phoenix: Indian Tribal Series, 1976.

Encyclopedia Britannica, 9th ed.

Euler, Robert C. *The Paiute People.* Phoenix: Indian Tribal Series, 1972.

————. *The Grand Canyon Up Close and Personal: Early Explorations of the Grand Canyon.* N.p.: Western Montana College Foundation, 1980.

Fisher, John S. *A Builder of the West.* Caldwell, Idaho: The Caxton Printers, Ltd., 1939. Reprint, New York: Arno Press, 1981.

Freeman, Lewis R. *The Colorado River, Yesterday, Today and Tomorrow.* New York: Dodd, Mead & Co., 1923.

Gamett, James, and Stanley W. Paher. *Nevada Post Offices.* Las Vegas: Nevada Publications, 1983.

Goldwater, Barry M. *Delightful Journey down the Green and Colorado Rivers.* Tempe: Arizona Historical Foundation, 1970. (With supplemental essay "Prehistoric Man in the Grand Canyon" by Robert C. Euler. Special consultant, O. Dock Marston.)

Hughes, J. Donald. *The Story of Man at Grand Canyon: Spanish Explorers.* Grand Canyon Natural History Association Bulletin 14. Grand Canyon, Ariz.: 1967.

James, George Wharton. *The Grand Canyon of Arizona.* Boston: Little, Brown & Co., 1910.

Jones, Anne Trinkle, and Robert C. Euler. *A Sketch of Grand Canyon Prehistory.* Grand Canyon, Ariz.: Grand Canyon Natural History Association, 1979.

Kolb, Ellsworth. *Through the Canyon from Wyoming to Mexico.* New York: Macmillan Publishing Co., 1914.

Lavender, David. *River Runners of the Grand Canyon.* Tucson: University of Arizona Press for the Grand Canyon Natural History Association, 1985.

Lingenfelter, Richard E. *First Through the Grand Canyon.* Los Angeles: Glen Dawson, 1958.

————. *Steamboats on the Colorado River.* Tucson: University of Arizona Press, 1978.

Lord, Walter. *Day of Infamy.* New York: Henry Holt, 1957.

McClintock, James H. *Mormon Settlement in Arizona.* Phoenix; 1921.

Paher, Stanley, ed. *Callville—Head of Navigation, Arizona Territory.* Las Vegas: Nevada Publications, 1981.

Palmer, William Jackson. *Report of Surveys across the Continent in 1867–68.* Philadelphia: W. B. Selheimer, 1869.

Powell, John Wesley. *Exploration of the Colorado River of the West and Its Tributaries Explored in 1869, 1870, 1871 and 1872 Under the Direction of the Secretary of the Smithsonian Institution.* Washington, D.C.: The Smithsonian Institution, 1875.

————. *First Through the Grand Canyon.* 1875. Reprint, New York: Outing Publishing Company, 1916.

————. *The Exploration of the Colorado and Its Canyons.* 1895. Reprint, New
    York: Dover Publications. 1961. (Originally titled *Canyons of the Colorado.*)
Ruffner, Budge. *All Hell Needs Is Water.* Tucson: University of Arizona Press,
    1972.
Stanton, Robert B. *Colorado River Controversies.* Edited by James M.
    Chalfant. New York: Dodd Mead & Co., 1932. Reprint, Boulder, Colo.:
    Westwater Books, 1982.
————. *Down the Colorado.* Norman: University of Oklahoma Press, 1965.
Stegner, Wallace. *Beyond the Hundredth Meridian.* Boston: Houghton Mifflin
    Co., 1953.
Twain, Mark. *Mark Twain in Virginia City, Nevada.* Edited by Stanley Paher.
    Las Vegas: Nevada Publications, 1985.
Welch, Vince, Cort Conley, and Brad Dimock. *The Doing of the Thing.*
    Flagstaff, Ariz.: Fretwater Press, 1998.

Newspaper and Periodical Articles

Once again, the major newspaper and magazine references for
White and his voyage came from Dock Marston. Despite Dock's haphazard method of passing on his research details, his offerings were
Xerox copies of actual, dated publications, and since many of them
were referred to in other books, I had no doubt of their authenticity.
What I do not generally have are page numbers, and while I regret that
omission, I do not believe the true scholar will have any trouble locat-
ing the references.

Newspapers

Alter, J. Cecil. "Tribune Travelogs." *Salt Lake Tribune,* 1922.
Beggs, William J. "Navigation of the Big Cañon, a Terrible Voyage." *Arizona
    Miner* (Prescott), 14 September 1867. Also published in *Deseret Evening
    News,* 27 January 1868.
————. "A Thrilling Adventure." *Rocky Mountain Herald* (Denver), 8 January
    1869.
Buhler, M. W. "James White Discovered the Grand Canyon (1867)." *New York
    Sun,* 11 November 1917.
Chicago Tribune, 16 September 1869.
Chicago Tribune, 21 September 1869.
Chronicle News (Trinidad, Colo.), 24 January 1917.
Chronicle News (Trinidad, Colo.), 14 January and 30 January 1927.
Daily Pantagraph (Bloomington, Ill.), 24 May 1869.
Grandin, E. B. Letter to Frank Alling (8 September 1867). *Alta California*
    (San Francisco), 24 September 1867.

"Half-Mile Below Ground." *New York Sun,* 10 June 1869.

Kenosha Telegraph (Wisconsin). 1 October 1868.

Kipp, J. B. Letter to Simon Wolff (10 September 1867). *Los Angeles News,* 20
     September 1867. Also published in *San Bernardino Guardian,* 21
     September 1867 and *San Francisco Bulletin,* 27 September 1867.

Meacham, R. "To the Public." *Arizona Miner* (Prescott), 14 September 1867.

Miller, Elder Henry W. In *The Deseret News of Great Salt Lake City,* 3 July
     1867.

Parry, C. C. "The Great Colorado of the West—Its Navigable Waters and Its
     Deep Canyons." *Weekly Gazette* (Davenport, Iowa), 19 February 1868.

Rocky Mountain Herald (Denver), 11 January 1913.

Rocky Mountain Herald (Denver), 8 January 1916.

Rocky Mountain News (Denver), 6 November 1867.

Rocky Mountain News (Denver), 23 June 1869.

"A Romantic Voyage," in "The Round Table." *Chicago Tribune,* 16 May 1869.

PERIODICALS

[Beggs, William J.] "A Terrible Voyage." *Lippincott's Magazine,* December
     1868.

Bulger, Dr. Harold A. "First Man through the Grand Canyon, a Review."
     Part 1. *Bulletin of the Missouri Historical Society* (July 1961).

Case, Robert Ormond. "Down the Colorado." Part of "Post True Stories of
     Daring and Adventure." *The Saturday Evening Post,* n.d. 1938.

Darrah, William Culp, ed. "George Y. Bradley's Journal." *Utah Historical
     Quarterly* 15 (1947).

———. "J. C. Sumner's Journal." *Utah Historical Quarterly* 15 (1947).

Dawson, Thomas F. In *The Trail,* February 1919.

Euler, Robert C. and Henry F. Dobyns. Review of *First Through the Grand
     Canyon,* by R. E. Lingenfelter. *Arizona and the West* 1 (autumn 1959).

Jones, Calico. "First through the Grand Canyon." *Real West Magazine,* May
     1967.

Keplinger, L. W. Correspondence. In *The Trail,* December 1920.

Lappin, Roy. Letter. *Deseret Magazine,* August 1953.

Lavender, David. "James White: First through the Grand Canyon?" *The
     American West* 19 (November–December 1982).

Lyon, William H. "Gentlemen of the Editorial Fraternity: Arizona's Fighting
     Pioneer Journalists." *The Journal of Arizona History* 31 (autumn 1990).

McConnell, Virginia. "Captain Baker and the San Juan Humbug." *The
     Colorado Magazine* 48 (1971). (Originally presented as a paper at the
     Colorado Historical Society meeting, Denver, September 1970.)

"Only God Knew the Way." Part of "Post True Stories of Daring and
     Adventure." *The Saturday Evening Post,* date unknown.

Parry, C. C. "Account of the Passage through the Great Canyon of the
    Colorado of the West, from above the Mouth of the Green River to
    the Head of Steamboat Navigation at Callville in the Months of August
    and September, 1867, by James White, Now Living at Callville."
    Transactions of the St. Louis Academy of Natural Science 2 (1868).
Stanton, Robert B. In *Engineering News,* 21 September 1889.
————. "The Alleged Journey and the Real Journey of James White, on the
    Colorado River, in 1861 [*sic*]." *The Trail,* September 1919.
"The Story of James White." *Outing Magazine,* April 1907.

U. S. GOVERNMENT DOCUMENTS

Congressional Globe. 40th Cong., 2d sess., 1868: 2563–66.
Dawson, Thomas F. *The Grand Canyon,* Senate Document No. 42.
    Washington, D.C.: GPO, 1917.
Ives, J. C. *Report on the Colorado River of the West.* Washington, D.C.: GPO,
    1861.
U.S. Army. "Further Proceedings of a General Court Martial Convened at
    Las Cruces, N.M. by Virtue of the Following Order, viz. Head Quarters
    Dept. of New Mexico, Santa Fe, N.M. 13 October 1864. Special Order
    No. 39. Eighth and Ninth Days: Trial of Private James White of
    Company H. 5th Inf. Cal. Col." RG 153, National Archives,
    Washington, D.C.
U.S. Army. Service Records. "James White, Fifth Infantry of California
    Volunteers, 1861–65." National Archives, Washington, D.C.
U.S. Congress. *Walapai Papers: Historical Reports, Documents, and Extracts from
    Publications Relating to the Walapai Indians of Arizona.* 74th Cong., 2d
    sess., 1936. Doc. 273.
Wheeler, Captain George M. *Geographical Report.* Vol. 1 of *U.S.G.S. Surveys
    West of the One Hundredth Meridian.* U.S. Army, Engineering Dept.
    Washington, D.C.: GPO, 1889.

DOCUMENTARY

Call of the Canyon. Produced by Dana Rouse. Pacific Mountain Network,
    1989. Videotape.

AUTHOR'S NOTE

> If you want to learn how much you can overlook or forget, just write a book.
>
> —Henry A. Pilsbry, *The Nautilus*, 1949

This homely truth is greatly magnified when you spend forty years writing a book without knowing that's what you're doing. You, the reader, have seen how a genetic accident handed this story to me on a silver platter and how I then coasted along on a serendipitous current of secondhand knowledge. I had a free ride, effortlessly acquiring the memories of my family, borrowing from the experience of river runners, and carelessly absorbing some of the expertise of Grand Canyon historians, all without firsthand responsibility. Participating in a three-way book with gentlemen vastly more knowledgeable than me meant I did not have to bother with such tedious activities as in-depth research and literary citations; I could leave it all up to them. I simply kept my little mountain of data in its haphazard order (surely an oxymoron, but in this case . . .) and enjoyed it for the gift it was. When I finally faced the reality of going it alone on this book, all those things I neglected so long ago came home to haunt me. I dismantled my mountain and reassembled it, and soldiered on, rediscovering along the way those who had provided my free ride. It is time to pay for my passage.

From the dim past, then, my first debt must be to my mother whose exceptional memory and tidy way with old letters and documents laid a firm foundation for the history of her father, and to my aunts and uncles whose recollections, once untangled, were so valuable. And of course to James White himself, whose survival made my life possible.

I owe another major debt to that remarkable gentleman, Otis "Dock" Marston, who, as you have seen, was the initiator and catalyst of this book. Were he alive today, he would denounce my arguments and conclusions, but such disagreement could not diminish his generosity with the time, energy, and affection he gave me over a twenty year period—a truly priceless gift.

This book is, in a way, a memorial to those long gone. If there is a Library in the Sky, I hope it will stock a copy or two for them.

Less distant is my good friend and once-collaborator, Robert C. Euler, whose scientific objectivity, integrity, and professionalism is evident in the book, and whose amazing detective work uncovered the magic needle of Moqui Canyon in the desert haystack.

Close to home is my immediate family. I once tried to persuade my son, Greg, to take over the project when it looked to be too much for me, but he told me that, after all those years of work, it had to be my book and then kept reminding me "You can do it, Mom." My daughter-in-law, Patti, and my granddaughter, Lauren, added their faith and encouragement. But most of all, I owe a huge debt to my husband and friend, Bob Adams. Without his unfailing, active, and generous participation in a thousand valuable ways, including the most difficult and tedious one of all—pushing me when I faltered, and that was often— I could never have completed the job. There are not enough words in any language to thank them.

To Brad Dimock I am indebted for his generous help and advice that led to a better direction for the book. I am grateful to Michael Clemans for his confirming research in the Marston Collection, as well as his unusual view of James White. And then, there is Dr. John Alley, editor nonpareil, whose middle name must surely be Patience. I am lucky to have received significant encouragement from Senator Barry Goldwater, research assistance from Laine Sutherland and James Knipmeyer, critiques from Al Holland, editing wisdom from Barbara Bannon, and the forebearance of friends like Kirk Cookson, Debra Winsberg, Yvonne Spens, Karen Peirolo, and others who read some or all of various versions of my manuscript with good grace; they are more than appreciated.

Many books and articles have made valuable contributions to the emerging picture of James White, his detractors, and his supporters, as well as the long-running controversy over him; however, there have been a host of substantive errors in the telling. I cannot think that I have escaped a similar fate, but while the flaws you may have found here are certainly mine, they are as unintentional as White's "passage through the Great Cañon of the Colorado of the West."